The Assault on Progress

The Assault on Progress

Technology and Time in American Literature

J. Adam Johns

THE UNIVERSITY OF ALABAMA PRESS
Tuscaloosa

Typeface: Perpetua

∞

The paper on which this book is printed meets the minimum requirements of American National Standard for Information Sciences-Permanence of Paper for Printed Library Materials, ANSI Z39.48-1984.

Library of Congress Cataloging-in-Publication Data

Johns, J. Adam.
The assault on progress : technology and time in American literature / J. Adam Johns.
p. cm.
Includes bibliographical references and index.
ISBN 978-0-8173-1625-9 (cloth : alk. paper) — ISBN 978-0-8173-8052-6 (electronic)
1. American literature—19th century—History and criticism. 2. Technology in literature. 3. American literature—20th century—History and criticism. 4. Literature and technology—United States—History—19th century. 5. Literature and technology—United States—History—20th century. 6. Time in literature. I. Title.
PS217.T43J64 2008
810.9′356—dc22

2008014005

For Trista and Cordelia,
with love and hope

Contents

Acknowledgments

This book would not have been possible without the assistance of many. I particularly thank several readers, who helped form the book in every way: Ronald Judy, Kirk Savage, Paul Bové, two extraordinary anonymous reviewers, and especially Phil Smith, who provided insight at every stage of composition. I also thank my students for their enthusiasm and even more for their skepticism, as they have faced the evolving ideas that became this book.

The Assault on Progress

Introduction

In *Israel Potter* (1855), possibly his least critically successful novel, Herman Melville addresses the problem of America: What is it, and what will it become? He explores this question through Israel Potter, who endures forty years of exile from the nation for which he gave everything, and through figures from the deadly, mercurial John Paul Jones to the pragmatic, duplicitous Benjamin Franklin. In this novel, one of America's possibilities is that it will become a nation of pirates—in our parlance, terrorists: "Sharing the same blood with England, and yet her proved foe in two wars; not wholly inclined at bottom to forget an old grudge: intrepid, unprincipled, reckless, predatory, with boundless ambition, civilized in externals but a savage at heart, America is, or may yet be, the Paul Jones of nations" (561). America's piracy is implicitly linked to the hubris and ambition of Captain Ahab, who usurps the will of his crew (a metaphorical nation), effectively turning them into machines. Yet Ahab, while mechanizing his crew, dreads mechanization: by yoking them to his own drive for freedom and power, he reveals the contingency of that freedom and power upon their oppression. Potter himself is caught for forty years in the mechanized hell of London, becoming a tiny cog in a vast mechanical civilization. *Israel Potter* is arguably a complex joke that derides the idea of progress at the heart of American ideology; Ahab's tragic struggle becomes a farce starring a spy-turned-brickmaker. America *am-*

biguously represents the advance of human freedom, as in one of the most famous passages from Melville's *White-Jacket* (1850): "we Americans are the peculiar, chosen people—the Israel of our time; we bear the ark of the liberties of the world. . . . We are the pioneers of the world" (506). The main subject of *White-Jacket,* despite such patriotic passages, is the common sailor's brutalization. America continually outruns its destiny, stumbling into slavery and brutality: in Melville's bizarre novel *Mardi* (1849), the island that represents America inscribes the reality of slavery for some and freedom for others in its very monumental architecture.

Melville helped create a tradition in American thought wherein the problem of freedom is inextricably bound up with questions of technology, architecture, and race. I briefly quote a startling example of this tradition from the polymath public intellectual Lewis Mumford's *The Pentagon of Power* (1970): "The Port of New York Authority's World Trade Center, 110 stories high, is a characteristic example of the purposeless giantism and technological exhibitionism that are now eviscerating the living tissue of every great city. . . . Dinosaurs were handicapped by insufficient brains, and the World Trade Center is only another dinosaur" (plate 20). The World Trade Center, Mumford argues, is a microcosm of "megatechnic ambition" as purposeless, brutal, and inhuman as the Egyptian pyramids that obsessed both Melville and Mumford. The problem for Mumford is blind faith in progress at the expense of "human values." His assault on progress is deeply indebted to Melville's interrogation of American ideology, yet Mumford misses the depths of Melville's project, because even he takes the reality of progress for granted, despite viewing it negatively.

Art removes veils, revealing realities otherwise unseen. Melville's interrogation of the relationship between freedom and technology, a theme spanning his career, preceded by a century, and helped to create, the architectural and technological criticism of Mumford, who launched the formalization of the former field (architectural criticism) and preceded the formalization of the latter field (technology criticism).

Novelists have anticipated philosophy and history in exploring and challenging our interlinked ways of understanding time, technology, and progress, especially in America. Mumford and his followers, important as they are, operated in literature's wake. It is vital that we draw upon this literary tradition more deeply; the ideology of progress that we embrace instinctively, even when we struggle to oppose it, is morally perilous and intellectually wrong, but its deep roots make it difficult to analyze, let alone oppose—a topic that leads me temporarily away from literature.

Western thought has been teleological at least since Christianity's institutionalization, possibly beginning with Aristotle or before. We imagine our universe as directed toward a *telos,* an end, the creation of the New Jerusalem or its secular equivalent. The details vary, but both secular and religious ideologies imagine human existence teleologically: take, for example, the state's eventual dissolution in orthodox Marxism. Teleology does not belong only to the religious. It has played a surprising role in physics, as with the influential anthropic principle, which in its strong form asserts that the universe *had* to eventually generate sentient life: the *telos* of the universe is scientific discovery itself.[1] Teleology has dominated modern biology, as the public intellectual and paleontologist Stephen Gould argued: science often asserts that humanity is the proper end of terrestrial life while ostensibly denying that very belief. Teleology dominates our thinking about technology and our relationship to it. "Modern" technology brings doom or salvation, a new world or the world's end; in short, we think of life eschatologically. Technology ends the world as we know it, destroying it or putting a new one in its place. This deeply American intertwining of eschatology and technology is perilous, both intellectually and politically.

Gould critiqued our conventional belief in biological progress, a belief he habitually linked to institutional racism, as in *The Mismeasure of Man* (1981). His main argument in *Full House* (1996) is that evolutionary progress, even in the limited sense of movement toward overall greater complexity, does not exist. Our complexity is a by-product of two simple facts. First, life can evolve toward either greater or lesser complexity; individual species are statistically more likely to be less complex rather than more complex than their ancestors, partially because parasitism, a common adaptation, generally implies simplification. Second, although there is no clear "right wall," or maximal complexity to life, there is a "left wall": life cannot become less complex than simple bacteria. Therefore, although life tends toward simplicity, at the numerically small (in terms of both individuals and species) right tail of the curve of life we see great and gathering complexity. Our prejudices teach us that this right tail is life's *telos,* but in reality we are not representative of life as a whole. We are a contingent statistical outlier, almost white noise. Gould sees his argument against progress (in life) as taking part in what Freud called the dethroning of human megalomania: we are not special or preordained; we do not result from or take part in a cosmic destiny; we are not avatars of progress or the universe's chosen children.

Yet Gould takes with one hand what he gives with the other. At the end of a tightly argued and important debunking of human megalomania, he offhandedly asserts that progress within human culture, especially technological progress, is perfectly real (*House* 219). What's good for the goose is not good for the gander: biological progress is an ideological trap, but technological progress, Gould asserts, is undeniably real. The person of our time who did the most to attack progress and teleology immediately let them in the back door. To appropriate Gould's terminology: his thought represents the wall of the ongoing struggle against human megalomania; few thinkers have approached, let alone surpassed, his attempt at "dethronement." His critique is, nonetheless, inadequate. The undergirding assumption of nearly all political and intellectual discourse, at least in the United States, is that progress, exemplified and led by technological progress, is real; implicitly, at least, we have a destiny, a *telos.* As an example, both George W. Bush and John Kerry engaged in teleological rhetoric in the final debate of the 2004 presidential campaign. The remarkable wording of Bush's invocation of teleological destiny speaks indirectly to my concerns; he spoke of a painting by Tom Lee of a mountain in West Texas that hangs in the Oval Office:

> He said, "Sara and I live on the east side of the mountain. It's the sunrise side, not the sunset side. It's the side to see the day that is coming, not to see the day that is gone."
>
> I love the optimism in that painting, because that's how I feel about America. And we've been through a lot together during the last 3 3/4 years. (United States, *Weekly Compendium* 18 Oct. 2004)

Bush grounds his closing affirmation of American optimism in nature, implicitly the frontier. He then moves from that image of the coming

American dawn to specific instances of progress under his administration, "No Child Left Behind" prominent among them. Then he gets around to destiny, rooted in "West Texas" optimism:

> I'm optimistic that we'll win the war on terror, but I understand it requires firm resolve and clear purpose. We must never waver in the face of this enemy that—these ideologues of hate.
>
> And as we pursue the enemy wherever it exists, we'll also spread freedom and liberty. We got [*sic*] great faith in the ability of liberty to transform societies, to convert a hostile world to a peaceful world. (United States, *Weekly Compendium* 18 Oct. 2004)

Rooted in the sunrise side of the mountain, we chase down evil wherever it lurks, spreading liberty in our wake, in the tradition of Ahab and Israel Potter. Bush implicitly asserts and defends the transformative effect of the Iraq War; the transformation will begin with the spread of the American ideology of progress to the oil fields. His appeal to optimism, to a future-oriented art and technology, could not be more banal; if one doubts its universality, one should note that Kerry engaged in a nearly identical (but characteristically bland) paean to progress.

In the candidates' shared ideology, the United States is oriented toward the future, not the past; its potential for progress, emphasizing technological progress, is boundless; it has a destiny and a mission among the nations to spread progress and freedom around the world (and beyond). Even Gould, whose career as a public intellectual was dedicated to an assault on the ideology of progress, reaffirms it where technology is concerned; he eats away at the scientific edges of the faith while embracing its technological core. The principle of human megalomania is conserved even by Gould, to say nothing of Bush.

The Western ideology of progress is an intellectual and moral disaster, as the presidential debate demonstrated beautifully. Both candidates shared the core belief that the United States has a *telos* as a technological city on the hill, illuminating the world: we are destined to produce or find whatever energy we need, and spread our blessings across the world; in America, David Nye argues in *Consuming Power,* power has been historically viewed as a commodity and right, and for us there is an equivalency between "rising energy and cultural advance" (1). Genuine alternatives become unimaginable.

This book is, however, essentially a work of literary criticism. I have tried here to demonstrate briefly something that chapter 1 will demonstrate at length, namely, that teleological progress is both central to our thinking (even when the best intellectuals try hardest to resist it) and profoundly dangerous. What, then, is to be done? I argue that a line of American literature that begins with Melville thoroughly critiques the ideology of progress; this tradition exposes our deep-rooted faith in progress, including the interdependence between our understandings of time and of technology. This tradition affirms *change* while rejecting *progress;* the challenge is to think history without a *telos,* time without progress. The idea of progress manifested in science, politics, and culture is moral and intellectual poison. It *is* human megalomania purified: not only is humanity the *telos* of history, but our particular moment is the fulcrum upon which world and time rotate.

Like George W. Bush's teleological vision of the American sunrise, my attack on teleological thought is rooted in art as much as technology. Teleology must be understood and attacked from all angles, and an understanding of the artistic tradition of anti-teleological thought is crucial for a broad critique. My arguments will draw on various disciplines, including the history and philosophy of technology and the history and philosophy of science, but my focus is American literature. My purpose is to show, first, that teleological thought is perilous; second, that a powerful tradition of American literature teaches us to resist it; and third, that part of the greatness of these literary works resides in their assault on teleology. Politics is art and art is politics—as, again, George W. Bush's closing statement demonstrates.

Chapter 1 begins with a lengthy critique of a classic of American literary criticism, Leo Marx's *The Machine in the Garden* (1960), in relation both to contemporary histories of technology and to various literary works, intertwined with a discussion of the deep historical and intellectual roots of our teleological understanding of time and technology, and our associated dread of the mechanization of humanity.

Chapters 2 and 3 concern the works of Herman Melville and Lewis Mumford, the latter of whom is famous both for his importance in the genesis of American studies and for his critiques of technology. I focus on Mumford's ongoing reading of Melville, from his early work on American culture and utopias through his various attempts at an autobiography. Through his work, but especially in the two-volume *The Myth of the Machine,* Mumford teeters on a knife's edge between abandoning all teleology and embracing a radical form of it. Both his own work and his readings of Melville (and, following him, the readings of most other critics) are ultimately eschatological; however, Mumford begins to show a way to read Melville, and through Melville all history and technology, non-teleologically and anti-eschatologically. His ambition is to abandon progress and to therefore reimagine history and time itself. One reason for Mumford's ultimate failure is his inability to link Melville's interest in "the machine's appearance" with Melville's interest in slavery; Mumford wants to understand history without race. My goal is to read Melville as Mumford tried (and failed) to read him.

Chapter 4 deals with William Faulkner, in whose work, many critics have thought, time is finished: we endure past the *eschatos.* Faulkner has often been read as a kind of romantic or Agrarian, but his "pastoral" southern landscapes are cluttered with airplanes, automobiles, and mechanical geniuses. The machine is integral to Faulkner's world and his conception of time; his understanding of both the machine and time are further linked, as with Melville, to his understanding of slavery and oppression. My contribution to Faulkner studies is to link his teleological understanding of time to his understanding of the machine. In Faulkner the self is threatened by and overwhelmed by mechanization precisely because Faulkner is unable to think of technology non-teleologically.

In chapter 5 I argue that Ralph Ellison achieves what Faulkner cannot: he *does* understand the long, even mythological duration of the relationship between self and machine. Ellison's political project articulates a counterfascist interaction between technology and myth. Although the Negro (in Ellison's terminology) has already been mechanized—or perhaps because of that fact—in Ellison's version of the story mechanization did not invade the garden suddenly; it is integral to the long histories of both enslavement and liberation. Although Ellison continually flirts with eschatology, he ultimately abandons it, becoming the pinnacle of the anti-teleological tradition in American literature.

The conclusion returns to a more theoretical mode, attempting to turn from the relationship between time and technology to the relationship between life (*bios*) and technology. This turn toward theory is also a turn toward biological thought, in anticipation of future works.

A few words about the book's title will help clarify my major goals and basic assumptions. The title *The Assault on Progress: Technology and Time in American Literature* references my main argument and several of my central terms. I argue that the hegemonic concept of technology in American (and indeed, Western) thought is radically teleological: technology threatens to kill time.

But is not American thought dominated by an *optimistic* account of technological progress, in which the very meaning of time is technological progress? Perhaps. Yet I argue that mainstream optimism and the dread of the technological system that runs through recent philosophical, critical, and ecological thought are mirror images of one another. In the optimistic American account, technology accelerates toward a final liberation (as in George W. Bush's version), which, as in Revelation, is *effectively* the death of time: events may indeed continue in some kind of sequence, following either a secular or religious *eschatos,* but further events are irrelevant once the story of history has been completed. The (often European) thinkers who fear technology are more forthrightly apocalyptic. Bernard Stiegler, following Martin Heidegger, Bertrand Gille, and Ernst Jünger, provides a dramatic but typical example: "Technics evolves *more quickly* than culture. . . . It is as if time has leapt outside itself" (15). In mainstream politics and academic philosophy, among the left and the right, technology threatens time (or *meaningful* time) itself.

What, then, is technology? The vagueness surrounding the term bears some responsibility for the eschatological freight it carries. Dictionary definitions hardly approach the uses to which we put it. Its etymology—*logos* (word, discourse) appended to *technē* (art, skill, craft, cunning)—would seem to indicate something like "discourses on arts, skills, and crafts." Yet we habitually use the word not to describe discourses but rather their objects. Furthermore, the word *technology,* as David Edgerton argues in *The Shock of the Old* (2007), is typically conflated with *invention;* we think and talk about technological innovation, not about the technologies we actually use (185). Edgerton urges that we think in terms of "technology-in-use," which will lead to "a rethinking of our notion of technological time, mapped as it is on innovation-based timelines" (xi). Our habitual usage of the term *technology,* then, is already infused with a particular understanding of time. It is appropriate, given the way its meaning tends to elide into *innovation,* that the term was coined only in 1828, early in the era of the American obsession with innovation (Nye, *Sublime* 45). Without trying to resist the fact that the word *technology* usually indicates objects rather than discourses (a meaning that Edgerton tacitly accepts), I argue that we need to resist the urge to accept a whole concept of time and history every time we use the word *technology:* I use the word to refer to discourses *and* their objects. Edgerton argues that we need to think more about use and less about innovation; in my related argument, we need to abandon technological teleology. Teleology, of course, originates in *telos* and *logos:* it refers to things that are directed toward ends, especially by internal forces but also by external ones. I argue that technology is not teleological: it is not directed toward any end, including the simple—but, as Edgerton points out, nearly universally accepted—end of innovation itself.

We have trouble thinking about technology without conceiving of it as being directed toward some end, which, subtly but seemingly inevitably, is ultimately the *eschatos,* the end of time. We need to think of time and technology differently (here my work parallels that of Edgerton and other historians of technology); my main argument is that a particular tradition in American literature teaches us how to do so by demonstrating that our teleological understanding of technology amounts to believing in the death of time itself, and by imagining the possibility of resisting that teleological, eschatological way of understanding technology.

1

The Garden in the Machine

The Sudden Machine

According to Leo Marx's *The Machine in the Garden,* American culture has been marked by the machine's sudden, traumatic entrance into the "garden," which is understood as the "middle state" of agricultural, tended nature: "What begins as a conventional tribute to the pleasures of withdrawal from the world—a simple pleasure fantasy—is transformed by the interruption of the machine into a far more complex state of mind. . . . More often than not in these episodes, the machine is made to appear with startling suddenness" (15). Many authors, argues Marx, contrast "the machine" with an ordered rural landscape to emphasize the former's artificiality, beginning with such romantics as Blake and Wordsworth (18). The machine comes upon Nathaniel Hawthorne as a "sudden, shocking intruder upon a fantasy of idyllic satisfaction" (29). In time, the machine's sudden appearance becomes a cliché (as in Frank Norris's novels), rooted in the fact of America's "unbelievably rapid industrialization" (343). Marx's book ends by asserting that artistic attempts to create a middle landscape have failed and that the "machine's sudden entrance into the garden presents a problem that ultimately belongs not to art but to politics" (365).

Marx insists on the machine's suddenness. It isn't imported piecemeal, nor does it evolve. It appears uproariously, a monster always already full-grown, what George Basalla describes sarcastically as a "masculine aggressiveness" contrasting with the "tender, feminine" landscape (29). The case for suddenness is aided by Marx's focus on steam locomotives, which often seem to embody irresistible technological determinism, as in Hawthorne's *The House of the Seven Gables* when Clifford and Hepzibah Pyncheon flee by railroad from any implication of complicity in their cousin's death: "this admirable invention of the railroad—with the vast and inevitable improvements to be looked for, both as to speed and convenience—is destined to do away with those stale ideas of home and fireside, and substitute something better. . . . These railroads . . . are positively the greatest blessing that the ages have wrought for us. They give us wings; they annihilate the toil and dust of pilgrimage; they spiritualize travel!" (574–75). In Hawthorne the miraculous railroad is ironically undercut: the Pyncheon siblings shortly return home to face their fate, which is reintegration *into* the landed aristocracy. Despite appearances, things don't change easily: "Shall we never, never get rid of the past? . . . It lies upon the Present like a giant's dead body!" (509). Hawthorne is skeptical about progress, but Marx speaks for many thinkers when he argues that the idea of history as "a record of more or less continuous progress" was popular "among the educated" in the eighteenth century and became pervasive across classes in the nineteenth, and that technological works, as well as natural events and wonders, became revered as sublime (*Machine* 197). The story of modernity becomes the story of people who believe in progress, specifically technological progress.

A curious contradiction stands revealed. The machine erupts suddenly onto the landscape as "the type and agent of an irreversible process . . . the implacable advance of history"; its speed "annihilates space and time" (*Machine* 252, 194). When it appears, everything changes; nature and the machine are at war. The locomotive is fast enough, argues Hawthorne's Clifford, to "return us to the nomadic state" (*House* 574). Yet Hawthorne's line is ironic; the Pyncheons return to their origins at the novel's end, which may explain why Marx ignores this novel in favor of simpler pieces like "The Celestial Railroad."

Yet, the "instantaneous" locomotive requires many professions, specialties, and mechanical parts, all of which evolve together. This complex process results in a new way of surveying the world and history: Descartes's theoretical spatialization of time becomes material. But despite the locomotive's annihilation of space and time, as well as human lives and material resources, and though it seemingly propels history, it is the *contingent* product of a slow historical process, driven by ideology more than economics; Basalla argues that it was totally unclear at the time railroads were spreading rapidly whether they would be economically competitive with (let alone superior to) canals. The concepts of the railroad and its annihilation of space and time, not sound economic sense, carried the day (Basalla 195–97). The locomotive propels history, seemingly, but is itself historically contingent. The concept of the locomotive as a finished artifact and a cultural reality erupts suddenly, moving with infinite speed, but the actual railroad, to say nothing of the technologies and workforce behind it, is centuries in the making. It took centuries of coal mining in England before the steam engine was developed; in fact, the development of the steam engine was driven by the need to find a power source for running the pumps to drain ever-deeper coal mines (Gimpel 81–84). The use of rails was already a commonplace in mines. Basalla argues in *The Evolution of Technology* that the "industrial revolution" was in no sense a revolution in the actual technologies, which developed incrementally. The revolution was in people's lives and worldviews; massive changes resulted from the widespread adoption of incrementally new machines and techniques (61). The very notion of an "industrial revolution," as Immanuel Wallerstein argues, is misleading, and "no amount of patchwork" can save it (*Expansion* 33). We should note, finally, that the very landscape upon which the locomotive erupted was shaped technologically, "using horses and oxen and a variety of machines" (Nye, *Power* 19). An incrementally achieved technology becomes revolutionary when perceived and distributed as a revolutionary advance: the ideology, not the machine, is the real revolutionary force.

I am not downplaying the importance of technology or of technologies, nor questioning the tendency of Marx and others to focus on the relationship between the railroad and American culture, a worthy subject. Rather, I mean to draw attention to the unexamined assumption that the railroad erupts suddenly onto the scene. Even what we perceive as historically sudden is often simply the settling, however violent, of accumulated historical sediments, as in Wallerstein's analysis of the French Revolution as "the moment when the ideological superstructure finally caught up with the economic base [of capitalism]" (*Expansion* 52). The technologies involved in the railroad's adoption are obviously incremental. Railroads require the mass production of wrought iron, which requires rolling mills. Building steam engines requires properly drilled cylinders. Massive quantities of coal are necessary to make rails and to fuel locomotives; extremely inefficient engines lead the way, since early steam engines are useful only in the depths of coal mines, at the source of the fuel they consume so prodigiously. Long-distance railroads are impractical without the telegraph, which requires practical batteries. These diverse technologies went through troublesome gestations (for a detailed discussion of these technologies see Arnold Pacey's *Technology in World Civilization* 108–17, 135–42). Ironically, the railroad *appears* sudden only after becoming an accomplished fact, even a reified object. In *The House of the Seven Gables,* Holgrave wants to be free of history: "the case is just as if a young giant were compelled to waste all his strength in carrying about the corpse of the old giant, his grandfather. . . . It will startle you to see what slaves we are to by-gone times—to Death" (509). Holgrave, a daguerrotypist, is deeply invested in technology, which he hopes will liberate him from the "dead giant" of history. His belief is ours: technology, being fundamentally discontinuous, frees us from history, leaping from one inventor to another, simultaneously freeing the inventor *from* history and making the inventor an important figure *in* history.

Basalla lists three sources for faith in the discontinuity of technology. First, antecedents to particular technologies are forgotten or concealed: the history of engineering is, in Siegfried Giedion's formulation, a largely anonymous history. Second, inventors of incremental improvements are promoted as heroes. When names do replace anonymity, they are inaccurate and late; moreover, innovators of the wrong racial backgrounds and social classes are habitually marginalized: masters were given legal credit for the inventions of their slaves (P. James 50). Third, technological change is confused with socioeconomic change, as with the railroad (Basalla 57). Socioeconomic changes are also sometimes incorrectly attributed to technological changes. For instance, the altered landscape usually attributed to industrialism was already radically different in

Thoreau's time from what it was before the arrival of Europeans: Thoreau wrote of a changed nature, including second- and third-growth timber, and the near-extinction of native species from deer and moose to bear (McMurry 33). We try to be shed of the dead giant by emphasizing discontinuity, particularly that of our own achievements, but history is a tenacious giant.

In reality, technology, rather than erupting, evolves. The incremental developments can be overwhelming, as with the railroad or hydrogen bomb, but as technological developments (and usually as socioeconomic developments) they remain incremental. Nonetheless, we tend to understand technology as erupting and, in its eruption, threatening all: the integrity of the human self and the future. As Marx implicitly argues, once we understand the machine's arrival as sudden and disruptive, we must see the scene upon which it arrives as disrupted. He discusses Alexander Hamilton's assistant Tench Coxe's positive use of the word *mechanism,* a usage that became impossible under romanticism's growing influence. We cannot "appreciate the dominant American attitude toward technology," he argues, if we project our ambiguous feelings about technology too far back (162). Sometime between Coxe and Hawthorne, Marx argues, the tables turned, and the border war between life and machine began slowly to define our understanding of technology.

Marx implicitly places both the beginning of the organic/mechanical conflict and the near-universal belief in techno-historical progress at roughly the beginning of the nineteenth century. The critical moment in the conflict, though, is his own, as the ending of the first edition of *The Machine in the Garden* shows: "The machine's sudden entrance into the garden presents a problem that ultimately belongs not to art but to politics" (365). At the end of the 2000 afterword he ironically notes that when writing the first edition he had believed that "the pastoral response to industrial society had almost certainly become anachronistic" (384), but later he witnessed the generation of the 1960s organize around allegedly pastoral ideals (although central figures like Herbert Marcuse and Abbie Hoffman believed not in a pastoral ideal but in industrialism's essentially infinite productivity), with later generations joining assorted green movements. Yet, after admitting his failure to understand the pastoral's ongoing power, the afterword closes with a variation on the previous ending: "Could it be that this kind of [green] oppositional politics is what the future now holds in store? If so, it is enlightening to recall that its emergence was foretold by American writers in their initial responses to the appearance of the new machine power in the national landscape" (385). The irony has repeated: the turning point of history and the organic/mechanical divide is *now*—although once Marx saw the pastoral dying, now he sees it as ascendant. Marx implies that we teeter at the brink of Western civilization's *telos.*

I begin with Marx not to attack him but because he is sufficiently historically astute to almost, but never quite, recognize his own teleology; he is troubled by the dominant vision of the world approaching a technological *telos,* but by accepting the machine's sudden arrival as a given he retains that teleology. For Marx, the *actual* suddenness of the machine drives the romantic perception of the machine's suddenness, which drives the problematic world-picture of the organic/mechanical divide, which is oriented toward the *telos* or *eschatos* at which the order of the world will be definitively determined.

The danger presented by the organic/mechanical conflict, for Marx and the authors he studies, is that the organic will be overcome and mechanized (at the moment of the *eschatos*). Interpreting Thoreau, and presumably under the influence of the Frankfurt school's critique of instrumental reasoning (best articulated in Horkheimer and Adorno's 1947 *Dialectic of Enlightenment*), Marx writes: "In the machinery of our collective existence, Thoreau says, we have 'constructed a fate, an *Atropos,* that we never will turn aside. And until we confront the unalterable . . . there can be no redemption from a system that makes men the tools of their tools" (*Machine* 354–55). Marx continues by showing that not only Thoreau but also Herman Melville, Mark Twain, Henry Adams, and F. Scott Fitzgerald see this danger in technological civilization. For all of his studied skepticism of the organic/mechanical divide, both endings to *The Machine in the Garden* and his uncritical acceptance of the machine's suddenness show that Marx essentially accepts this conflict as the *telos* of Western civilization. Mankind stands in danger of becoming a tool to its tools, of being subsumed within a mechanical historical determinism.

The Mechanized Self

The idea of a mechanized self predates romanticism; the concepts of progress, a mechanical universe, and "man the machine" are conventionally assigned to Enlightenment thinkers and institutions, as in Michel Foucault's *Discipline and Punish,* which argues that human mechanization took place in both "anatomico-metaphysical" and "technico-political registers," written, respectively, by "physicians and philosophers" starting with Descartes and by "regulations and by empirical and calculated methods relating to the army, the school and the hospital, for controlling or correcting the operations of the body" (136). Romanticism's organic/mechanical divide responded to already-dominant ideas about a mechanical universe. These mechanical philosophers looked back to even earlier concepts of a crafted universe; James Lennox argues that Robert Boyle (1627–91) referred to Plato's Demiurge-crafted universe when formulating his own specifically mechanical theory of the universe. Industrialism greatly preceded the "industrial revolution" (a claim I will detail), as did the concept of the mechanical universe. There are important literary and philosophical antecedents to the formal concept of the mechanical universe; I will examine a selection, including Shakespeare, Edmund Spenser, Thomas Hobbes, and (predictably) René Descartes, leading up to a discussion of Mary Shelley, to demonstrate the age and continuity of ideas about a mechanical self. This discussion is inexhaustive and deliberately canonical. I am making absolutely no Bloomian claim that Shakespeare or Spenser invented the mechanical self. To the contrary, I mean to show that the concept has a long history and was already well formed when Shakespeare put it to use.

In the fifth act of *Coriolanus* (1608), Coriolanus, mightiest and most terrible of Shakespeare's heroes, seems to two old friends to have undergone a metamorphosis, as they anticipate his imminent assault on Rome, despite the presence therein of his mother and friends: "When he walks, he moves *like an engine,* and the ground shrinks before his treading. He is able to pierce a corslet with his eye, talks like a *knell,* and his *'hmh!' is a battery.* He sits in his state as *a thing made for Alexander.* What he bids be done is finished with his bidding. He wants nothing of a god but eternity and a heaven to throne in" (5.4.1–20; emphasis added). Shakespeare blends fate, godhead, and technology. The extremity of Coriolanus's power cannot be expressed merely by likening him to a god or demon: only reifying him into multiple machines and objects reveals his power. To hold ultimate power, one must be a thing, not a man. Coriolanus the war-engine arrives as suddenly as Leo Marx's locomotive. Rome's only hope is to derail him from his purpose; it can no more resist his actions, compressed into the moment of his bidding, than wheat can stand against a McCormick reaper; in his person "time leaps ahead of itself." Coriolanus's mother derails his eschatological purpose; he is then promptly destroyed, being unable to help himself after leaving the predetermined track of his power. Coriolanus is vital to Rome's success, then to the Volscians', but he is powerful *only* as a resource, unable to claim his power in a new and different way, and as bereft of "authentic" possibilities as the technologically dominated mankind which concerns the Frankfurt school. His mechanical power makes him like "a thing made for Alexander"; *because of* his power, he is without options, a clockwork soldier, like those Foucault discusses in reference to the *eighteenth* century (*Discipline* 135). Coriolanus is his mother's creation, not merely by birth but by *craft;* the military machine of the French Revolution is implicit in Coriolanus, as Wallerstein might recognize.

The power of Spenser's Talus is greater, and his options proportionally more restricted, for Talus is literally a machine, an outright possession, where Coriolanus is theoretically a man. Talus plays a large role in the fifth book of *The Faerie Queene* (1596), where he is the "yron man" who serves Artegall and Britomart as protector and guide. He is a mechanical man, a machine of justice, but with thoughts and feelings, as when he hesitates before giving Britomart bad news (790; bk. 5, canto 6, stanzas 9–11). Despite his gentle feelings, his brutal mechanical power is unrivaled, as when he attacks the defeated warriors fleeing from Britomart's rescue of Artegall from the Amazon Radigund: "a piteous slaughter did begin: / For all that euer came within his reach, / He with his yron flale did thresh so thin, / That he no worke at all left for the leach: / Like to an hideous storme, which nothing may empeach" (807; bk. 5, canto 7, stanza 35). No fine feelings interfere with Talus's execution of his duty, which is figured naturalistically and economically: the mechanical man's wrath is like a farmer threshing and also like a storm. His wrath is both sublime and businesslike. Talus is given to Artegall to "doe what euer thing he did intend. / His name was Talus, made of yron mould, / Immoueable, resistlesse, without end. / Who in his hand an yron flale did hould, / With which he thresth out falshood, and did truth vnfould" (730; bk. 5, canto 1, stanza 12). Talus is iron, made in an iron mold, remorseless, irresistible, perfectly obedient, and dedicated to truth. He is justice personified, a machine of truth, imagined in the late sixteenth century in a country that had made heavy use of mills and clockwork for centuries, which was centuries into one stage of "industrial revolution," although we conventionally date the "Industrial Revolution" much later; London itself had suffered air pollution from coal since the thirteenth century, and England was about to enter into a new coal era driven by the discovery that coke can reduce iron ore (Gimpel 81–82). Shakespeare's and Spenser's Britain was not "pre-industrial"; if it was less industrialized than that of the romantics, the difference was in degree, not in kind. Spenser's imagination, preceding what we call mechanical philosophy but operating in what had long been an industrial society, flirts with the reduction of human agency to mechanical determinacy and forthrightly describes a world wherein the boundary between man and machine is permeable, in which a machine can wield power that ordinary people cannot match.

Discussing William Stidger's 1923 hagiography of Henry Ford, David Nye writes: "Kant saw the sublime in a hurricane; Stidger sees the steel mill as a man-made cataract of flame and fury. Kant's natural forces reduce man to a feeling of weakness; Stidger feels intoxicated by the revelation of human mastery" (*Sublime* 131). In Nye's account, the sublime proper is characterized by its humbling of the human: the technological sublime, however, exalts the human *while* humbling it; the technological sublime may be beyond the human scale, but is also the work of human hands. Yet, before Kant wrote on the sublime, Talus already exemplified the technological sublime. Dating the arrival of the technological sublime, then, is as problematic as dating the "industrial revolution" itself.

"But when they thought on Talus hands to lay, / He with his yron flaile amongst them thondred / . . . That th'heaps of those, which he did wound and slay, / Besides the rest dismayd, might not be nombred" (777; bk. 5, canto 5, stanza 19). Talus's violence is promiscuous, mass-producing death (despite his gentle feelings) as brilliantly as a guillotine or a Chicago slaughterhouse, or "disassembly line" (Edgerton 174). Talus doubly embodies the end of human agency. First, he is ambiguously machine and man, with human feelings but fully subject to another's will—he is arguably a slave, in an empire deeply indebted to the slave trade. Second, by dispensing truth and unfolding justice mechanically (he fights with a flail: war and justice have become economic and industrial activities), he reduces the world to a deterministic (and eschatological, given the poem's background of Protestant-Catholic conflict, often framed apocalyptically by Protestant writers) mechanical order. He is mechanical and mechanizing, a forerunner to various science fiction robots, along with the cyborgs, starting with Captain Ahab, who populate nineteenth-century American literature, according to Klaus Benesch's *Romantic Cyborgs* (2002).

Shakespeare and Spenser were well in advance of the thinkers who mechanized and regularized the universe as a whole: philosophy followed in literature's wake. The mechanical philosophers are habitually discussed as a set group, as Benesch does in *Romantic Cyborgs,* writing on the American romantic backlash against mechanical philosophy: "the writers of the American Renaissance adopted the imagery of the man-machine, which was handed on to them through the lingering influence of mechanical philosophy" (12). Hobbes's concept of the state as an artificial man in a mechanical universe is one vital example of this mechanical philosophy, as we see in the opening to *Leviathan* (1651):

> NATURE (the art whereby God hath made and governs the world) is by the *art* of man, as in many other things, so in this also imitated, that it can make an artificial animal. For seeing life is but a motion of limbs, the beginning whereof is in some principal part within; why may we not say, that all *automata* (engines that move themselves by springs and wheels as doth a watch) have an artificial life? For what is the *heart,* but a *spring;* and the *nerves,* but so many *strings;* and the *joints,* but so many *wheels,* giving motion to the whole body, such as was intended by the artificer? *Art* goes yet *further,* imitating that rational and most excellent work of nature, *man.* For by art

> is created that great LEVIATHAN called a COMMONWEALTH, or STATE, (in Latin Civitas) which is but an artificial man. (7, emphasis in source)

For Hobbes, no clear line demarcates organic from mechanical: a blast furnace, a musket, a dog, and a man are equally machines; given sufficient knowledge, we could make Talus. Nature is God's art (*technē*), a larger and better version of human art. Interestingly, despite the lack of a single motive physical power behind the individual parts that compose a state, Hobbes still sees the state as an artificial—which is not clearly distinguished from natural!—man. Talus is a single, localized machine for compelling obedience or "administering justice"; Hobbes's Commonwealth is a pervasive, non-localized machine with the same goals: the "subjects" of the "sovereign power" heading the Commonwealth are "bound by covenant, to own the actions, and judgements of one, cannot lawfully make a new covenant, amongst themselves, to be obedient to any others, in any thing whatsoever, without his permission" (115). Already with Hobbes we are dealing with cyborgs, humans interfaced with machines in ways that make distinctions and boundaries between human and machine meaningless. The true project of romanticism (to leap ahead of myself) is not to oppose the machine's recent, sudden arrival but to deal with its entrenched facticity, as a socio-technological presence and a philosophical-literary concept: the romantic garden is what erupts onto the mechanical stage.

Descartes (1596–1650) takes a path similar to Hobbes's, arguing that the human body is a machine distinct from other machines in its perfection, not its fundamental nature; it is a machine controlled by reason, whereas animals are purely machines, such that a well-designed machine could be indistinguishable from an animal (44). A human being, for Descartes, can theoretically only be distinguished from a humanoid automaton by speech and reason, the "universal instrument which can be used in all kinds of situations" (44). Descartes anticipates the "Turing Test" for artificial intelligence, according to which a computer is intelligent when an observer having a written conversation with a computer and a person can't tell which is which; Descartes couldn't believe (or safely say) that intelligence can be viewed as mechanically as life can be. The difference between life and machine is eroded if, like Turing, we imagine a machine capable of Cartesian rationality, but the difference is eroded earlier and more thoroughly if rationality itself is questioned, as by David Hume, for whom reason is really repetition: the death of reason as such implies no abandonment of a mechanical world-picture. Katherine Hayles has argued that, with the arrival of the Turing test, the possibility of a posthuman subjectivity has arrived; ironically, one might be better off dating the arrival of the posthuman, then, to the Cartesian anticipation of the Turing test: posthuman subjectivity, then, arrives with the Enlightenment—that is, with the human as we know it (*Posthuman* xi–xiv). In all fairness, of course, Hayles's book, following Bruno Latour, closes with precisely this observation, that "we have always been posthuman" (291).

One distinguishing characteristic of the Cartesian mechanical or clockwork universe is that it can represent time in space. This characteristic of Cartesian or Enlightenment thought has received wide commentary. For Foucault, for instance, one characteristic of the Enlightenment is that its disciplinary methods involve continually more microscopic management of time, forming a "machine in time as well as in space" (*Discipline* 162, 164). Understanding the world as clockwork enables a fine-grained, detailed control that extends through both time and space.

Despite the claims of romanticism and its descendants, which imagine an apocalyptic battle between the organic and the mechanical (in which the current moment is *the* fulcrum on which history turns), we should be skeptical: by pretending that the machine belongs to a *new* order, romanticism justified a return to the "old order"—the revolutionary Holgrave's return to the landed aristocracy in *The House of the Seven Gables*—as a response to the machine's eschatological arrival. Romanticism permits something that even Hobbes doesn't: the old order becomes *natural,* a problem central to *Frankenstein,* the prototypical cautionary tale about science and technology and one of the major works of literary romanticism.

As Foucault might predict, Victor Frankenstein works in the finest increments of time and space. "I saw how the worm inherited the wonders of the eye and brain. I paused, examining and analyzing all the minutiae of causation, as exemplified in the change from life to death, and death to life, until from the midst of this darkness a sudden light broke in upon me" (Shelley 51). The key to life and death is *minute* observation, small transitions; the universe is mechanical in the sense that, like clockwork, all processes can be reversed—one can move back and forth between life and death if one attends to the finest details. To connect this to romanticism as a whole: we have lost the garden to the machine, but all processes are reversible, if only through the *eschatos.* Romanticism inherits mechanical philosophy's faith in reversibility, which Henri Bergson derides: "Change *must* be reducible to an arrangement or rearrangement of parts; the irreversibility of time *must* be an appearance relative to our ignorance; the impossibility of turning back *must* be only the inability of man to put things back in place" (*Creative* 17). For Frankenstein, as for Bergson's internal metaphysician, every transition must be discretely caused in a discrete moment, and therefore be reversible.

One might argue that, since Frankenstein's method *works,* Mary Shelley is in Descartes and Hobbes's camp, not Bergson's. True, Frankenstein mechanically creates life, but the behavior of his creation is anything but mechanical; the monster is not calculable, nor are the actions of Frankenstein himself, who is congenitally unable to pursue his own best interests and remains thoroughly entrenched in an old order, even while establishing the basis for a new one.

Frankenstein aims to create a race of superior beings who "would bless me as its creator and source. . . . No father should claim the gratitude of his child so completely as I should" (52). Frankenstein then drifts into a fantasy of reversing death: change *must* be reducible to an arrangement of parts. Frankenstein does not dream of a family of children, but of a race; not of affection, but of boundless gratitude; not of equality, but of duties claimed. He dreams of a fully spatialized—and hence reversible—time, and of near-infinite power administered first upon and then through his creations.

But his calculated creation doesn't merely fall apart; it disintegrates as it begins, at the moment his mastery of the "minutiae of causation" summons his monster to life. His creation's sublimity seems like ugliness: "breathless horror and disgust" fill him. The monster pursues him, presenting not the aspect of an obedient Talus but of a babbling baby: "His jaws opened, and he muttered some inarticulate sounds, while a grin wrinkled his cheeks" (57). Frankenstein flees from this aspect of his "machine," causing the chain of disasters and tragedies constituting the rest of the book. Despite Frankenstein's ability to create life and his ambition to resurrect the dead, thus metaphorically reversing time, his life is transformed by one irreversible moment. The future is incalculable, the past ineradicable; Frankenstein's new world order dissolves as he first articulates it. The only "outsider" affected by the novel, Captain Walton, takes away one lesson: that he should return to the household, the *oikos,* rejecting the irrational rationalism of the power quest. The *telos* of history is a return to the garden, the cultivated middle landscape of the landed aristocracy.

The Mechanical Self in the "Industrial Revolution"

Two eschatological fears seem ubiquitous in nineteenth- and twentieth-century writing: that worldly mechanization will bring the mechanization of the self, and that this mechanization is uniquely contemporary. Here and through the rest of this book I will use the term *mechanization* not only to indicate the transition of labor-intensive industries to highly automated ones but also to refer to the process by which a free subject becomes an automaton.

Karl Marx's book-length chapter "Machinery and Large-Scale Industry," in *Capital* (1867), illustrates the age's obsession with the machine's sudden appearance and with the automation of the self. Marx argues that "fully developed" machines consist of three parts: motor, transmitting mechanisms, and a "tool or working machine"; with the third, "the industrial revolution of the eighteenth century begins" (494). Although he acknowledges continuity between tool and machine, Marx (following Hegel) emphasizes the latter's apocalyptic suddenness: "In handicrafts and manufacture, the worker makes use of a tool; in the factory, the machine makes use of him. There the movements of the instrument of labor proceed from him, here it is the movements of the machine that he must follow. In manufacture the workers are the parts of a living mechanism. In the factory we have a lifeless mechanism which is independent of the workers, who are incorporated into it as its living appendages" (548). Life is subordinated to the machine, under which people serve a lifetime bound "to a single specialized operation. At the same time, the capitalist form of large-scale industry reproduces this same division of labor in a still more monstrous shape" (614). The power of this unliving monster is tied to invention, and in particular to the steam engine, "an antagonist that enabled the capitalists to tread underfoot" the workers' demands (562). The steam engine "makes history," in Robert Heilbroner's classic formation. For Marx, "modern industry" is essentially revolutionary, while earlier forms of production are conservative (617).

Marx draws an eschatological line, roughly coinciding with the adoption of the steam engine, at which battle is joined between capitalist and worker, organism and machine. Marxism is clearly continuous with a long line of teleological-historical thinking, as Lyotard argues in *Postmodern Fables;* Marx's eschatology is fixated on the machine's eruption onto history as the equivalent of the arrival of the Beast of Revelation (*Fables* 97).

Thomas Carlyle's 1829 essay "Signs of the Times" also argues that the self is mechanized in the wake of mechanical production. His age is a mechanical age, which, with "its whole undivided mights, forwards, teaches and practices the great art of adapting means to ends. . . . [A]ll is by rule and calculated contrivance" (34). An artificial order suddenly violates a natural order, although if we attend to mechanical philosophy (and its artistic antecedents) we might argue, contra Carlyle, that the artificial (*technē*) actually precedes the organic.

Carlyle argues that both the "external and physical" and "the internal and spiritual" are managed mechanically (35). Education, religion, government, and science all operate mechanically, not "dynamically" (organically). "Men are grown mechanical in head and in heart, as well as in hand. They have lost faith in individual endeavor, and in natural force, of any kind" (37). The mechanical age's enormous physical power leads to great deeds, but "in true dignity of soul and character, we are perhaps inferior to most civilized ages" (46). For Carlyle, the solution to internal mechanization is simple: we must return to cultivating the individual spirit rather than the world: "the only solid . . . reformation, is what each begins and perfects on himself" (54). As Leo Marx emphasizes, for Carlyle mechanization represents a change not only in tools and techniques but most of all in world-picture (*Machine* 174). More interiority, not different politics, is the key for Carlyle. Leo Marx argues that Karl Marx's concept of alienation—created in large part by machine technology—parallels Ralph Emerson's and Carlyle's critiques of the subordination of the "dynamic" to the "mechanical" (*Machine* 176–78). Romanticism and Marxism see history teleologically: history, unlike in mechanical philosophy, begins with nature and ends with the conflict between nature and the machine.

In American literature the conflict between the organic and the mechanical has generated utopian and dystopian eschatologies: the machine can be a savior, Christ as *logos,* rather than the Beast of Revelation; the machine's saving power *is* democracy's saving power. Leo Marx gives the example of Timothy Walker, who wrote a "Defense of Mechanical Philosophy" in response to Carlyle (*Machine* 181–82). In *Civilizing the Machine,* John Kasson discusses American utopian ideas about mechanizing world, landscape, and self. For instance, Benjamin Rush, following Tench Coxe and Alexander Hamilton, argued that American education should generate "republican machines," that is, citizens (32). This line of utopian mechanistic thinking has many exemplars, from Edward Bellamy to the admirers of Lowell's textile mills, organized by physical and moral machinery, where the lives of unmarried women workers were regulated on many levels (Kasson 100). In America, battle lines have often been drawn over whether the mechanization of industry and the self supports or undermines the republican order; is it a romantic or mechanistic republic? Nye argues that by the Jacksonian era it was a commonplace to understand various technological improvements (especially sublime ones) like the Erie Canal as components of a "moral machine" that "ensure not only the prosperity but also the democracy and the moral health of the nation" (*Sublime* 39). Interestingly, Nye argues that the media-orchestrated spectacles of the technological sublime in the late twentieth century lacked political content, no longer making the "claim that a new technology was a moral machine that would elevate the people," but instead that they were raw displays of power "as a sign of national greatness" (280). Nye charts a technological rhetoric that shifts from emphasizing individual improvement to collective power.

Perhaps the most cited example of the theory behind mechanizing the self is Frederick Winslow Taylor's *The Principles of Scientific Management* (1911). Taylor, an early-twentieth-century efficiency expert, broke workers' movements into components that could be arranged algorithmically. He argues that employers' duties and opportunities lie in "systematically cooperating to train and to make this competent man, instead of in hunting for a man whom some one else has trained" (iii). Efficiency requires rigid standardization of techniques and motions, enforced by management, with the compensation of increased wages (41). Taylor argues that great freedom can be realized within a worker's ever more restricted movements:

> When through teaching and this minute instruction the work is apparently made so smooth and easy for the workman, the first impression is that this all tends to make him a mere automaton. . . . The same criticism and objection, however, can be raised against all other modern subdivision of labor. . . . [T]he modern surgeon is [not] any more narrow or wooden a man than the early settler of this country. The frontiersman, however, had to be not only a surgeon, but also an architect, house-builder, lumberman, farmer, soldier, and doctor. . . . The workman who is cooperating with his many teachers under scientific management has an opportunity to develop which is . . . generally better than that which he had when the whole problem was "up to him" and he did his work entirely unaided. (65–66)

Freedom and progress lie in further refining a mechanized self: "Maximum prosperity can exist only as a result of maximum productivity" (2). Maximum productivity exists only under scientific management; under maximum productivity, "prosperity will be permanent" (1). The utopian *telos* of humanity is eternal prosperity driven by ongoing refinement of scientific management's control of human motion.

Because of his embrace of the mechanized self, Taylor is often seen by friends *and* foes as standing in his era's history-producing vanguard. But the study and mechanization of movement was not new; at most, he formalized an old process. The creation of clockwork soldiers, as detailed in Foucault's *Discipline and Punish,* Manuel De Landa's *War in the Age of Intelligent Machines,* and Arnold Pacey's *Meaning in Technology,* is based on musical rhythms, enabled partially by the mechanization of music, as composers began to recommend metronome settings late in the eighteenth century, such that "music might sometimes be played—and armies might be drilled—by the precise rhythms of a machine," while rhythmic musket-loading ensured that "Reloading was carried out more quickly and the soldiers made fewer errors" (Pacey, *Meaning* 19, 27). The rigidly mechanized Greek phalanx, along with the musical rhythms of slavery and serfdom, also precede Taylor's techniques. The mechanistic mastery of motion is not essentially a contemporary phenomenon.

Siegfried Giedion (1888–1968) places the origins of the assembly line not with Henry Ford or Frederick Taylor but with largely non-mechanical (dis)assembly lines in butchery and biscuit making, starting as early as 1804 (77–78, 87). The factory, whether for disassembling pigs or assembling biscuits, doesn't necessarily require, and isn't necessarily driven by, actual machines: mechanical rhythms can precede the machine, as in the slaughterhouse, or follow it, as with some of Taylor's "innovations." In Upton Sinclair's *The Jungle* (1906), Jurgis, the protagonist, marvels at being a "cog in this marvelous machine" *before* seeing any of the slaughterhouse's actual machines, which in any case are secondary. The wonder of the scene is its human element: Jurgis wonders at seeing a hog "dressed by several hundred men. It was like a wonderful poem" (37). As with the steam engine, the historical reality of the (dis)assembly line in the slaughterhouse greatly precedes its own sudden, earthshaking arrival in the automobile industry.

The intellectual process by which the machine's incremental arrival is displaced by suddenness is aided by technology's anonymity, its tendency to devour its own history: "Henry Ford does not mention Taylor. He is the self-taught man, who does everything for himself" (Giedion 115). Innovators want to *be* innovators, revolutionaries to *be* revolutionaries. The crisis must be unfolding *now,* not gradually through the course of history.

Further visions of a technological *eschatos* abound. Take the writings of Lafcadio Hearn (1850–1904), who, after emigrating from the United States to Japan, predicted and hoped for the sake of humanity that Japan would triumph over mechanical Western civilization, which he assails:

> These leagues of palaces, of warehouses, of business structures, of buildings describable and indescribable, are not beautiful, but sinister. One feels depressed by the mere sensation of the enormous life which created them, life without sympathy; of their prodigious manifestation of power, power without pity. They are the architectural utterance of the new industrial age. And there is no halt in the thunder of wheels, in the storming of hoofs and of human feet. . . . The unaccustomed feels the sensation of being in a panic, in a tempest, in a cyclone. Yet all this is order. (15)

Hearn argues that the West is doomed by its obsession with order and stability; modern architecture causes cultural ossification. Japanese civilization is distinguished by its focus on impermanency, the necessity and perpetuity of change. "Yet all this is order," he writes ironically, amidst his vision of the mechanized and mechanizing horrors of the West. The result of Hamilton, Rush, and Taylor's civilization, in which every movement is regulated, is spiritual chaos amidst mechanical order; for Hearn, Taylor's "endless prosperity" causes the loss of "the power of independent movement" and a "useless multiplicity of daily wants" (24, 27). The *telos* of Western history is total mechanization, which must be vigorously resisted by other civilizations and values. By embracing an implicitly organic "change" over mechanical "order," Hearn reveals his own romantic roots, but he also anticipates Bergson's vision of evolution, to which I will return (30). For Hearn a concept of endless flux has the potential to dethrone Western teleology.

The enormous power of the Western system in Hearn's work is matched and exceeded by the all-devouring power of Henry Adams's dynamo, which explicitly threatens history itself. When facing the dynamo at the end of *The Education,* Adams does everything but declare the *eschatos:* "Here was a breach of continuity—a rupture in historical sequence! Was it real, or only apparent?" (340). The machine, although a product of historical process, arrives with infinite suddenness, moves with infinite speed. "One lingered long among the dynamos, for they were new, and they gave to history a new phase. . . . The historical mind can think only in historical processes, and probably this was the first time since historians existed, that any of them had sat down helpless before a mechanical sequence" (342). *This* mechanical determinism threatens time itself, rendering sequence incomprehensible: causality is troubled, leaving the historian as mute and aghast as if the seventh seal in Revelation were opened: "When the Lamb opened the seventh seal, there was silence in heaven for about half an hour" (Revelation 8:1). Thus the pairing of dynamo and Virgin: one *eschatos* displaces another, leaving the old eschatology destroyed, yet strangely intact; as when Lyotard comments on Marxism, the eschatological principle is conserved (*Fables* 92). To Adams the "dynamo became a symbol of infinity. . . . [H]e began to feel the forty-foot dynamos as a moral force, much as the early Christians felt the Cross" (380). Early Christianity was, of course, oriented toward the imminent, utter remaking of the world. "Before the end," writes Adams, "one began to pray to it; inherited instinct taught the natural expression of man before silent and infinite force" (380). The new world is fundamentally unlike the old: "In these seven years man had translated himself into a new universe which had no common scale of measurement with the old" (381). Adams echoes the discontinuity of the New Jerusalem with the Old: "The city lies foursquare, its length the same as its width; and he measured the city with his rod, fifteen hundred miles; its length and width and height are equal" (Revelation 21:16).

For a historian of technology, Adams's understanding of technology, in particular the dynamo's rupturing effect upon history, is a kind of romanticism, as Lynn White argues in *Medieval Religion and Technology* (108). But the most interesting aspect of Adams's technological *eschatos* is its representivity: the rupturing, apocalyptic nature of technological change is assumed by both technology's critics and its admirers, without regard for the granular, evolutionary nature of actual technological change. The *image* of the locomotive or dynamo's arrival devours its own historical contingency.

Leo Marx argues that *The Education* demonstrates the dialectical nature of the American novel, because Adams endorses *and* recoils from the technological determinism that has separated him from his family traditions (*Machine* 346). The Virgin and the dynamo "figure an all-embracing conflict: a clash between past and present, unity and diversity, love and power. In his Manichaean fashion he marshals all conceivable values" (347). Marx argues that "the apocalyptic image of the Dynamo and the Virgin is the ultimate expression of the tragic doubleness that Adams locates at the center of modern history" (349)—a doubleness between organic and machine which Lee Quinby argues is also the dualism of seasons that begins the book and the dualism of gender that pervades it (*Anti-Apocalypse* 84). Leo Marx recognizes Adams's apocalyptic mode without seeing that he, too, by accepting the machine's suddenness, writes in the same mode. Quinby argues that Adams's "ironic apocalypse" is paradigmatic for twentieth-century apocalypses, which operate by "restoring a totalizing vision while denying unity and totality of vision" (77, 78). Quinby's and White's readings of Adams show his work as essentially united with the technological apocalypses that precede and follow him.

Has American literature always been dominated by the machine as *telos*? Must the machine-garden dialectic begin with an earth-shattering event that threatens finally to destroy time? Must change be understood as progress toward a *telos,* like Bacon's understanding of technological progress as the means to hasten the Antichrist's coming and the end of history?

In Leo Marx's words, *The Education* begins with "a variant of the pastoral design in describing the rhythmic alternation between the seasonal attitudes toward nature and civilization he had known as a boy" (*Machine* 348). Similarly, near the beginning of his own book Marx envisions the action of Shakespeare's *The Tempest* as the movement of a pendulum between the "poles of nature and civilization," with Prospero's goal being to still the pendulum, thus achieving a harmonious middle state (*Machine* 66). The flaw beneath this conception of the pendulum's sway between nature and civilization/machine is that the machine is old; there was never a time innocent of it. The image of the pendulum is not useless, however; it becomes more useful if we envision it moving between competing technologies and visions of time, representing a conflict between different technological determinisms, different historical visions.

Poe's "Pendulum" and the Sublime

Edgar Allan Poe's "The Pit and the Pendulum" opens with an epitaph rejoicing in the destruction of the Jacobins and thus, implicitly, in the old regime's restoration. Yet, the narrator is no exemplar of traditional values, but a "recusant," a religious dissenter, who is rescued from the Inquisition by General Lasalle, one of Napoleon's generals. The story ends with the old order's destruction—"The Inquisition was in the hands of its enemies"—but *begins* with its (later) restoration (207). It recounts multiple overthrows and reversals, on the historical level of revolution and counterrevolution and the personal level of the narrator's repeated escapes from death. Consider the narrator's response to his death sentence: "[The] inquisitorial voices seemed merged in one dreamy indeterminate hum. It conveyed to my soul the idea of *revolution*—perhaps from its association in fancy with the burr of a mill-wheel" (212). The inquisitors sound like a mill-wheel revolving; this literal, physical revolution is implicitly connected to the political revolution that destroys the Inquisition at the story's end. Revolution qua physical, rotating machine implies revolution qua political transformation. Interestingly, the story was written in 1843 and revised in 1845, at the brink of the revolutions of 1848. The wheel rotates, from old regime to Jacobins to Napoleon to restoration to revolution again.

Clearly, most eighteenth- and nineteenth-century intellectuals believed that science and technology progress and that this material progress largely goes hand in hand with moral and intellectual progress, romanticism's criticism of mechanization notwithstanding. Our conventional wisdom about mainstream Enlightenment thought goes something like this: "The intellectual heritage of technological determinism can be traced to the enthusiasm and faith in technology as a liberating force expressed by leaders of the eighteenth-century Enlightenment" (Smith 2). Benjamin Franklin, for instance, represents belief in technology's positive transformative power, with Carlyle representing belief in its negative transformative power (Smith 3). In either case, the newness of technology is critical, offering a sudden, transforming threat or promise. Franklin's stove, for instance, promised radically more efficient heating—

such a pure and admirable advance that Franklin wanted no remuneration for his invention (*Writings* 1417–18). That same unalloyed good, though, was a threat to Hawthorne, for whom Franklin's wondrous stove threatened to drain the soul from fire (*Tales* 841–48).

From either viewpoint, mechanical innovation drives history. In Robert Heilbroner's formulation, the fact that "machines make history in some sense—that the level of technology has a direct bearing on the human drama—is of course obvious" (54). Technology moves us toward some point, or we use technology to approach some point or moment, depending on how deterministically one formulates it. What are we moving to? Two concepts of this movement are, writes Malcolm Bull, "scientific projections of universal catastrophe" and "the Kantian dream of unending progress" (1). Our mechanical ingenuity may destroy the world through nuclear war or global warming, or we may progress eternally in a science fiction utopia: endless night and endless progress are conventionally our secular possibilities. In religious thought, the significance of technological innovation can be that it hastens the literal *telos* of Christ's return. "Ego to alpha kai to omega, ho protos kai ho eschatos, hē archē kai to telos," announces Christ near the close of Revelation (Aland et al., Revelation 22:13): "I am the alpha and the omega, the first and the last, the beginning and the end." For Bacon, improved technology will hasten the apocalypse and provide weapons against the Antichrist (Pacey, *Maze* 30).

Technology conventionally offers or threatens a new, potentially eternal order. "The Pit and the Pendulum" plays with and problematizes the convention. In Poe's story, we aren't presented with *a* mechanical *telos,* but with *two;* this duality, mirroring the duality of self that torments his fiction, changes everything. Each competing notion of "history" in "The Pit and the Pendulum" proposes its own first (*protos*) and last (*eschatos*), its own beginning (*archē*) and end (*telos*), but the larger story is of a rhythmic motion between these sets of possibilities.

Poe's Inquisition is variously mechanized: the narrator's contact with it is "as if I had touched the wire of a galvanic battery" (213). The dungeon is a technological wonder, with hinged iron walls that can be uniformly heated while in motion. The pendulum can be freely lowered and raised while in motion. The pendulum's appearance is striking: "It was the painted figure of Time as he is commonly represented, save that, in lieu of a scythe, he held what, at a casual glance, I supposed to be the pictured image of a huge pendulum such as we see on antique clocks" (220). The pendulum resembles an antique clock, but is also a guillotine-like killing machine. Like any clock, it spatializes and demarcates time—in particular, the time before death. This spatialization of death-time is a mechanical model of eschatological history, in which events that are measured and driven by technology accelerate to the *eschatos.* The pendulum's death-time is a scale model of God's own death-time: the clockwork universe ends in a clockwork apocalypse, if the Inquisition understands history correctly. Like Bacon, the Inquisition presumably hopes to compress the time before the *eschatos* through technological innovation. God's judgment, like the Inquisition's, is *timed,* even if only he "knows the hour." Frederick Winslow Taylor's rhythmic control of workers' movements in time resembles the way Poe's Inquisition has mastered time; both are directly rooted in the supervisory understanding of time established in Revelation.[1]

But despite its mechanical ingenuity, the Inquisition understands history incompletely. The narrator's multiple escapes do not, in themselves, cause difficulties; they simply reflect the element of free will within the larger deterministic picture. The narrator's revolutionary methodology is more problematic. He deals with his imprisonment by making "effort to exercise my reason," and he "deduces" his real condition (215). He makes a "circuit"—a revolution—of his cell, measuring it deliberately; these "researches" are driven only by a "vague curiosity" (216). Despite his terror before the pendulum's death-time, he suddenly masters himself: "For the first time during many hours . . . I *thought,*" which leads to him manipulating rats into freeing him (223–24). His calculated, Enlightenment-style reasoning doesn't free him from his prison, but because it exists within a larger political context, in which the overall cause of the Enlightenment/revolution is advancing, he gains enough time to be freed by the Enlightenment's revolutionary representatives.

Is an Enlightenment-teleological concept of time and technology then victorious over the Christian-teleological concept? Hardly. Despite the French Revolution's "innovations" (really, as Wallerstein argues, the rationalization of an existing system), such as total warfare and the guillotine's industrialization of execution (a version of Giedion's disassembly line), the counterrevolution crushes it at the *beginning* of the story. The mill-wheel revolves: presumably the wheel of history will turn again, replacing the Christian-teleological understanding of time and technology with the Kantian-teleological understanding once more. Poe, typically, refuses to turn two into one: he adheres to no single stable concept of time and technology. That dualistic suspension is his characteristic form of the sublime.

Poe treats machinery as gothic, not modern: the pendulum is like a painting of a pendulum, dominated by the image of Father Time. Technology has not *erupted* into history, but is embedded in the medieval *and* the modern; rather than disrupting history, it *has* history. Deliberately or not, Poe's gothic technology makes a vital historical point: to whatever extent machines make history, they have been doing so for a very long time. The spinning mill-wheel Poe invokes at the story's beginning was, although important to nineteenth-century industry, not a creation of it. The *Domesday Book* lists 5,624 mills for three thousand English communities in 1086 (White, *Social Change* 84). Medieval power technology was so pervasive that some have argued that there was a *medieval* industrial revolution; Jean Gimpel argues that there were as many as one mill for every fifty households in eleventh-century England (12). Then as now, technology was used for social control as well as economic gain: powered grain mills and cathedrals centralized and symbolized power (Pacey, *Maze* 4). The church was not opposed to power technology, contrary to stereotypes: the Cistercian order particularly was at the forefront of developing and disseminating power technology; water-powered model factories on the same scale as the church were universal features of Cistercian monasteries (Gimpel 67). The medieval church and civilization were anything but technologically backward: they were arguably industrialized. Moreover, despite the arrival of the steam engine, Nye argues that steam had hardly begun to displace the old-fashioned mill wheel until late in the nineteenth century, only overtaking it about 1890 (*Power* 82). In other words, the characteristic medieval technology continued to dominate American industry long after Poe's death.

Poe's association of the old regime, the gothic, and medieval religion with mechanical ingenuity is no anachronism. Even as the mill-wheel of history brings revolution and counterrevolution cyclically to power, neither one is unfamiliar with sophisticated technology, as the dual death machines of pendulum and guillotine demonstrate. Neither in actual history nor in "The Pit and the Pendulum" is the machine a sudden arrival in the eighteenth and nineteenth centuries. The conflict in Poe's story is not between a progressive, revolutionary, technological world-picture and an atavistic, medieval world-picture, as one might expect in a story about a "recusant" trapped by the Inquisition. Rather, it concerns a repeating, oscillating conflict between two concepts of time, technology, and progress: a Christian-teleological concept and a Kantian-teleological concept. History is not driven by *one* technological determinism, but *two.* Industry and technology are medieval *and* modern, American, European, and other. The cyclical contest between two models of history, one leading to the Christian *telos,* the other leading endlessly upward in "purposefulness without purpose," driven by a Kantian teleology, hints that both concepts of history are ideas (monads?) trapped within a larger cyclic history. Can either of these radically different linear models of history break free from cyclic history?

The dueling world-pictures are associated with death machines: the pendulum and the guillotine. In both deterministic models, human potentiality is subordinated to mechanical processes; yet the narrator is saved, because *neither* linear-mechanical world-picture is dominant within the larger revolutions of history. The oscillation between revolution and counterrevolution opens a space for meaningful action and an approximation of free will, almost anticipating Ralph Ellison's accomplishment in *Invisible Man.* Either form of technological determinism would individually eliminate human freedom; together, they allow motion beyond what either Taylorism or monasticism permits.

Nye's *American Technological Sublime* is concerned precisely with the awe inspired by technology—an awe that confronts us both in the tools of the Inquisition and, with a deeper reading, in Poe's clashing technological systems, each sublime in its own way. Nye would find no incompatibility between the Inquisition and the technological sublime: "an essentially religious feeling," the technological sublime is "an integral part of contemporary consciousness, and its emergence and exfoliation into several distinct forms during the past two centuries is inscribed within public life" (xiii). Nye is focused on exploring the varieties of the technological sublime, from the early variety, stimulated partially by works such as the Erie Canal, which formed a "moral machine," to later, corporate varieties that were "sanitized and safe"—the sublime of Disneyland (213).

Nye is concerned with the shifting, distinctive nature of the American sublime. At a particular historical moment, with the commercialization of Niagara Falls, the American public began to acquire a taste for the sublime; from the beginning, the "natural" sublime was linked with consumption, with thc wilderness being "appropriated as a natural symbol of the nation while . . . being transformed into a man-made landscape" (37). With the appropriation and destruction of nature, in other words, comes the appreciation of nature as sublime. The work of other critics interested in the sublime has followed Nye especially in one critical way; Lee Rozelle writes that the "sublime is itself a system, one that morphs and adapts to each period's critical caprice" (5). There is a sublime for every era, in other words. Rozelle argues that the ecosublime belongs to us—or perhaps better, we to it. The ecosublime "can be defined as the awe and terror of heightened awareness of the ecological home"—an awe and terror that arises when the house is burning (1).

Both Nye and Rozelle emphasize the shifting nature of the sublime, which adjusts to meet the needs of every historical moment. Both make their arguments in convincing detail. Laying aside the significant details of the technological sublime and the ecological sublime themselves—worthy subjects detailed in the two books—I turn to a question in line with my own project. Granted that the sublime continually shifts, what does that very fluidity (as in Poe's case) mean? Nye's understanding of technology is nuanced and historically complex; part of my evidence for the granularity of technological change, in fact, comes from his work. His analysis of the technological sublime is not an analysis of machines as such but of the "social context" of technology (xv). In other words, his analysis of the sublime is another confirmation of the fact that technology is continually experienced as abrupt, even apocalyptic: the self is overwhelmed by the technological object and the ecological home.

And yet, Spenser and Shakespeare elaborated visions of that technological sublime before it supposedly existed. Poe's opposed technological systems articulate not only the technological sublime but also the clash between two different versions of it, one medieval (in which awe in the face of technology inspires repentance) and one "revolutionary." The very fluidity of the technological sublime illustrates its continuity and long duration, to anticipate my eventual turn to Bergson—as well as the way in which literature (Poe) anticipates theory (Nye, Rozelle) where technology is concerned.

The Question Concerning Time and Technology

Recall that in *Frankenstein* "the organic" wins a tentative victory against "the machine." This victory is neither conclusive nor heartwarming. When Frankenstein and the monster try to negotiate a settlement, the monster plans a pastoral future: "I will go to the vast wilds of South America. My food is not that of man; I do not destroy the lamb and the kid to glut my appetite. . . . We shall make our bed of dried leaves" (Shelley 141). The monster rejects the machine for the garden. Curiously, Leo Marx, although working with the idea that in America the pastoral can be (re)discovered, does not discuss Shelley substantively (*Machine* 100). Instead, he casually references "stock expressions" of "the Frankenstein fable: the story of the robot that destroys its heartless creator" (184). This conventional simplification makes *Frankenstein* into a symbol of the organic/mechanical conflict. But this "machine" only wants to enter a garden: *Frankenstein* is the story of a creator too undisciplined, too unmechanical to impose mechanical discipline on his creation, and of a creation ("robot") who *never from the beginning* acts predictably or mechanically.

Marx's failure to attend to *Frankenstein*'s complexities, to say nothing of Poe's peculiar technological sublime, is significant. Instead of dealing with the long presence or complexity of the machine, Marx emphasizes its abruptness: "the sudden appearance of machine technology in the underdeveloped 'new world' provided the sensory components of a—perhaps the—great central figurative conception of nineteenth-century American culture." Marx acknowledges that the Industrial Revolution is preceded by the philosophy of "Newton, Descartes, and Bacon," but he insists that the ideal of the pastoral was upheld by the "exponents of the Romantic recoil" (*Machine* 376). He mentions the machine's origins only to emphasize its suddenness, never to question it.

Despite considerable knowledge of the history of technology, Marx is trapped into seeing the machine's arrival as sudden and recent, downplaying the fact that "industrialization" and "mechanization" are long historical processes under way by the eleventh century, if not earlier (all "industrial revolutions" are footnotes to the slow agricultural revolution of the Neolithic). Even the technologies critical to the subduing of the "Wild West" were well within the practical reach of medieval engineering (Basalla 51; White, *Religion* 112–20). The long, textured history of the machine is important in understanding such "gothic" writers as Mary Shelley and Poe. For Shelley, Frankenstein's hypermodern work is rooted in discredited alchemy; for Poe, "the machine" belongs as much to the Inquisition as to the Enlightenment.

Why are the ideas of the "industrial revolution" and the machine's sudden appearance on the pastoral landscape so powerful? Why is mechanization's long history, which is better understood through Braudel and Wallerstein's adaptation of Bergson's *longue durée* than through the convulsions of Whiggish history, buried and replaced with the urgency—utopian, dystopian, or ambivalent—of the machine's abrupt arrival? Our dominant accounts of the machine are teleological, and often eschatological. The machine makes history; the machine brings a new order; it hastens the Antichrist's coming, or allows us to spread liberal democracy across the universe. Perhaps the machine does "drive history"; I don't deny the importance of the hydrogen bomb or the McCormick reaper. But the machine that drives history is also driven *by* history, that is, by our understanding of history and time. "We" do not simply observe the machine's suddenness, or merely create it; we insist that it be sudden, and we create an account of the machine that renders its role as *telos* clear.

I return to a central irony of *The Machine in the Garden:* Marx believed that the conflict between the organic and the mechanical was ending: "I closed the book . . . with the implication that today (1964), in the era of high technology, the pastoral response to industrial society almost certainly had become anachronistic, and that it soon might be expected to lose its hold on the minds of disaffected Americans" (383–84). For an apocalyptic writer, *now* is always the fulcrum on which time turns; history is *now* being swallowed by a new world (the apocalyptic and the sublime are related). In his late essay "The Idea of 'Technology' and Postmodern Pessimism" Marx recognizes that "the progressive world picture," based in the "late-eighteenth-century idea that modern history itself is a record of progress," is problematic; yet this notion of progress lies behind his 1964 belief that the pastoral was passing (239). Marx, following his intellectual grandfather Lewis Mumford, is enmeshed in the same teleology he wants to reject, and he never disentangles his acceptance from his rejection. What is to be done? How can we authentically question the machine as *telos* and *eschatos* and thereby broadly question teleology and eschatology? This issue demands an understanding of the relationship between time and technology: Why is technology persistently linked to "the end," and can it be understood differently? These questions occupy this whole book; this section is an initial attempt at a theoretical answer.

Following a long tradition of eschatological philosophy and history, Max Horkheimer and Theodor Adorno blame the desolation of modernity on the tradition of Enlightenment, most famously in *Dialectic of Enlightenment,* which begins: "Enlightenment, understood in the widest sense as the advance of thought, has always aimed at liberating human beings from fear and installing them as masters. Yet the wholly enlightened earth is radiant with triumphant calamity. Enlightenment's program was the disenchantment of the world" (1). A disenchanted world is a world enslaved: "Technology is the essence of knowledge. . . . What human beings seek to learn from nature is how to use it to dominate wholly both it and human beings" (2). Under Enlightenment, animism is destroyed and meaning abandoned; all "Gods and qualities" are destroyed; the whole universe is reduced to man's prey (3–6). In the "mathematization of nature," traced back to Galileo, "Thought is reified as an autonomous, automatic process, aping the machine it has itself produced, so that it can finally be replaced by the machine" (19). Reason becomes purely instrumental, serving "as a universal tool for the fabrication of all other tools, rigidly purpose-directed" (23). Reason enslaves the world, rendering it an undifferentiated heap of matter and energy: Enlightenment, technological reason, becomes only a means, yet this means is enthroned as the only possible end. Doom seems complete, although the messianic promise of Horkheimer and Adorno's colleague Walter Benjamin's philosophy of history remains dimly alive. In "Theses on the Philosophy of

History," Benjamin assails the enslavement of nature in favor of its transformation, praising Fourier against vulgar Marxism:

> The new conception of labor amounts to the exploitation of nature, which with naïve complacency is contrasted with the exploitation of the proletariat. According to Fourier, as a result of efficient cooperative labor, four moons would illuminate the earthly night, the ice would recede from the poles, sea water would no longer taste salty, and beasts of prey would do man's bidding. All this illustrates a kind of labor which, far from exploiting nature, is capable of delivering her of the creations which lie dormant in her womb as potentials. (*Illuminations* 259)

In Benjamin's messianic thought, spurred by fascism and technological domination, the world cries for redemption: "A historical materialist approaches a historical subject only when he encounters it as a monad. In this structure, he recognizes the sign of a Messianic cessation of happening, or, put differently, a revolutionary chance in the fight for the oppressed past" (262–63). "Arresting of happening," the "crystallization of the monad" allows the flow of time to be mastered: technological reason can be confronted by arresting it in thought, which will lead to the utopian transformation of humanity, nature, and the earth itself (262–63).

Benjamin's messianic moment (monad), like the dominant biblical messianic moments (but unlike, following Frank Kermode, the *original* gospel of Mark), is complete, closed, and wholly self-sufficient, such that, following Leibniz's *Monadology,* "Every present state in a simple substance [Monad][2] is a natural consequence of its preceding state, in such a way that its present is big with its future" (256). The crystallization of Benjamin's messianic moment is, as with the messianic moment of Revelation (Christ's "Ego to alpha kai to omega, ho protos kai ho eschatos, hē archē kai to telos"), the crystallization (spatialization) of *all time.*

While Benjamin asserts that a new kind of labor will "deliver" nature of her creations rather than exploiting her, the difference between a future in which nature is "exploited" and one in which beasts of prey "do man's bidding" is unclear. In Benjamin's messianic moment, time is frozen and known: the earth is remade, transformed to bring forth its full potential. Is this not domination?

Tellingly, when Horkheimer and Adorno assail Francis Bacon as the originator of nature's disenchantment and enslavement, they omit Bacon's dream of using "disenchanted nature" to hasten the Antichrist's coming (1, 34; Pacey, *Maze* 30). Bacon's vision of technological domination, like Benjamin's "deliverance," is explicitly eschatological: nature will be made new, in a particular way. How different is Bacon's *eschatos* from Benjamin's? The manner in which Benjamin's eschatology mirrors other technological eschatologies may explain Horkheimer and Adorno's reluctance to create their own technological-utopian fantasy—but even they step in that direction when discussing the literal insanity of "political reality": "the abundance of goods which could be produced everywhere and simultaneously makes the struggle for raw materials and markets seem ever more anachronistic" (169).

While our industrial accomplishments are impressive, the claim that struggles over raw materials and markets are anachronistic shows boundless, teleological faith precisely in technological domination—a faith we should resist. The ability of nature to deliver the goods should always be in doubt: all technological wizardry aside, wartime Britain and Germany could hardly feed themselves. "Nature" does not answer all questions that are put to it in the affirmative, as should be clear in an era in which, in Roy Porter's dry words, "the Darwinian evolutionary battle between mankind and microbes is itself unpredictable" (*Benefit* 715). Faith in our potentially boundless productivity is what Andrew McMurry, writing in *Environmental Renaissance,* has sarcastically called "the liberal formula, hearkening always ahead to the age of postscarcity" (23). My own work, while not ecocriticism as such, is congruent with much ecocriticism: one aspect of the technological teleology I analyze is precisely the groundless faith in an always-imminent era of postscarcity. A well-founded ecocritical and ecological vision demands the abandonment of the eschatological dream of the end of scarcity; the Frankfurt school, despite appearances, offers a problematic foundation for any ecological vision.

Although Martin Heidegger was ideologically and politically vastly different from the Frankfurt school, his critique of technology, developed during the same period as theirs, is markedly similar: even political and philosophical opponents tend to share ideological presumptions about technology as a kind of ideological substrate. Heidegger's terminology is distinctive, but his understanding of technology is substantially familiar; Rüdiger Safranski's intellectual biography of Heidegger places him in a lineage that sees Hobbesian mechanical materialism as a ruinous choice, while Heidegger's Germany was saturated by visions of a technological apocalypse, for instance in Oswald Spengler's *Decline of the West* (31, 92). In *Heidegger's Confrontation with Modernity,* Michael Zimmerman analyzes Heidegger's indebtedness to various reactionary thinkers who predicted technological apocalypses, especially Ernst Jünger (46–47). Heidegger, while following Jünger and in step with Nazism, believed that "humanity must submit to the technological *Gestalt*" yet that one need not accept oneself as an object or an instrument; rather, we must open to the suffering "associated with the technological domination of humanity and the earth," so that technological destiny could be fulfilled and a new start made (89–90).

Heidegger's embrace of Nazism was partially fueled by his belief that Nazism could oppose the Russo-American "technological frenzy"; Nazism offered an organic world-picture, not a mechanical one. In *Introduction to Metaphysics,* Heidegger argues that Russia and America share "the same hopeless frenzy of unchained technology and of the rootless organization of the average man. When the farthest corner of the globe has been conquered technologically and can be exploited economically; when any incident you like, in any place you like, at any time you like, becomes instantly accessible . . . when time is nothing but speed, instantaneity, and simultaneity, and time as history has vanished from all Dasein of all peoples . . . what then?" (40). The problem with technology is that it flattens time, eliminating true historical Being. Anticipating the anti-globalization movement, Heidegger argued later in his career that "dwelling occurs only when entities are 'gathered' (*versammelt*) into a world in which the integrity of things is preserved. Such a world would be intrinsically 'local,' bound up with place in a way wholly foreign to the planetary reach of modern technology" (Zimmerman 151). Modern technology is wrong because it destroys connections, turning all things and people into mere instruments. Because technology threatens to displace time as it is normally understood, resisting it demands deep transformation—in Heidegger's case, a rediscovery of an early Greek orientation toward the world. Heidegger assumes that the spatialization of time can be literalized, that history really can be destroyed, that we really are standing on the brink of doom. The correctness or applicability of teleology and spatialized time to all things never comes under question, and hence, inevitably, Heidegger anticipates the *eschatos.*

By the war's end, Heidegger understood that he'd been wrong to see Nazism as the true hope against the machine's sudden entry into the garden. He still hoped for "the Occidental," the organic, but, according to Safranski, he came to believe that "Official Germany can no longer be its location, for there, as Heidegger keeps reiterating, the 'machine economy' and man's degradation into mere material have been victorious" (329). Technological domination, for Heidegger, as for Horkheimer and Adorno, seems inescapable.

In his postwar essay "The Question Concerning Technology," Heidegger assumes that modern technology is essentially different from previous technologies: "The revealing that rules in modern technology is a challenging, which puts to nature the unreasonable demand that it supply energy that can be extracted and stored as such. But does this not hold for the old windmill as well? No. Its sails do indeed turn in the wind; they are left entirely to the wind's blowing. But the windmill does not unlock energy from the air currents in order to store it. . . . The work of the peasant does not challenge the soil of the field" (14–15). Heidegger assumes the otherness of "modern" technology: the hydroelectric dam and the steam engine are *essentially* different from the windmill; the peasant's farm is *essentially* different from the mine (one interesting aspect of Nye's *Consuming Power* is his analysis of the persistence of "old" power systems under the regime of "new" ones). But mining, like agriculture, has been a human activity for millennia. If mining is modern technology, then modernity, like peasantry, dates to the late Neolithic. Coal had been used in European industry for many centuries, while the steam engine, understood within its original mining context, is continuous with earlier mining technologies. As Arnold Pacey details, Leo Marx's "middle landscape"—equivalent to Heidegger's pastoral ideal, rooted in Hölderin and the German peasantry—was always technological: "The middle landscape was essentially a remade garden, harmonizing with nature to a degree, but artificial in its control of planting and wildlife and its use of machines. Moreover, the early phases of industrialization could often fit neatly into this middle landscape" (*Meaning* 139). Medieval Europe was sufficiently mechanized, argues Lynn White, that it rested not "on the back of sweating slaves or coolies but primarily on non-human power" (*Religion* 22). Medieval European technology is fully continuous with earlier technologies and the technologies of other parts of the world, from the Middle East to China and India (Pacey, *World*). The machine is rooted in what Heidegger sees as the garden. Heidegger, like many romantics before him, attacks modern technology from an ahistorical understanding of peasant life: the late German model of agriculture becomes the model for authentic Being itself; curiously, Heidegger and others ignore the tremendous transformation wrought by agriculture and water mills. The same is true, albeit to a lesser extent, for Horkheimer, Adorno, and Marcuse.

Heidegger's eschatology calls for a "turn," emerging from the heart of technology itself: the way out is through, and time's fulcrum is *now:* "when destining reigns in the mode of Enframing, it is the supreme danger. . . . As soon as what is unconcealed no longer concerns man even as object, but does so, rather, exclusively as standing-reserve, and man in the midst of objectlessness is nothing but the orderer of the standing-reserve, he then comes to the brink of a precipitous fall . . . to the point where he himself will have to be taken as standing-reserve. Meanwhile man . . . exalts himself to the posture of lord of the earth" ("Question" 26–27). We can be saved only in technology's "coming to presence" which harbors "the possible arising of the saving power" (32). Grace descends at the omega moment: a familiar story. Heidegger's saving power is based in a primordial connection between art and technology: "There was a time when it was not technology alone that bore the name *technē*. . . . Once there was a time when the bringing-forth of the true into the beautiful was called *technē*. And the *poiēsis* of the fine arts was also called *technē*" (34). The original meaning of *technē* can be restored through art, driven by the "frenziedness of technology," such that "the essence of technology may come to presence." Only through art, which is both akin to and alien from technology, can true reflection upon technology take place, but "only if reflection on art . . . does not shut its eyes to the constellation of truth after which we are *questioning*" (35).

For Heidegger, an abyss divides modern technology from premodern technology and from its own essence, which can only be understood through art, an argument much like Marcuse's in *One-Dimensional Man* (238). For Heidegger, unlike Marcuse, the "turn" is not essentially political, but ontological: it deals with technology's essence, not mere means and ends; as Zimmerman argues, for Heidegger modern technology is not "a development within the history of humanity" but within the history of Being (166).

Despite the complexities of Heidegger's and the Frankfurt school's understandings of technology, both ultimately idealize the same "middle state." Their apparent divergence is really unity, as best demonstrated by the work of Marcuse. Marcuse went from being a Marxist to being one of Heidegger's students to being a member of the Frankfurt school, partially in response to Heidegger's embrace of Nazism; intellectually, he remained in productive tension with Heidegger, as John Abromeit details in "Marcuse's Critical Encounter with Heidegger."

In his 1941 article "Some Social Implications of Modern Technology," published in the Frankfurt Institute's journal *Studies in Philosophy and Social Science,* Marcuse argues that all human spontaneity has been transferred to machinery, with individual achievement being transformed into "standardized efficiency" (*One-Dimensional* 44). He warns against those who criticize particular technologies rather than the technological system, which assumes its totalizing, dominating character by creating and enforcing scarcity. What is the "technological system," though, and why is it clearly distinct from individual technologies?

> Technology is taken as a social process in which Technics proper (that is, the technical apparatus of industry, transportation, communication) is but a partial factor. We do not ask for the influence or effect of technology on the human individuals. For they are themselves an integral part and factor of technology. . . . Technology, as a mode of production, as the totality of instruments, devices and

> contrivances which characterize the machine age is thus at the same time a mode of organizing and perpetuating (or changing) social relationships, a manifestation of prevalent thought and behavior patters, an instrument for control and domination. (41)

The core of Marcuse's argument—which is implicit in most other critics of technology, Heidegger, Horkheimer, and Adorno foremost—is the unexamined assumption that at some recent moment technics proper enabled "technology" as a system of domination. This assertion is undefended, as it is from Carlyle to Heidegger. The "special historical form" in which "technics is utilized" is so readily apparent that it doesn't even need to be defined. The division between *this* historical moment and all prior historical moments is so abrupt, so absolute, that only those blind to the eschatological event could fail to perceive it.

Under technological domination as the Frankfurt school understands it, time is bifurcated into "before technology" and "after technology": the culture industry threatens to replace art, manipulated abundance replaces true scarcity, domination replaces a contingent freedom. These tendencies, already well developed in the work of Horkheimer, Adorno, and Marcuse in the 1940s, acquire a prophetic glow in Marcuse's *One-Dimensional Man,* which argues (as does Heidegger) that under technological domination, a potential utopia grows:

> The technological processes of mechanization and standardization might release individual energy into a yet uncharted realm of freedom beyond necessity. The very structure of human existence would be altered; the individual would be liberated from the work world's imposing upon him alien needs and alien possibilities. . . . If the productive apparatus could be organized and directed toward the satisfaction of the vital needs, its control might well be centralized; such control would not prevent individual autonomy, but render it possible. (2)

The possibility of the nearly effortless satisfaction of vital needs is simply asserted; we have entered into McMurry's realm of "postscarcity." The efficacy of technological domination is known and trusted, and it is as obvious as the very gulf between technological and pre-technological civilization.

In *Heidegger and Marcuse: The Catastrophe and Redemption of History* (2005), Andrew Feenberg argues that Marcuse "emphasizes that reason is bound to civilizational projects but he cannot explain concretely how this actually plays out because he confuses two very different levels of rationality. The level of natural scientific abstractions must be distinguished from the concrete technical disciplines through which those abstractions become historically active" (132). Marcuse never successfully distinguishes between technics and technology, or between technics and science, despite his sporadic attempts to do so, and if he cannot show how particular technics relate to technology (as domination) as a whole, then he cannot show that the technological system belongs to any particular time—that is, our time.

In "Some Social Implications of Modern Technology," Marcuse asserts, as does Heidegger in "The Question Concerning Technology," that the essence of technological civilization belongs to no particular technology. Technological domination emerges from a technological worldview, rooted in Western science and metaphysics, that "freed nature from inherent ends and stripped matter of all but quantifiable qualities" (*One-Dimensional* 157). This technological worldview does not develop from technology itself but from the history of philosophy, including the use of slave labor in ancient Greece and Plato's prioritization of *logos* over *eros* (147). The technological worldview, although tied to no particular technology, is related to the total impact and potential of all technologies, which enables the strengthening of domination even as its yoke seems to lift. At a critical moment in *One-Dimensional Man,* Marcuse writes:

> The domination of man by man is still the historical continuum that links pre-technological and technological Reason. However, the society which projects and undertakes the technological transformation of nature alters the base of domination by gradually replacing personal dependence . . . with dependence on the "objective order of things." . . . domination now generates a higher rationality—that

> of a society which sustains its hierarchic structure while exploiting ever more efficiently the natural and mental resources, and distributing the benefits of this exploitation on an ever-larger scale. (144)

Despite his opposition to technological reason, Marcuse believes that it generates a *higher* rationality; the abrupt rupture between pre-technological and technological thought is also an ascension, if only into tyranny, that opens the possibility of a utopian turn, as in Heidegger. Marcuse implicitly criticizes technological reason as *in*sufficiently directional and linear, for stripping nature of an internal teleology (147). He accepts without question that the technological worldview is essentially Western and contemporary, that we can speak objectively of contemporary technology and technological reason being *more* than other technologies and reasons, that science drives technology and metaphysics drives science.

But the histories of science and technology are *not* one, and the assumed relationship is wrong; technology, even "machine technology," is old, and while eliding science and technology together may serve political purposes, it is historically problematic: "Contemporary technology seems to have had a greater effect on science than the other way around, and one needs to be wary of concluding that the modern alliance of science and technology appeared with the Scientific Revolution" (Dorn and McClellan 269). The largely anonymous history of technology is easily devoured by the histories of philosophy and science, which have no such reticence. Marcuse comes closer to grappling with the reality of technology than most of its critics, but his attempt, while successfully bridging Heidegger and the Frankfurt school, is insufficiently historical: it is yet another exercise in teleology and eschatology, with essentially no element of technological history.

"Technology has replaced ontology," Marcuse asserts in "From Ontology to Technology." Bridging Heidegger and the Frankfurt school, he asserts that technology has violated or displaced authentic being—and yet this argument depends on the undefended and essentially incorrect belief in technology's eruption onto a pastoral scene. Right and left alike, the great critics of technology fall into incoherence on the most basic of historical issues.

Why do "we" intellectuals generally understand technological change eschatologically and teleologically? Why do "we" make radical distinctions between past and present technologies? There is no true discontinuity between "traditional" and "modern" technology: the machine arrives incrementally, not abruptly, and if a worldview (call it enframing) characterizes modern technology, there is no reason to see that worldview as itself abrupt. "Our" habit of speaking of modern technology's "essence" or "nature" is fundamentally a prejudice, albeit one with a long pedigree. Modern technology has distinctive characteristics, but the devil is in the details, not in the "essence."

Heidegger demonstrates one peril of belief in a mechanical eschatology: horror of the "frenziedness" of American and Russian technology drove him to see the Nazis as the garden's defenders, against the Soviet-American machine. Heidegger's error is clear: if the war had anything to do with opposing technological systems, these systems are more like the historically specific (yet sublime) opposing technologies of Poe's "The Pit and the Pendulum" than they are like the Virgin/dynamo divide of Henry Adams's *Education*.

We labor under heavy misconceptions: machine technology is as rooted in medieval Europe as it is in the nineteenth century; our obsessions with mechanical artifacts and especially weapons rather than technique-tool-container complexes lead to underestimating non-Western technologies; technology and literature precede the "mechanistic" philosophies of science that supposedly generate them. Belief in the machine's time-shattering entry into the garden is ideological, not historical. Yet critics and enthusiasts, leftists and reactionaries, subscribe to shared beliefs: technology is sudden, its moment is now, and it drives toward some end, whether wondrous or terrible.

Even those who view technology deterministically usually acknowledge that it should be a human means for human ends; deep confidence that technology can be regulated by reason lies, for instance, at the heart of Jürgen Habermas's *The Future of Human Nature,* a meditation on genetic engineering. Habermas's ever-careful and measured argument ends on a Kantian note: "Would not the first human being to determine, *at his own discretion,* the natural essence of another human being at the same time destroy the equal freedoms that exist among persons of equal birth in order to ensure their difference?" (115). This supremely, even sublimely liberal critique of unrestrained gene manipulation (which retains confidence in limited, regulated gene manipulation) ends on Leo Marx's divide between organism and machine: we must draw the line in genetic engineering at making the essence of another human being. Human "essence" must not be manufactured, that is, *technē;* liberals and reactionaries alike reject crossing that line.

Yet dividing *bios* from *technē,* "natural" from manufactured life, modern from premodern technology, is impossible. Life makes and is made; contemporary humanity manipulates its environment in distinctive ways, but all environments are made by life, as Richard Lewontin (a geneticist who writes on the deterministic, capitalist ideology at work in contemporary biology) argues in *Biology as Ideology:* "Organisms do not experience environments. They create them" (109). Life creates its world, and it mutually creates the life around it. Genetic engineering is perilous—far more so than Habermas acknowledges—but it threatens no "essence."

In their influential essay "Autopoiesis: The Organization of the Living," Humberto Maturana and Francisco Varela advance the notion that life is best defined as an autopoietic machine, that is, a machine that "continuously generates and specifies its own organization through its operation as a system of production of its own components"; it is a homeostatic system that "has its own organization . . . as the fundamental variable which it maintains constant" (79). That is, in some sense, living organisms are self-producing machines: *bios* is a special form of *technē.* Although the concept of autopoiesis has its uses, and has been deployed to considerable effect in the social sciences and humanities, I find this conceptual framework both problematic and illuminating. This is a concept of life that deliberately sidelines its most interesting aspects: the fact that all life interacts with other life, creating an environment in the process. Each organism, under the regime of autopoiesis, becomes a monad; Maturana and Varela's struggles to explain how "autopoietic machines" interact with one another mirror Leibniz's similar struggles in *Monadology.* In the process, they debunk teleology and emphasize the inner connection of *bios* and *technē.* A full engagement with their texts is beyond the scope of this project, but my fundamental divergence from their work is that they see *bios* as a particular form of *technē,* a self-generating technique, whereas I see *technē* as a *universal* attribute of *bios. Technē* is what *bios does,* not what it *is;* it is an attribute, not (as for Maturana and Varela) a full description of *bios.*

Earlier I wrote briefly on the convergence of this project with what I see as the mainstream of ecocriticism; here I must mark a point of divergence. Most ecocritics are too ready to accept the reality of "nature" as a given. I take Andrew McMurry as an example: "I want to think about how primary, nonhumanized nature . . . has been *systematically* expunged from the world, to be replaced by what Marx called 'second nature' " (5). Politically, this rhetoric serves legitimate purposes (including promoting our own survival), but it is theoretically flawed, rooted in an eschatological way of thinking that ignores the fact that life, by its very nature, always makes its own environment. "Second nature" was always already with us, even before humanity. Even the notion of "species" has become problematic, badly undercutting "essence" as anything but an intellectual chimera. And this takes me to a thinker who resists thinking in terms of essence and speciation.

The assertion that modern thought spatializes time is central to most philosophical critiques of technology; a curious attribute of this critique is that it necessarily accepts the spatialization it critiques, by radically demarcating modernity. Critics of spatialized time generally accept that it *works.* One remarkable exception is Henri Bergson, who criticizes not the ontological or ethical impact of spatialized time but rather the accuracy of the model. Bergson argues that it is easier and more natural to think in terms of discrete change and spatialized time than in terms of evolution: "In vain, therefore, does life evolve before our eyes as continuous creations of unforeseeable form: the idea always persists that form, unforseeability and continuity are mere appearance—the outward reflection of our own ignorance. What is presented to the senses as a continuous history would break up, we are told, into a series of successive states" (*Creative* 30). Thinking in spatialized time and discrete change is natural—and wrong. It is natural, for instance, to assume that the machine arrived suddenly, that we *switch* from Virgin to dynamo, from nature to "second nature": natural, but wrong.

For Bergson, spatialized time and instrumental thought are fundamental not merely to modernity but to the biological mind. In *Creative Evolution* he critiques the very applicability of a spatialized time to life: "in astronomy, physics, and chemistry . . . certain aspects of the present, important for science, are calculable as functions of the immediate past. Nothing of the sort in the domain of life. . . . [T]he present moment of a living body does not find its explanation in the moment immediately before, [all] the past of the organism must be added to that moment, its heredity—in fact, the whole of a very long history" (20). Spatialized time is useful but inapplicable to life, and it has a complex history, rather than being defined by linear equations (here Bergson anticipates De Landa's Deleuzian deployment of chaos theory). To solve problems we must think instrumentally, but by doing so we reduce the universe to raw materials and empty space.

Bergson analyzes reason from an angle problematic for positivism, by arguing that reason specifically and primordially exists for changing the world (environment, in Lewontin's terminology). Reason *is* instrumentality itself; abstract reasoning exists only on the margins of thought: "Our intellect has been cast in the mold of action. Speculation is a luxury, while action is a necessity. . . . We are born artisans as we are born geometricians, and indeed we are geometricians only because we are artisans. Thus the human intellect, inasmuch as it is fashioned for the needs of human action . . . proceeds at the same time by intention and by calculation, by adapting means to ends and by thinking out mechanisms of more and more geometrical form" (*Creative* 44–45). Physical science must treat the universe mechanically, but philosophy must not; yet, attempting to approach the universe non-instrumentally violates the nature of reason. Life is oriented toward "an effort to engraft on to the necessity of physical forces the largest possible amount of *indetermination,*" that is, freedom (114). Life gathers energy from matter and releases it: life can be regarded as a machine, but as one that produces freedom or indeterminacy (115). To appropriate Heidegger's terminology, all life arrays the universe as standing-reserve. Paradoxically, intelligence exists *for* generating freedom, but it does so by treating the universe instrumentally, fixing on forms that can be controlled and altered. Intelligence is inextricably linked with manufacture; mankind would be better called *Homo faber* than *Homo sapiens,* and intelligence is characterized originally by tool making (139).

Bergson does not justify instrumental reasoning, but he does explain its pervasiveness, which derives from the fundamental orientation of life toward shaping its environment. He argues that we live time as "duration" but think it spatially, incrementally: "Just as we separate in space, we fix in time. The intellect is not made to think *evolution*. . . . [T]he intellect represents *becoming* as a series of *states,* each of which is homogeneous with itself and consequently does not change" (163). Life—and particularly consciousness—is paradoxical, existing "to create with matter, which is necessity itself, an instrument of freedom, to make a machine which should triumph over mechanism, and to use the determinism of nature to pass through the meshes of the net which this very determinism had spread" (264). The mind is not suddenly, eschatologically threatened by modern technology, although Bergson acknowledges that the steam engine is *the* characteristic of his era (139). Rather, life is an ongoing struggle between consciousness and "automatism" (264). For Bergson, what many see as the crisis of modernity—technology's threat to time and the mind—constitutes life. Life struggles to act in a universe with limited resources, to be aware despite a universal tendency toward automatism. Consciousness, which is the freedom toward which life urges, is conflicted, for in its very freedom it perceives the universe instrumentally: "We are at ease only in the discontinuous, in the immobile, in the dead" (29). The machine's assault on time is equiprimordial with thought. The conflict between organism and machine is real, but it is enduring and internal rather than external and abrupt.

Even Bergson eventually takes an eschatological turn on technology. Despite his skepticism about suddenness and abruptness, he believes in progress: life evolves *up,* and this belief conditions his understanding of technology. Anticipating cybernetic theorists and critics, Bergson sees continuity between organs and tools (also a theme in Heidegger's *Being and Time*): "If our organs are natural instruments, our instruments must then be artificial organs" (*Sources* 298). This leads to a distinctive understanding of modernity, which posthumanist theory would do well to attend to. Because our tools have grown enormously in scale and complexity, we don't measure up to them; our extended bodies outgrow our spirit: "the body, now larger, calls for a bigger soul. . . . Machinery will find its true vocation again, it will render services in proportion to its power, only if mankind, which it has bowed still lower to the earth, can succeed, through it, in standing erect and looking heavenwards" (*Sources* 299). Unlike most other thinkers, Bergson rejects the idea of sudden change in the human self leading to or caused by power machinery; he rejects the illusions of discreteness and suddenness in technological development, as in the self. In other words, he rejects the machine's sudden entry into the garden. Nonetheless, he retains a teleological confidence in progress: mechanization is integral to the progress of life and human consciousness.

Bergson illustrates philosophically a lesson that contemporary historians of technology, as well as other historians, including Braudel and Wallerstein with their emphasis on the *longue durée,* have demonstrated empirically: assuming the suddenness and newness of technological change (or simply change, in the case of Braudel and Wallerstein) is both problematic and fundamentally ideological; furthermore, mainstream attempts to criticize "modern" technology embrace the most fundamental notions of the lines of thought that they attempt to attack: they accept that the fulcrum of time and human being is *now.* Even Bergson's thought is poisoned by progress, which ends apocalyptically, with a mystical, mechanized humanity reaching for the stars.

This project aims to go beyond Bergson, toward the complete abandonment of teleology and eschatology, without denying the reality of change and duration. Even Bergson insists upon the illusion of unambiguous, teleological progress, both technological and spiritual—despite the fact that he, perhaps more than any other philosopher, struggles to oppose a worldview focused on suddenness and the special status of our era.

Following Bergson, I argue that change, even directional change, is not progress. Bergson shows theoretically (as Basalla and Pacey show empirically) that the "modern" relationship between humanity and technology is primordial; yet even Bergson messianically asserts that this problematic relationship will blossom like a flower. My view is otherwise: technological change, like all change, is ambiguous and irreversible—it is an evolution that may tend in certain directions, but that direction is never simply toward the good or bad.

This book questions progress—not its desirability, but its reality. More particularly, I argue that a line of thinking in American literature has questioned progress more radically than Bergson, or even contemporary theorists of biology and technology, beginning with Melville and continuing through the works of Ralph Ellison into the present. In this narrative tradition, the machine both unfolds *over* and projects *into* time; it does not represent "progress"; it is not a *telos,* nor does it result from one; the technological self continually opens and forecloses possibilities, rather than reducing all possibility to an already-calculated moment.

2
Melville, the Pyramid, and the Machine

The idea that Melville's works critique Western imperialism, metaphysics, industrialization, and capitalism has almost become a cliché; interest in this aspect of his work has fueled the ongoing bull market in Melville criticism. In this chapter and the next I will add to that literature, and to the limited literature on Melville's role in the works of Lewis Mumford, the historian and theorist of technology, architecture, and the city. I will show that a Mumford-influenced reading of Melville combined with a Melville-influenced reading of Mumford can articulate an understanding of the relationship between time and technology that is neither eschatological nor teleological. The immediate subjects of these two chapters are Melville and Mumford, but they are also the means to a further end.

In this chapter I will first analyze the relationship of Queequeg (of *Moby-Dick*) to technologies of war, which has received little critical attention. Second, I will discuss Melville's obsession with Egypt and its monumental architecture, which will illuminate his understanding of time. Third, I will detail Melville's portrayal of the mechanization of humanity, partially in relationship to his portrayal of "actual" physical technologies. This chapter prepares the way for the following chapter, which explores the influence of Melville's thought on Lewis Mumford.

Queequeg's Technology, Queequeg's War

In an oft-quoted passage from the chapter "Biographical," Ishmael relates his understanding of why the "savage" Queequeg has abandoned his ancestral royal home for the sea. He imagines Queequeg boarding his first whaling ship:

> Struck by his desperate dauntlessness, and his wild desire to visit Christendom, the captain at last relented. . . . But this fine young savage—this sea Prince of Wales, never saw the captain's cabin. They put him down among the sailors, and made a whaleman of him. But like Czar Peter content to toil in the shipyards of foreign cities, Queequeg disdained no seeming ignominy, if thereby he might haply gain the power of enlightening his untutored countrymen. For at bottom . . . he was actuated by a profound desire to learn among the Christians, the arts whereby to make his people still happier than they were; and more than that, still better than they were. But alas! the practices of whalemen soon convinced him that even Christians could be both miserable and wicked. (56)

Queequeg yearns to visit Christendom, but this is no conversion narrative. He wants to visit Christendom and learn Christian arts (*technē*); Christianity itself goes unmentioned, which is unsurprising for the Queequeg who listens to part of Father Mapple's famously logocentric, Hellenistic sermon but leaves "before the benediction some time" (49).[1] From Ishmael's phrasing, we might believe that Christian wickedness was a surprise to Queequeg, but Queequeg is not *really* surprised by Christian corruption, as the purpose of his voyage reveals.

"Like Czar Peter," Queequeg is willing to "suffer ignominy" to enlighten his countrymen. Recall the purpose of Peter the Great's two famous trips to Europe in 1697–98 and 1717: the first voyage involved his attempt to learn "navigation, but . . . also other technical skills and crafts" and to form a coalition against the Ottoman Empire; the second was motivated by his need for allies against Sweden (Riasanovsky 242–45). Czar Peter focused on technologies of war: navigation, shipbuilding, ballistics.

Ishmael's Peter is a warrior-king serving a technological apprenticeship vital both for Russia's wars of expansion and for its ability to stand toe-to-toe with the European states, which, if smaller, were more sophisticated as war machines.[2] Queequeg is no innocent full of illusions about Christendom. He is at war; the purpose of his mission, following Ishmael's hint, is to bring Western technologies of war to his people. Navigation, shipbuilding, ballistics, gunsmithing: these are the arts by which Queequeg plans to "make his people still happier than they were"—through security.

Three of Melville's five novels before *Moby-Dick* were partially accounts of Western military power; Joyce Adler argues that the colonialist wars waged in the South Pacific are "the real, though not the external story of *Typee/Omoo*" (7). Western power is unambiguously condemned and racialized in *Typee:* "The fiend-like skill we display in the invention of all manner of death-dealing engines, the vindictiveness with which we carry on our wars, and the misery and desolation that follow in their train . . . distinguish the white civilized man as the most ferocious animal on the face of the earth. . . . His remorseless cruelty is seen in many of the institutions of our own favoured land" (150). "White civilized" man is distinguished not by religion, science, or culture but by a peculiar aptitude for war and its technologies, as well as for related techniques of oppression; Melville's ongoing, proto-Foucaultian critique of the American penal system has been detailed in Michael C. Berthold's "The Prison World of Melville's *Pierre* and 'Bartleby' " (1987) and Carol Colatrerra's *Literature and Moral Reform* (2002). The fact that Western "superiority" amounts to superior technologies of war is underlined repeatedly in *Typee*. The chiefs of the Typees account Tommo an "inferior sort of white man" because of his lack of knowledge of gunsmithing, but he arms them with the best weapon he can devise: popguns (219, 172). This seems like a joke, especially given Melville's lengthy description of the Typees' antics chasing and ambushing each other with the popguns, except for the fact that the same chapter carefully details one of the principal native crafts of tapa-making (tapa being a fabric), thus contrasting a "civilized" art of war with a "savage" art of peace.

Typee and *Omoo* fall, Adler argues, under the shadow of French warships (6). Tommo's fumbling attempts at martial technologies are a projection of the real war machine from which he emerges. The Typees don't know it yet, but their days are numbered. The crimes committed against the people of Tahiti and Hawaii (enumerated in *Typee* and *Omoo*) will be committed against them in turn.

It's easy to see Queequeg as representing anti-Western values. Adler argues that Queequeg stands for "values of life" against Ahab's "values of death" (61). On one level, who could deny it? Queequeg's tattoos, the visionary system of a native prophet, represent a "complete theory of heavens and the earth"; his love saves Ishmael's spirit as his coffin saves Ishmael's body (481). Nonetheless, Queequeg's project is Czar Peter's: to oppose the Western war machine, he adopts the technologies and techniques that compose it. No wonder that he has become too corrupt to assume the throne: "he was fearful Christianity, or rather Christians, had unfitted him for ascending the pure and undefiled throne. . . . [H]e would return,—as soon as he had been baptized again. . . . They had made a harpooner of him, and that barbed iron was in lieu of a sceptre now" (56). Queequeg has been corrupted not by Christianity, which he rejects, but by the whaling industry, itself a variety of war, as Melville continually makes clear, run by "fighting Quakers . . . Quakers with a vengeance" (73). Whaling is a peculiarly Quaker form of warfare, even as the American prison and asylum are arguably peculiarly Quaker disciplinary institutions.

For all of his tattooed otherness and halting speech, Queequeg willingly joins Ahab's mad quest, even giving his blood to temper Ahab's steel. Like Ishmael, who "could perceive a horror, and still be social with it," Queequeg is able to learn at the feet of that which he most opposes (7; ch 1). Ahab in all his world-ordering megalomania is both what Queequeg has gone to sea to oppose and the very image of what he, like Czar Peter, seeks to become.

If Ishmael is saved from the *Pequod*'s wreckage because he has been transformed by his encounter with Queequeg, Queequeg is destroyed because he has been transformed by his encounter with Ahab: because his end, his *telos,* is to assume the Ahabian power of the West, he shares in the West's own *telos.* When Queequeg plans to die and be set adrift in a ritual vessel rooted in his own people's practices, he has an opportunity to escape Ahab's vision. Standing over the dying Queequeg, Pip extemporizes on Queequeg's contradictions: "Poor rover! will ye never have done with all this weary roving? where go ye now. . . . Form two and two! Let's make a General of him! Ho, where's his harpoon?" (479). Queequeg is a rover-general, lying in a coffin modeled and furnished after the customs of his people but by Western techniques, holding a harpoon that is a technological microcosm, and yet wielded by "savages." He is a wandering general without an army, unable to save his people without destroying himself. If the fundamental dilemma of *Typee,* as Daneen Wardrop has argued, is whether Tommo, a "renegade from his signifying culture," will "honor the logos of his birth culture with its attendant cruelties" or embrace "the superior pre-signifying culture of the Typees," then Queequeg's dilemma is that of a renegade *into* signifying culture, who takes up the ways of what Melville named "the war-world" to oppose that war-world (143).

After Pip's words, Queequeg lies still, "as if in a dream," then rises, having decided to live because "he had just recalled a little duty ashore, which he was leaving undone; and therefore had changed his mind about dying" (480). What duty does the rover-general remember?

After Pip names Queequeg a general, he praises his courage, while execrating himself for cowardice. Pip reminds Queequeg that he is both a rover and a general; for a rover, his choice of spontaneous death may be appropriate, but for a general it is foolishness—Pip's character continually draws attention to reversed and confused values. The duty Queequeg remembers is his duty as a kind of Czar Peter. But by embracing this mission, although it is originally defensive in character, he embraces its *telos,* incarnate in Ahab. Ishmael has become just savage enough, for all of his contradictions, to be saved; Queequeg is just civilized enough, for all of *his* contradictions, to be damned.

Queequeg's war does not end with his death. His tattooed coffin delivers Ishmael, who becomes a tattooed wanderer in turn: investigating, refining, and spreading the story of revolution in "The Town-Ho's Story"; owing allegiance to "The King of the Cannibals," learning of both "savage" life and whaling life, continually mocking and reviling Western values. Ishmael, as signified by his oriental warrior's name, now wages Queequeg's war.

In *Typee* and *Omoo,* white sailors who submit to tattooing are permanently marked as outsiders; Tommo dreads the fate of a man who had his "face damaged for life, for the cursed heathens tattooed a broad patch clean across his figure-head" (47). Later, the fear of tattooing is a primary motivation for Tommo's escape. In *Omoo* the narrator comes upon "a stranger, a renegado from Christendom and humanity—a white man, in the South Sea girdle, and tattooed in the face" (353). The "civilizing" of Tahiti is marked by a law forbidding tattooing—a law that is part of the process which Melville names the "denationalizing" of the Tahitians (509). For Wardrop, Tommo's fear of tattooing manifests a fear of "his own forced acculturation into a community he has not fully embraced at the same time that he is fated ineluctably to wield the Lacanian Name-of-the-Father, the heritage of his white, logocentric culture" (136). Ishmael, following the model of Queequeg's own acculturation, is able to make the leap that Tommo cannot, and accepts this mark of a cannibal and outcast from "Christendom and Humanity." Ironically, he even uses his now marked and savage body to record the measurements of a whale: the weighing, measuring, and delimiting of Western technology is displaced onto a body-become-savage (451). Logocentrism is a tool in an assault on logocentrism, as in the chapter "Cetology," where Ishmael endlessly itemizes the varieties of whales, real and legendary, before arguing that only a draft of this knowledge is either possible or desirable. "God keep me from ever completing anything," he writes, in a systematic attack upon system building, which he imagines in the form of the incomplete cathedral of Cologne (145). Elisa New shows that this very cathedral, which Ishmael praises for its eternal incompleteness, was "particularly galling" to Goethe, precisely because it lacked and implicitly denied all unity; she argues that this passage advocates Hebraism against Goethe's Hellenistic logocentrism (298). The Ishmael who mocks Goethe, who advocates Hebraism and opposes logocentrism, who urges us to cast Kant and Locke overboard, is a work in progress himself, but a work in progress radically altered, or better, remade, by his encounter with Queequeg—who has himself adopted Western technologies and logocentrism.

The Ishmael who is projected beyond the novel's apocalyptic ending by Queequeg's coffin, marked with the "hieroglyphs" that Queequeg has copied from his own body, is essentially projected beyond the apocalyptic end of time, past the *eschatos*—but he does not enter into a New Jerusalem where "time is no more." Rather, as New writes, "if allegory is finally, for Melville, an apocalyptic mode . . . his Ecclesiast toils on, living through the apocalypse of metaphor" (301). For Eric Wilson, also writing on Ishmael's passage beyond the end, we have reached "the passing of imperialistic metaphysics, the violent dream of anthropocentric thought; the emerging of conjunctive thought, conjugation, a new earth gathering primitive and civilized, a new heaven of natural culture" ("Nomad" 241). For Wilson, Ishmael is moving back to an earlier and better world, like the Eden that "out-Edens Eden" for Wardrop (Wardrop 141). Many other writers have made similar observations about *Moby-Dick*'s "ending."

Yet, Ishmael isn't merely an escaping free agent with a fresh worldview; he has been *hurled* by Queequeg, whose harpoon never misses. Pip awakened Queequeg-the-general, who then carved his coffin with his own tattoos, establishing it as the buoy that becomes Ishmael's deliverance. This projection beyond the end is anticipated at the beginning of the novel, in the chapter "The Spouter-Inn," in the painting of a whale and a whaling ship: "It's a Hyperborean winter scene.—It's the breaking-up of the icebound stream of Time. But at last all these fancies yielded to that one portentous something in the picture's midst. *That* once found out, and all the rest were plain. But stop; does it not bear a faint resemblance to a gigantic fish? even the great leviathan himself?" (13). An apocalypse *should* end time, freezing or annihilating it, but under Queequeg's tutelage and because of his actions, icebound time is violently broken. Queequeg's Petrine mission to arm his people with Western technologies of war is an embrace of apocalyptic time (hence Queequeg's impurity and death at the novel's "apocalyptic" "end"), which also simultaneously enables him to hurl Ishmael (named after the biblical "wild man" whose hand is "against every man") beyond that apocalypse, creating an ongoing history.

We should not sentimentalize the history into which Ishmael is cast. It is hardly a "new heaven of natural culture," but a battlefield, in which Ishmael sets the priests of the Arsacides violently against one another in order to make the measurements with which his body will be tattooed, and in which he goes mockingly among the Dons of Peru in "The Town-Ho's Story," prophesying their doom (448–51, 242–59). This is not apocalyptic, finished time, but neither is it Edenic, stable time. Ishmael is a violent projection into a violent future. When the icebound stream of time melts, it floods.

In "The Mat-Maker"—mat making is, incidentally, a craft differing little between the "civilized" and "savages"—Ishmael serves as Queequeg's page (i.e., apprentice knight), providing his own arms as the shuttle to accompany Queequeg's heavy wooden sword. Ishmael grows dreamy:

> it seemed as if this were the Loom of Time, and I myself were a shuttle mechanically weaving and weaving away at the Fates. . . . Meantime, Queequeg's impulsive, indifferent sword, sometimes hitting the woof slantingly, or crookedly, or strongly, or weakly, as the case might be; and by this difference in the concluding blow producing a corresponding contrast in the final aspect of the completed fabric; this savage's sword, thought I, which thus finally shapes and fashions both warp and woof; this easy, indifferent sword must be chance—aye, chance, free will, and necessity—nowise incompatible—all interweavingly working together. (214–15)

Queequeg's sword shapes time chaotically and spastically, in stark contrast to Ahab's vision of time, in which his "one cogged circle fits into all their various wheels, and they revolve" (167). Ahab's world is an engine hurtling toward a fixed destination. Queequeg's time, though—which is both the time into which he hurls Ishmael, and Ishmael himself, as signaled by Ishmael's arm's role as the very woof of time—is fluid time, tumultuous and violent, forever unfinished. Most of all, it is a *manufactured* time, anti-apocalyptic and anti-teleological, which answers Ahab's equally manufactured apocalyptic time; it is not "organic," "natural," or "cyclical." It is as random, perilous, and treacherous as the post-apocalyptic Ishmael himself.

Joseph Andriano argues in "Brother to Dragons: Race and Evolution in *Moby-Dick*" that Melville's novel undercuts both the hierarchies of "white over non-white and of human over animal" (141). Categories are continually challenged: Starbuck is superstitious (savage), interpreting a giant squid as a portent, while Queequeg naturalistically deduces from it that they will soon find whales (282). Ishmael and Queequeg see the universe as driven by the essentially evolutionary struggle for survival, not by transcendental good and evil, unlike the teleology-minded Ahab. *Moby-Dick,* especially the characters of Queequeg and Ishmael, anticipates Darwinian evolution by, in Eric Wilson's words, being a harbinger of Darwin's "momentous dissolution of the great chain of being" ("Great Chain" 132). The novel partakes in the Darwinian assault on human megalomania. But while Wilson recognizes Ishmael's affiliation with evolution, he can't resist a tendency to make that very affiliation transcendental: "Ishmael devolves to the source of the *scala naturae,* primal water, rising again, baptized, to repeople an earth without chains" (148). Wilson's use of "baptized" is significant; Queequeg could not return to his people until he was baptized, born again: his baptism has been realized not directly but through Ishmael, "owning no allegiance but to the King of the Cannibals; and ready at any moment to rebel against him" (270).

Ishmael's rebirth, if we call it that, doesn't simply signify the end of political, racial, or biological hierarchies. It signifies an assault on temporal hierarchies, upon which the other hierarchies are based. Melville's time, anticipating Bergson's, leaves a bite: it is irreversible, never permitting a return to an Edenic or organic innocence (Queequeg can't go home), never fully calculable (as we see in the repeated failures of Ahab's ambitions), and ultimately counter-apocalyptic: the Hellenistic *telos* is achieved, but a new time, generated by the deliberate, treacherous, Petrine encounter of the "savage" mind with the tools and techniques of a teleological mind, has been created. When the icebound stream of time melts, it sweeps both teleological and "natural" cyclic time before it.

Shekinah Intolerably Bright: God as *Techne*

Melville's critics and biographers have often tried to explain his "silence": his retreat away from fiction and publicity into the New York customhouse and poetry. For Raymond Weaver, Melville's first full biographer, the silent years, during which Melville "scorned the world," are so irrelevant as to be like death—although he admits that the "silent" years may have been Melville's happiest (16). For Lewis Mumford, Melville's next biographer, Melville's "silent" years involve a reconnection with nature and family: after the long torment of his creativity, Melville embraced organic values (*Melville* 351–52).

Contemporary critics and biographers tend to acknowledge that Melville's poetry is a substantial and perhaps even worthy body of work, deserving some attention. Nonetheless, most criticism implicitly accepts, even while explicitly denying, that Melville's poetry is silence. Gilles Deleuze writes that "Bartleby" "announces the long silence, broken only by the music of poems, into which Melville will enter and from which, except for *Billy Budd,* he will never emerge" (*Essays* 72–73). The poetry is *other* than the prose, which conveniently allows one to neglect continuities between the two, mirroring the inattention given to Melville's early novels: most Melville criticism lops the head and the tail from his corpus.

There is a customary Melville canon: *Moby-Dick* and the short fiction garner most attention; *Pierre, Typee,* and perhaps *The Confidence-Man* much less; the other texts are nearly ignored. The worst problem with this implicit canon is that critics feel free to focus on the "major" texts without addressing connected themes and issues in the "minor" ones; the individual texts become, through custom, more independent than they truly are. This is particularly problematic for the novels; Melville published his first six novels between 1846 and 1851 and the rest of his fiction (excluding *Billy Budd*) by 1857, exceeding in compression even Faulkner's "one matchless time" of 1928 to 1942. After this excess of fiction it is unsurprising that its cessation seems like "silence" and that many critics think some of Melville's novels bear marks of sloppy writing. These judgments, though, lead to a hermeneutical obsession with a limited number of texts that more properly flow and blur into the "minor" texts. Consequently, one of my concerns is to work through a particular set of orientalist themes across the *full* body of Melville's work.

Two recent books on American orientalism, Malini Johar Schueller's *U.S. Orientalisms* (which steps beyond the mainstream by focusing on *Clarel*) and Scott Trafton's *Egypt Land,* both carefully mention Melville's use of Egypt in a famous passage from "Bartleby the Scrivener," immediately after the narrator-advocate notices that Bartleby has died: "The Egyptian character of the masonry weighed upon me with its gloom. But a soft imprisoned turf grew under foot. The heart of the eternal pyramids, it seemed, wherein, by some strange magic, through the clefts, grass-seed, dropped by birds, had sprung" ("Bartleby" 671).

Bartleby is trapped in the Tombs, New York City's infamous prison with pseudo-Egyptian architecture, one of many buildings where, as Trafton argues (echoing Mumford's 1924 *Sticks and Stones*), "the iconography of empire—that of its wielders as well as its resisters—was lavishly drawn from that of ancient Egypt" (2). Egyptian imagery symbolized raw American power from the Washington Monument to the Tombs, but the iconography of Egypt and the escape from it were equally vital to the "resisters," including slaves and abolitionists. Moreover, Trafton argues, the "wielders" were aware of the ambiguity of their symbol, rooted in the fact that the story of Egypt in Exodus focuses on its *defeat;* thus, those who used Egyptian history and iconography to justify American hierarchies, especially racial hierarchies, had to replace the biblical story of nations with one based on a protofascist interpretation of Egyptian history and artifacts (9, 51). Egypt represented power, empire, and the projection of that power and empire into the distant future, but the iconography of Egypt carried anxiety, including racial anxiety, along with it. Even the nicknaming of the Halls of Justice and House of Detention as "The Tombs" displays this ambivalence, which Trafton attributes to American Egyptomania in general: "The nickname marks a central feature of American Egyptomania: an interest in containment joined with a fear of escape, a desire for entombment combined with a fascination with excavation, a relief at interment mixed with a hope for resurrection" (149).

Bartleby, despite his astonishing passive resistance, is obliterated by the legal and economic machinery of a culture in which he can be only a cog. He is casually annihilated in "the heart of the pyramid," but his death is accompanied by the impossible penetration of the pyramid by grass seeds. The pyramid's victory is total yet troubled; the narrator has been touched despite himself. Schueller argues that "Bartleby's hermeneutical impenetrability . . . is explicitly tied to the resistance of the Near Eastern Orient to Western inquiry" (127). Bartleby can be destroyed but never *known* in the ways so necessary to orientalist inquiry; the narrator's probing, penetrating questions are rebuffed, his charity rejected, and his posthumous investigations reveal little.

Schueller argues that this impenetrable otherness is developed in Melville's journal of his 1856–57 journey to Egypt and Palestine, and especially in *Clarel* (1876). In both works the westerner confronted with the Orient is powerlessness and confused: "The process through which the New World hero saves or defines the Near East . . . gives way in *Clarel* to a more pronounced process of desire and identification, an attempt to deny any separation between self and Other" (139). This attempt to create an erotics of confusion or impenetrability, displacing the "powerful, male, heteronormative, and raced discourses of imperialism," is reflected back to the New World and its own imperialist wars in the Pacific and on the western frontier (138–39). Melville's earlier critique of the growing Pacific empires of France, Britain, and the United States is carried on by way of Egypt.

Schueller's reading of "Bartleby" and *Clarel* as "subversive Orientalism" is nuanced and convincing, as are similar readings, for instance, in Christopher Sten's "Melville's Cosmopolitanism: A Map for Living in a (Post-) Colonialist World." My purpose is not to alter or extend what Trafton and especially Schueller have said about Melville's "subversive Orientalism." Instead, I want to tell a story of Melville's life's work that revolves around the experience of the pyramid, a story illuminating Melville's understanding of time and technology. The staggering confrontation of the self with the pyramid recurs through the body of Melville's work, "major" and "minor" alike. This pervasive, enduring moment has, as such, received no prior critical attention.

In *Typee,* Tommo, although dwelling among "untutored savages," faces the remnants of a monumental architecture that generate more awe in him than "if I had stood musing at the mighty base of the Pyramid of Cheops. There are no inscriptions, no sculpture, no clue, by which to conjecture its history: nothing but the dumb stones" (185). He speculates that the island housed an advanced civilization contemporaneous with Egypt's, and wonders if these monuments could have been constructed by the "indolent" savages who now inhabit it. If their ancestors did construct them, the descendants have "sadly deteriorated in their knowledge of the mechanic arts" (186). The romantic, Edenic savagery of the Typees is not eternal, but undergirded and preceded by a monumental, technological civilization that is repeatedly compared to Egypt's.

The islanders' tattoos are called hieroglyphs, hinting again at the preceding technological-monumental civilization. Contra Wardrop and others, then, the Typees don't exist in a pre-signification Eden—if anything, their "Eden" is *post*-signification.

In *Mardi* we are reminded, in a book peppered with references to Egypt, pyramids, and hieroglyphic tattoos, that the eternity of the pyramids is founded in a deeper eternity: "duration is not of the future, but of the past; and eternity is eternal, because it has been; and though a strong new monument be builded to-day, it only is lasting because its blocks are old as the sun. It is not the Pyramids that are ancient, but the eternal granite whereof they are made" (890).

"Duration is not of the future, but of the past." From the dawn of civilization, *nothing* has been new. The technologies of monumental architecture reach back, not forward, aspiring for the old, not the new, even as the Egyptian and Hellenistic monumental architectures of Melville's United States find their source and power in the same past that renders them, as in "Bartleby," so horrific.

In an oft-quoted passage in *White-Jacket,* White-Jacket famously urges America not to be bound by the past: "Israel of old did not follow after the ways of the Egyptians. To her was given an express dispensation; to her were given new things under the sun. And we Americans are the peculiar, chosen people—the Israel of our time; we bear the ark of the liberties of the world. . . . We are the pioneers of the world; the advance-guard, sent on through the wilderness of untried things, to break a new path in the New World that is ours" (506). Ironically, White-Jacket's plea for America to become the new Israel comes in a book that exposes the American warship itself as an oriental work of architecture: "the canvas on the main-mast and fore-mast presented the appearance of majestic, tapering pyramids, more than a hundred feet broad at the base, and terminating in the clouds. . . . The three shrouded masts looked like the apparitions of three gigantic Turkish Emirs striding over the ocean" (676). The ship becomes a pyramid at sea; the sailors are cogs subordinated to a cruel war machine. The ship becomes, by analogy, a "world-frigate"; its amputations, beatings, rapes, and state of perpetual war are the world's condition. The book's central metaphor is that the world, like the ship, is a war machine sailing into the unknown. White-Jacket, when making his plea for abused soldiers, plays the good son, naming America as the Hebrew to the Old World's Egypt. But the ship's real condition is that of the pyramid itself. Melville uses Egypt as a figure for the extremity and tyranny of American power (Trafford's "wielders" and "resisters" are both represented), but with an unsettling tendency to literalize the figure. The pyramid's power is actual, not symbolic.

In *Moby-Dick,* Melville uses Egypt relentlessly, to the point where John Birk argues that the *Pequod*'s crew represents the Egyptian gods. Regardless, Ahab, *Moby-Dick,* and sperm whales in general are webbed in Egyptological references. Ishmael jokingly refers to "those huge bake-houses the pyramids"; this is a joke in a novel wherein laughter belongs most to the hyena, in the chapter named after him. The sperm whale's "pyramidical silence" is proof of his genius; when Stubb dreams of being utterly overwhelmed by Ahab's power, "Ahab seemed a pyramid"; his feeble attempts to resist Ahab are figured as "stubbing my silly toes against that cursed pyramid"; Stubb's laughter, too, is akin to the hyena's (347, 131–33). The Egyptians were, according to Ishmael, masthead standers who built the pyramids for astronomical purposes—note that in *Moby-Dick* the stars are a source of power to be embraced or resisted, not merely objects to be studied (154–55). The chapter "Moby-Dick" emphasizes his "pyramidical hump" (183). Mechanical outlines or impressions of the whale are no more useful than "taking the profile of a pyramid" (267). The markings on a whale's skin are literally hieroglyphs: "These are hieroglyphical; that is, if you call those mysterious cyphers on the walls of pyramids hieroglyphics, then that is the proper word to use in the present connexion. By my retentive memory of the hieroglyphics upon one Sperm Whale in particular, I was much struck with a plate representing the old Indian characters chiselled on the famous hieroglyphic palisades on the banks of the Upper Mississippi. Like those mystic rocks, too, the mystic-marked whale remains undecipherable" (306). As in *Clarel* (following Schueller), the Orient's unreadability is linked with that of the American West (which was, as Melville was well aware, the site of various monumental civilizations) but also to the whale; the American project becomes not the Roman or Greek project but the Egyptian project. Undecipherable languages and technologies lie everywhere just beneath the surface; Queequeg's lost innocence may be the discovery that he and Ahab share the same past, for a "vital strength lurked in his [Ahab's] Egyptian chest" (185).

In *Moby-Dick* the pyramid signifies technology, inscrutability, and power. Stubb is like Bartleby, trapped in the pyramid's heart, yet even Ahab shares the same situation. Ahab thinks to own the crew utterly, to mechanize them. By the novel's end they are "ground to finest dust . . . in the clamped mortar of Ahab's iron soul. Like machines, they dumbly moved about the deck" (536). Despite Ahab's ability to mechanize the crew, his own attempt to withstand Moby-Dick is merely like kicking a pyramid in turn.

The trajectory of Melville's fascination with the pyramid eventually took him there in person. I quote at length from his 1857 journal:

> Nothing in Nature gives such an idea of vastness. . . . Old man with the spirits of youth—long looked for this chance—tried the ascent, half way—fainted—brought down. Tried to go into the interior—fainted—brought out—leaned against the pyramid by the entrance—pale as death. Nothing so pathetic. Too much for him; oppressed by the massiveness & mystery of the pyramids. I myself too. A feeling of awe & terror came over me. Dread of the Arabs. Offering to lead me into a side-hole. The Dust. Long arched way,—then down as in a coal shaft. . . . I shudder at idea of ancient Egyptians. It was in these pyramids that was conceived the idea of Jehovah. Terrible mixture of the cunning and awful. Moses learned in all the lore of the Egyptians. The idea of Jehovah was born here. . . . Entrance of pyramids like a shoot [*sic*] for coal or timber. Horrible place for assassination. As long as earth endure some vestige will remain of the pyramids. (*Journals* 75)

In David Nye's analysis of the technological sublime, the railroad's sublimity lies in its annihilation of space and time; for some of Melville's contemporaries, the steamboat transcended the pyramids, and the Brooklyn Bridge was later compared positively to the pyramids (*Sublime* 53, 57, 85). According to Nye, the technological sublime, unlike the Kantian sublime, "exalted the conquest of nature" (152). Remarkably, Melville doesn't simply elaborate the standard comparison between America's technological wonders and the wonders of the ancient world, contrasting the sublime to the technological sublime; for him, the pyramid *is* the technological sublime: hence the image of the pyramid's entrance as a coal chute.

This pyramid is a machine. For what purpose? To make power; to make a god. This machine, to paraphrase *Mardi,* operates from the past into the present and the future; like the mysterious ruins in *Typee,* it underlies the contemporary world, "civilized" and "savage" alike. This machine is, as in *White-Jacket,* a war machine, or world-machine, gliding among the stars. Nature is not being conquered *now,* as the disciples of the railroad and the suspension bridge would have it: nature was conquered long ago.

In *Pierre,* Pierre's attempts at self-discovery are figured as pyramid robbery: "By vast pains we mine into the pyramid; by horrible gropings we come to the central room; with joy we espy the sarcophagus; but we lift the lid—and no body is there!—appallingly vacant as vast is the soul of a man!" (*Pierre* 332). The pyramid's endless power, like Ahab's and Moby-Dick's, masks an emptiness at its heart.

In book 2, canto 11 of *Clarel,* titled "Of Deserts," Melville follows up on "Bartleby" and his journals by associating modernity and the pyramids. Near the beginning of the canto he refers to Darwin's interest in Shelley, then compares "Western counties all in grain" to the Egyptian desert; later in the canto he returns to the pyramids:

> When comes the sun up over Nile
> In cloudlessness, what cloud is cast
> O'er Lybia? Thou shadow vast
> Of Cheops' indissoluble pile,
> Typ'st thou the imperishable Past
> In empire's posthumous and reaching sway
> Projected far across to time's remotest day? (2.11, 168–69)

The pyramid casts its shadow over the Libyan desert, previously associated with the American West; the empire is posthumous but still reaches; it is projected into the past—but is not the projection ambiguous? Is it not, being imperishable, projected into (or from) the future? Darwin's and Shelley's dread of the wilderness is associated with a monumental work of architecture, overlooking and dominating history, paradoxically from the wilderness. Egypt and the pyramids are again associated with America's destiny, but in this version America is dwarfed by the monument that is conventionally supposed to figure its power. That monument projects onto and beyond the present; its shadow is our very being.

Melville's final book, *Timoleon* (1891), developed partially out of dialogue with the orientalist painter Elihu Vedder: it was dedicated to Vedder, and Melville's wife sent him a copy after Melville's death, as Dorsey Kleitz has documented. Melville and Vedder practiced an orientalism that was not a closed, tyrannical system—"as seen in Melville's interest in Vedder, Melville looks to the Orient not so much as a site where answers are found, but as a site where questions are asked" (Kleitz 461). "The Great Pyramid," the book's penultimate poem, gives another version of an encounter with the pyramid. The poem's first stanza blurs the categories of the technological and natural sublimes: "Your masonry—and is it man's? / More like some Cosmic artisan's. / Your courses as in strata rise, / Beget you do a blind surmise / Like Grampians" (*Poems* 339). This masonry is indistinguishable from a mountain range, the Grampians of Scotland. If there is a difference between the natural and the artificial, it is irrelevant, as in what Nye terms "the electrical sublime," wherein the erasure of the line dividing the natural and the artificial creates "a synthetic environment infused with mystery" (*Sublime* 152). But Melville discovers this "electrical" sublime in the pyramid alone, with no modern intrusion; it belongs to the ancient as much as to the modern. The final stanza reads: "Craftsmen, in dateless quarries dim, / Stones formless into form did trim, / Usurped on Nature's self with Art, / And bade this dumb I AM to start, / Imposing him." The "I AM"—that is, Jehovah speaking "I am that I am" out of the fire—is a human creation, formed by craftsmen out of stone; he is both architecture and automaton: Jehovah as golem. God, the spirit, who in the previous poem ("In the Desert") emits light and fire—"Holy, holy, holy Light! / immaterial incandescence, / Of God the effluence of the essence, / Shekinah intolerably bright!"—is created with—or *is*—the pyramid that is the pinnacle of *material* sublimity (*Poems* 338–39). The presence of God (Shekinah) is one with the imponderable and utterly material power of the pyramid. In short, the divine *logos* is a machine that dominates time: "Time's future infinite you dare, / While, for the past, 'tis you that wear / Eld's diadem," ends "The Great Pyramid" (339). The pyramid (or God) owns and supervises time.

Ahab's apocalyptic time, the time that destroys Bartleby and underlies *Typee,* the time that Queequeg embraces, betrays, and hurls Ishmael beyond, is the pyramid's time. It is a time in which all is already calculated and destined. It is as spatialized and demarcated as the very blocks from which the pyramids were constructed.

The idea that Melville resists the Western philosophical, teleological tradition may have become a cliché in Melville criticism, but the cliché still bears repeating. In *Cosmopolis and Truth: Melville's Critique of Modernity* (1996), Bernhard Radloff defines the modernity opposed by Melville thus: "The final triumph of universal Reason over the limitations hitherto imposed on humanity by tradition is the telos of history conceived as the movement of the progressive emancipation of mankind in its collective, social being. . . . [T]he 'critique of modernity' . . . questions the premises of this project in essential respects" (1). Ahab's leadership attempts "to give sense to the sense-lessness of the modern economic enterprise and the atomistic social order of Lockean isolatoes" (2); rationality is appropriated for a mad, ungrounded purpose. Radloff argues that *Pierre* and *The Confidence-Man* challenge the possibility of finding a grounding, political or personal, in "classical ideas" of truth and self-knowledge (5). In *The Piazza Tales* the "imperial" nature of truth is demonstrated; that is, the true is "stable, upright, self-certain and secure," that is, monumental. History and historiography are not truly rational but "mythological" and "monumental" (7–8). Melville becomes a postmodernist battling logocentrism: "What remains . . . is the potential of sacrifice to institute a new beginning, and [of] language to let the originary speak without representing it" (233). I have discussed similar ideas, from New's argument that Melville takes a Hebraic stand against Hellenism and its *telos,* to Eric Wilson's apocalyptic vision of the passing of Western metaphysics. For William Spanos in *The Errant Art of Moby-Dick,* Melville "proleptically delegitimized the discourse of the New World Order. I mean the ontologically grounded and dialectically propelled discourse of the post–Cold War, the 'end-of-history' discourse that is essentially beyond the critical reach of the New Historicism of the New Americanists" (278). Melville's work (i.e., mostly *Moby-Dick*) is persistently interpreted as an articulate response to Western metaphysics and teleology, offering something in its place: Sacrifice? Evolution? Being-in-Itself? I am in sympathy with this tendency of theory-minded critics, and also with the urge to understand Melville as a "subversive Orientalist." My own argument is that Melville's response to teleology and Western metaphysics is of a part with his "subversive Orientalism." The shadow of the pyramid looms behind Western metaphysics and teleology; in effect, the pyramid *is* the *telos* toward which Western thought inevitably hurtles, *and* its secret origin.

Lyotard has argued that Marxism and Enlightenment "conserve the eschatological principle of Christian thought" (*Fables* 97). Melville proleptically outbids Lyotard: for Melville, Christian eschatology emerges from the pyramid—which predates even the "natural" world of the Typees—under which God was created. The Enlightenment is a pasteboard mask, as is the Christian eschatology that Lyotard sees beneath the Enlightenment. When we attain a "little lower layer," in Ahab's words, we discover that Egypt's technologies and monumental architecture are identical with Western metaphysics, eschatology, and teleology, that is, with the deadening, mechanizing experience of modernity. Melville's (counter)orientalism is his (post)modernism: the eternal heart of the pyramids is modernity. "Shekinah intolerably bright" is not a Demiurge, a crafts(wo)man, but is herself a technological product. The experience of being reified and mechanized belongs to the invention of monumental history and the generation of teleological time (at the pyramid's construction) as much it belongs to the present, over which the pyramid still looms, surveying all time.

Melville's Automatons

Melville's works betray a fascination not only with technology and humanity individually but with mechanized humanity and humanized technology: automata and cyborgs. Melville's critique of colonialism and warfare is also a critique of technology. Young Polynesians are not "filled with envyings of each other's charms . . . nor yet moving in whalebone corsets, like so many automatons, but free, inartificially happy, and unconstrained" (*Typee* 152). Ironically, the automaton-women at home *are* constricted by whalebone corsets: the industry that rapes and murders

Polynesian women mechanizes white women. While the islanders live under the threat of asymmetrical warfare, the very process of colonization (in the case of whalers) and its products (corsets) enslave and mechanize the perpetrators and alleged beneficiaries of this warfare.

Omoo is packed with references to mechanized and mechanizing humanity. Unskilled sailors are like machines: "Regarded in the light of a mechanical power, whenever there is any plain, hard work to be done, he is put to it like a lever; every one giving him a pry" (380). Westerners mechanize the world, the natives, and themselves, as when an attempt is made to introduce weaving machinery to Afrehitoo; the natives work for a time as a novelty, then the machinery is abandoned (517). One imagines that the next time machinery is introduced, military force will back it. Long Ghost, the narrator's companion, plans to settle in Polynesia: "I'll put up a banana-leaf as physician from London—deliver lectures on Polynesian antiquities—teach English in five lessons . . . establish power-looms for the manufacture of tapa—lay out a public park in the middle of the village" (573). The doctor jokingly envisions himself as teacher, engineer, and architect, building a park in a tropical paradise, instantly mechanizing the preeminent native craft, and educating natives about their own artifacts. He aspires to place the whole village under the discipline of scientific management. He himself does not escape this vision of an engineered world, but imagines himself as a cyborg: "Oh, that one's joints were but provided with holes to drop a little oil through" (560). On another occasion he wakes after a night of drinking "ArvaTee," saying: "Heavens! my head's all wheels and springs, like the automaton chess-player! What's to be done, Paul! I'm poisoned!" (603). Although the doctor is theoretically an intellectual laborer, less vulnerable than an ordinary sailor to becoming a "lever," he considers even himself mechanically. In *Omoo,* Polynesians, sailors, and upper-class Anglo-Saxon women are equally threatened by a seemingly inevitable mechanization of the self that moves in tandem with mechanized industry. Ishmael's later line "Who ain't a slave?" could be rephrased "Who ain't a machine?"

The mechanized self pervades *Mardi.* Sailors' swinging hammocks are figured as pendulums: "Time, and time-pieces! How many centuries did my hammock tell, as pendulum-like it swung to the ship's dull roll" (665). Pendulums make possible the creation of precision chronometers "necessary for determining longitude at sea" (Mayr 14). The sailors, like the chronometers, are precision instruments. The narrator mourns that he can't make these machines rebel, for "There was no soul a magnet to mine. . . . [T]here was naught to strike fire from their steel" (664–65). Later in the novel, a philosopher wonders: "Who put together this marvelous mechanism of mine; and wound it up, to go for three score years and ten; when it runs out, and strikes Time's hours no more? . . . What keeps up the perpetual telegraphic communication between my outpost toes and digits, and that domed grandee up aloft, my brain?" (1195). This passage is seemingly within the Cartesian tradition, in which the clockwork body is controlled by a free soul. But the souls of the sailors, figured as chronometers, are unfree: even as the digits are telegraphically controlled by the grandee of the brain, so most people are controlled by literal grandees. In *Mardi,* as Wai-Chee Dimock has demonstrated, freedom for one (for Dimock, the author's tyrannical ego) means imperialism for others.

Mardi's obsessions with automatons and chronometers dovetail: according to Mayr, the creation of clocks and automata was one craft, more political than practical in nature: clocks existed to perform and demonstrate power, through automata performances. Melville wrote when the clock-as-chronometer was displacing the clock-as-automaton but before the association between the two had been broken. Early clocks and automata were primarily symbols of power, subordinating "the public life of the whole town to a common schedule," organizing the citizenry in "more and more tightly interlocking patterns," and "placed in the center of utopian town designs" (Mayr 15). Accurate timekeeping was not the purpose of early clocks, which often had to be set using sundials (Mayr 10). Early clocks regulated the world, illustrating (or even creating) a deterministic worldview and authoritarian centralization.[3] Manuel De Landa discusses the connection between automata and the mechanization of warfare: "These rigid squares of men and weapons, incapable of exercising any individual initiative on the battlefield, resembled a well-oiled clockwork mechanism. The time when the phalanx reached its peak . . . was also the time when technology had extended the clockwork paradigm to its ultimate consequences, as can be seen in the elaborate mechanical gardens and toy automata of the period" (65). The mechanization and alienation of the individual under modernity are also the mechanization and alienation of modern war. What Dimock and others have seen as *Mardi*'s strident egoism is undermined by intense anxiety about the self's subordination to the war machine; Adler, again, has discussed the novel's obsession with war at length (15–16).

In *Redburn,* too, the narrator is an automaton. When the ship sails through a fog, "the chronometer pronounced it noon," but the fog was so dense that "I, poor Wellingborough, mounted aloft . . . tolling the ship's bell, as if for a funeral" (108). Elsewhere in the novel the human body is compared to a ship, and the narrator imagines "classes of men in the world, who bear the same relation to society at large, that the wheels do to a coach: and are just as indispensable" (77, 153). A large swath of the world's population exists as machines, Redburn among them.

In *White-Jacket* life is endlessly mechanized. For each occasion there is a station and task for every man; because of "this endless subdivision of duties in a man-of-war," sailors have "need of a good memory. . . . White-Jacket, for one, was a long time rapt in calculations, concerning the various 'numbers' allotted him" (358). Given labor's subdivision and names' replacement with numbers, *White-Jacket* resembles Zamyatin's *We* and similar dystopias. The narrator is nearly flogged for being in the wrong place during an exercise; by *not knowing his place* he has wandered outside disciplinary, regimented time. Foucault writes on how time, bodies, and forces are regulated, leading, in his terminology, to the creation of "man-the-machine":

> The disciplines, which analyze space, break up and rearrange activities, must also be understood as machinery for adding up and capitalizing time. . . . 1. Divide duration into successive or parallel segments. . . . 2. Organize these threads according to an analytical plan. . . . 3. Finalize these temporal segments, decide on how long each will last and conclude it with an examination. . . . 4. Draw up series of series; lay down for each individual . . . the exercises that are suited to him. . . . [I]t is a disciplinary polyphony of exercises. (*Discipline* 157–59)

White-Jacket must know his place during all the ship's "polyphony of exercises" in accordance with the "series of series" assigned to him, or he'll be disciplined *into* his place for desegmenting, demechanizing, and despatializing time.

The captain's authority is absolute. He is "lord and master of the sun," controlling even time itself, since "it is not twelve o'clock till he says so" (*White-Jacket* 371). The captain is the master chronometer. Living in a man-of-war is like "living in a large manufactory" or "a market" (384). The sailor-automaton of this dystopia has no privacy, no possessions other than what fits in a canvas bag accessible only at appointed hours. As an interchangeable part in a war machine he stands ready to manufacture death. The hearts of the sailors beat "like sledgehammers in those hot smithies, our bosoms . . . let them feel of our generous pulses, and swear that they go off like thirty-two-pounders" (427). An elderly commodore spends his time directing naval exercises, as Charles V diverted himself "watching the gyrations of the springs and cogs of a long row of clocks" (550). The sailors are so disciplined that "like their own guns, they have fought without a thought" (687). The sailor is nearly indistinguishable from the cannon. Melville describes the man-of-war as a complete system of discipline: "The whole body of this discipline is emphatically a system of cruel cogs and wheels, systematically grinding up in one common hopper all that might minister to the moral well-being of the crew" (742). The crew is a collection of disciplined and mastered bodies forming one mechanism subject to the captain's will. Their bodies are docile under what Foucault calls a "mechanics of power," which "defined how one may have a hold over others' bodies, not only so that they may do what one wishes, but . . . with the techniques, the speed and the efficiency that one determines" (*Discipline* 138).

In *White-Jacket* humanity is fully mechanized, despite scattered resistance. Melville anticipates Foucault in his early works and outbids him in later ones by placing the mechanization of humanity into the deep past. Melville does not excuse discipline as a necessary corollary to democracy, as Benjamin Rush does (see chapter 2); for him a republican machine is only another name for a war machine.

Two extracts at the beginning of *Moby-Dick* portray the Leviathan as a machine or artificial man. Melville quotes from Hobbes's *Leviathan:* "By art is created that great Leviathan, called a Commonwealth or State . . . which is but an artificial man" (xx). This wildly rich allusion makes the Leviathan out to be state, automaton, and whale all in one. The preceding extract, from Waller's *Battle of the Summer Islands,* deepens the allusion: "Like Spencer's Talus with his iron flail, / He threatens ruin with his ponderous tail / . . . / Their fixed jav'lins in his side he wears, / And on his back a grove of pikes appears" (xx). The spears in the creatures's back mark it as a whale, which is then linked to Talus of *The Faerie Queene,* the iron man who serves Artegall, the knight of justice, with perfect, inhuman obedience. The Talus whom Melville invokes is a true clockwork soldier, the perfect "army of one"; he is like Moby-Dick, but also like Ahab and the automatons of the crew. The quote from Waller compares a whale and an automaton; the one from Hobbes calls the Leviathan an artificial man. The three concepts of whale, mechanical man/soldier, and state fuse: the technological fantasy of a mechanical man springs from and results in the state's mechanization of humanity.

The theme of the automaton thus appears *before* the beginning of *Moby-Dick.* Stephen Ausband documents the theme's persistence in "The Whale and the Machine." David Mitchell has demonstrated that Ahab is critically shaped by his dismemberment and the inflexible prosthetic leg that replaces his natural leg (19). Ahab's disability renders him dependent on mechanical contrivances, as when he needs to go to another ship. Perhaps, as Mitchell argues, this makes him see himself more inflexibly. He *does* view himself mechanically, for instance in "The Symphony": "Is it I, God, or who, that lifts this arm. . . . By heaven, man, we are turned round and round in this world, like yonder windlass, and Fate is the handspike" (545). The image of the self as a machine is connected to a generalized mechanical determinism. Ahab envisions himself as a windlass, as dominated by outside forces, and as in need of repair by a blacksmith (488).

Ahab figures his totalitarian triumph mechanically: "my one cogged circle fits into all their various wheels, and they revolve . . . . [L]ike so many anthills of powder, they all stand before me; and I their match" (167–68). Ahab dominates a system of machines but regrets that he must become a machine to do so, and he rebels against the condition of the world that reveals him as mechanical even while imposing a mechanical order.

Starbuck sees himself as a mine and a clock: "he drilled deep down, and blasted all my reason out. . . . [M]y whole clock's run down" (169). The crew experience themselves as machines, especially as clocks. Lynn White argues that the near-universal introduction of the mechanical clock is connected not only to the regulation of humanity but especially to temperance, the great bourgeois virtue (*Religion* 181–204). Ahab, note, usurps the ship's clockwork for *in*temperate purposes, reversing the classic meaning of the clock (a reversal begun in *White-Jacket,* with the captain's whim). The temperance that the clock is supposed to generate is replaced by what Radloff calls the "rootlessness of desire" (40). The clock still represents power, but Melville mocks temperance and associated virtues, including in his various satires of Benjamin Franklin and his (in)temperance in *Israel Potter,* "The Lightning-Rod Man," and *The Confidence-Man.*

When Melville mocks temperance by linking the clock's regulatory power to Ahab's rootless desire, he is not merely responding to the Enlightenment and liberalism, as most critics would have it; the mechanized world originates in the deep time evoked by Melville's Egyptological references. In "The Candles" Ahab's encounter with the divine is mediated by technological artifacts; the masts, boat, and harpoon are electrified in sequence; a decision must be made to deploy or not deploy the lightning rods. When the corpusants (St. Elmo's fire) illuminate the ship, Ahab admits but defies their power: "thou art but my fiery father; my sweet mother, I know not. Oh, cruel! what hast thou done with her? There lies my puzzle; but thine is greater. Thou knowest not how came ye, hence callest thyself unbegotten; certainly knowest not thy beginning, hence callest thyself unbegun. . . . There is some unsuffusing thing beyond thee, thou clear spirit, to whom all thy eternity is but time, all thy creativeness mechanical" (508). Etsuko Taketani discusses this passage's Gnostic provenance: "The visible fire is the representation of Jehovah (the Demiurge) who made man. Beyond the fiery father, Ahab's Gnostic discourse invents the presence of another father, the Unknown God" (130). Despite Ahab's defiance, his "Gnostic manipulation of discourse, however, seems impotent in altering the material history" (131). Ahab attempts a Gnostic rebellion against teleology and Western historiography, invoking a divine mother (Sophia) against the divine father, and a spiritual realm against the Demiurge's mechanical, material realm. But Ahab also seeks a *telos;* his obsession with the pure origin behind the Demiurge is also an obsession with destroying the Demiurge. Hence the significance of Fedallah, whose unflagging loyalty to Ahab's quest against the Demiurge is remarkable when understood in the full context of his "Parsee" (Zoroastrian) origins: Zoroastrianism's belief in a precise, precalculated duration to history, which is an ordered battlefield between good and evil, precedes Christianity. Fedallah's faith is, like Ahab's Christian/Enlightenment beliefs, both eschatological and technological; far from being savages, Parsis were in the forefront of Indian shipbuilding and other native capitalist industries (Pacey, *World* 67–68). Given the sophistication of Melville's knowledge of Indian shipbuilding in *Redburn,* it seems likely that he was aware of the Parsi role in this industry. Gnosticism, which owes its dualism and concept of history partially to Zoroastrianism, is the embrace of a secret spiritual world behind the treacherous material one, which is at best a problematic rebellion against teleological history: if it rejects the pyramid (i.e., Jehovah or the Demiurge, a wicked or ignorant god and the world's creator), it still finds redemption only in the end of history and the Demiurge's final defeat. In Ahab's Gnostic worldview, time is only teleological and the world can only be mechanical, until world and time are destroyed. In attacking "salvation history," the half-mechanical and all-mechanizing Ahab seeks only salvation *from* (but never *in*) history: since time is not a machine he controls, he must destroy it, just as he destroys the quadrant in "The Quadrant."

As a prosthesis-using mechanical man, a product of and rebel against teleology and the war machine, a technological Faust to Fedallah's devil, Ahab is a cyborg, "simultaneously animal and machine, who populate worlds ambiguously natural and created" (Haraway, *Simians* 149). Haraway writes: "Modern war is a cyborg orgy, coded by C^{3}I, Command-control-communication intelligence" (150). Ahab, the prosthetic man, does not control the crew through physical strength but through C^{3}I; recall the captain in *White-Jacket,* who is the master of time itself; Ahab's domination is both subtler and more thorough. "The cyborg is resolutely committed to partiality, irony, intimacy, and perversity. It is oppositional, utopian, and completely without innocence," writes Haraway "Unlike the hopes of Frankenstein's monster, the cyborg does not expect its father to save it through a restoration of the garden. . . . [Cyborgs] are the illegitimate offspring of militarism and patriarchal capitalism. . . . But illegitimate offspring are often exceedingly unfaithful to their origins" (*Simians* 151). Could there be a better description of Ahab, traitorous heir of capitalism and the war machine, a totalitarian desperate for freedom, as C. L. R. James argues, who pursues an irrational war regardless of consequences for the crew, but loves Pip, the lowliest member of it, who follows in Victor Frankenstein's footsteps but equally in the footsteps of Frankenstein's monster?[4]

The category of the cyborg is not intended for nineteenth-century figures like Ahab any more than Nye's "technological sublime" is supposed to reach back into prehistory; it is thus all the more significant that Ahab plays the part so well. Historians of technology like Lynn White urge us to reconsider the history of technology, pushing the "industrial revolution" farther back into the "middle ages," while acknowledging that America's conquest of the West used essentially medieval technology (White, *Religion* 22, 109, 120). We must acknowledge that the "cybernetic age" did not begin suddenly with, say, the invention of the computer. In *When Information Came of Age,* Daniel Headrick argues that the "information revolution" has been under way for centuries, with one example being the development of cataloging techniques and statistics, which are both foundational for and continuous with contemporary techniques and technologies. The cybernetic age is *old;* it is exemplified in Ahab's desire to create a legion of mechanical men to serve his purposes. The ship's carpenter is an "unreasoning wheel," the smith a "manmaker"; Ahab tells the carpenter to order the smith to make him a mechanical man: "I'll order a complete man after a desirable pattern. Imprimis, fifty feet high in his socks . . . no heart at all, brass forehead, and about a quarter of an acre of fine brains" (470). The carpenter, machine-like himself, hardly understands that Ahab has requested a mechanical man with immense computational abilities: the Pentagon's dream man-machine.

Moby-Dick's apparent vision of technology and time is now commonplace: physical and disciplinary technologies lead both to a mechanized war machine and a mechanized self; together, the two are the West's *telos.* This understanding of Melville is compatible with that of most contemporary critics, who, willingly or not, follow Leo Marx. But there is in *Moby-Dick* a countermovement that develops further in *The Confidence-Man* and Melville's late poetry, in which physical and disciplinary technologies do not lead to a *telos,* because they *precede* history. Traditional criticism has seen Queequeg as waging a border war against technology, linear time, and the West on the behalf of nature, cyclic time, and aboriginal cultures, but his war against the former makes him betray the latter, which opens up a vision of time and technology as pure flux, as in *The Confidence-Man* and the late poetry.

When Melville shifted to writing about life ashore, he increasingly literalized his mechanical men. In *The Confidence-Man* an herb-doctor accuses a cripple of being "a demoniac unfortunate. . . . [a] Regular infernal machine" (940). Shortly thereafter the herb-doctor encounters a Missourian, who complains of being "embezzled" by nature and remembers with loathing the last boy who worked his farm: "I am now started to get me made some kind of machine to do the sort of work which boys are supposed to be fitted for" (955). The Missourian refuses to keep either slaves or white servants. Later he encounters a "Philosophical Intelligence Officer" (a philosopher or member of a military intelligence apparatus?) who offers to help the Missourian find a boy; the Missourian refuses emphatically: "I'm now on the road to get me made some sort of machine to do my work. Machines for me. . . . cider-mill, mowing-machine, corn-husker—all faithfully attend to their business. . . . shining examples that virtue is its own reward. . . . Start my soul-bolts, what a difference, in a moral point of view, between a corn-husker and a boy! Sir, a corn-husker, for its patient continuance in well-doing, might not unfitly go to heaven. Do you suppose a boy will?" (963). Replacing boys with machines, the Missourian mechanizes himself—"start my soul-bolts," he says, repeating Stubb's words from *Moby-Dick.* As Radloff argues, the concept of virtue in the "confidence world" rests entirely on virtue as "automatism of habit": "Confidence is faith in the rational transparency of a calculable agent—this is the very basis of the commercial contract. If the money lenders of this world thought that their debtors were as liable to kill themselves, or kill them, or burn their assets . . . the calculating brain of the Leviathan would burn out," he concludes (30). The Missourian has adopted the Calvinist economic virtues of temperance, thrift, and so forth so thoroughly that mechanical efficiency has become, in his eyes, the only virtue. A teleological history, with heaven looming at its end, can be endured only by machines. The human animal is a "losing animal," destined for mechanical replacement: "that the day is at hand, when, prompted to it by law, I shall shoulder this gun and go out a boy-shooting" (964). The Missourian envisions a future of landowners ordering the standing-reserve of the machinery, with the lower classes being eliminated. He is Ahab become nauseatingly ordinary. Eventually, the Philosophical Intelligence Office convinces the Missourian to try another boy, who has been phrenologically examined: this boy, being thoroughly investigated and *known,* is sufficiently mechanized to do a machine's work.

In "The Paradise of Bachelors and the Tartarus of Maids," Melville describes a paper mill where the workers are "girls" of all ages, unmarried and infantilized. They never speak; they have "pallid faces" and are repeatedly described as cold; Melville satirizes didactic novels and stories about mill girls, which generally focused on the struggle to maintain agrarian virtues while earning enough money to get married, put one's brother through school, and so forth. The narrator envisions the girls as mechanical products: "awe now stole over me, as I gazed upon this inflexible iron animal. . . . [W]hat made [it] terrible to me was the metallic necessity, the unbudging fatality which governed it. . . . Before my eyes—there, passing in slow procession along the wheeling cylinders, I seemed to see, glued to the pallid incipience of the pulp, the yet more pallid faces of all the pallid girls I had eyed that heavy day. Slowly, mournfully, beseechingly, yet unresistingly, they gleamed along, their agony dimly outlined on the imperfect paper" (1277). Klaus Benesch argues that Melville's critique of mechanized labor was unusual for his time, but Philip Young argues that the story is "an unapologetic testament of fruitless anger at the 'metallic necessity' that governs the reproduction of the species"—precisely the feeling that leads Victor Frankenstein to his own act of creation (Benesch, "Technology" 66; Young 224). Whether the narrator sees the girls as mechanical or dreads the mechanism of human reproduction, the mechanical woman walks among us, ordered as standing-reserve by "Old Bach" (a reference to the mechanization of music), who controls the factory. Bach is another little Ahab whose factory produces both paper and mechanized women, that is, "girls."

As if to underline his interest in the relationship between time and technology, Melville creates a literal mechanical man in "The Bell-Tower," in which the "mechanician" Bannadonna is "reputed to be an architect" and is building the highest bell tower in Italy, which will include all the functions of a clock tower (819). He is establishing an architectural edifice that will help regulate the population and show the power of church and state (Mayr), while reminding the people of the virtues, especially the virtue of temperance (White). When Bannadonna casts the largest bell for the tower, one of his workers balks, and Bannadonna kills him without consequence. Beyond the ordinary clock and automata, he is creating a forbidden "something for the belfry" (821). Like Victor Frankenstein, he is absorbed in his forbidden, Promethean work; he is too sovereign, too Promethean, to be punished by any save his creation, the mechanical man whom the few visitors to the tower sometimes hear. When the hour approaches for the bell to be rung, there is only a muffled sound. Soldiers break into the tower to find an automaton standing over Bannadonna, having killed him with the mace that was supposed to strike the bell: Bannadonna, indifferent to the mechanical time he was creating, was standing before the bell at the appointed time, and his creation, as obedient as Spenser's Talus, strikes where and when it is supposed to strike. The automaton that kills him was either to be the prototype for a more complete mechanical man, or else that creation had already been made: "He still bent his efforts upon the locomotive figure for the belfry, but only as a partial type of an ulterior creature, a sort of elephantine Helot . . . [to further] the universal conveniences and glories of humanity; supplying nothing less than a supplement to the Six Days' Work; stocking the earth with a new serf. . . . Talus was to have been the all-accomplished Helot's name. Talus, iron slave to Bannadonna, and through him, to man" (830). This is Ahab's and the Missourian's dream: to have a perfectly obedient automaton, wiser and more capable than man. We even hear echoes of Ahab's totalitarian power, for Talus is not to serve humanity directly, but *through* Bannadonna. Remember: Spenser's Talus is first and foremost a war machine! The desire for efficiency and the threat of absolute, totalitarian power merge; one might connect this to the development of scientific management, as well as to slavery, as in *Benito Cereno.*[5]

Much of the narrator's unease in "Bartleby" comes from the extremity of Bartleby's mechanization. A mechanized man is convenient for the narrator to a point, but beyond that point he feels his world teetering: "He ran a day and night line, copying by sun-light and by candle-light. I should have been quite delighted with his application, had he been cheerfully industrious. But he wrote on silently, palely, mechanically" ("Bartleby" 642). Bartleby is a human copying machine, yet he rebels against mechanization and refuses work. He will not do the efficient, mechanical job of verifying the quadruplicate copies he has made. Other characters are described mechanically: Turkey sits "glowing like a brass boiler," for instance (647). The clerks are paid by the piece, like factory workers. Bartleby is so mechanized that he never leaves the place of his work, and he never seems to move except when commanded or forced; yet this very refusal to depart is an act of rebellion. When the narrator finds him intolerable he is a "millstone" (657). When Bartleby refuses to serve, he suffers the same fate as Pierre: he is delivered to the Tombs, the monument to death that is the Egyptian *telos* of history and the product of all the story's machinery.

Throughout his work, Melville dwells on the problem of the mechanization of humanity, although in his later work (the poetry and *Billy Budd*) the focus on machinery as such is largely transformed into a focus on monumental architecture. In Melville there is always the question of whether "modern" industry and economic practices have mechanized humanity itself. This issue has been widely addressed, although I have made some additional comments on it. But for Melville the question of mechanization isn't mainly a problem of the modern, despite his interest in modern industry. He is more essentially concerned with mechanization as an enduring way of thinking and being; Bartleby's mechanization is grounded in the pyramid as well as Wall Street, and Ahab's mechanization (as both victim and victimizer) is grounded as much in the pyramid and in early Christian and pre-Christian eschatologies as in the immediate realities of the whaling industry. This tendency to focus on mechanization as a way of thinking and being is visible even in *Typee,* even if that novel foregrounds Melville's concern with a material war machine; over the course of his career, though, the image of the pyramid as the soul of mechanization grows increasingly important, and his career fittingly ends with this image in the closing poems of *Timoleon*.

3
Mumford, Melville, and Megatechnics

Defining the Megamachine

At the end of his much-criticized *Herman Melville* (1929), Lewis Mumford struggles with questions central to his attempt to canonize Melville: Why is Melville important, and why is he so much more important now than he was to his contemporaries? Although Mumford's research has been legitimately criticized, his answer to these crucial questions anticipates the course subsequently taken by much of Melville criticism: "Herman Melville's world is our world, magnificently bodied and dimensioned: our synthesis must include and sublimate that very quest of power which Melville portrayed with such unique skill. . . . Melville's life warns us not to stop here: men must test their strength in surrender as well as in lonely conquest" (365). Ahab's problem is power's necessity and its impossibility. For Mumford, writing before depression and war, the quest for power has a legitimate place *within* a proper, life-oriented context, but valuing power as an end in itself leads to our appalling civilization, which displays "its aimlessness, its grand attempt to conceal its emptiness by extending concrete roads and asphalted streets and vacuum cleaners to more and more remote terrains" (364). Melville represents organic values against the larger culture's materialism. Following the predilections of his generation of critics and anticipating those of future generations, Mumford centers his discussion of Melville around *Moby-Dick,* which for him achieves a synthesis that opens doors for all of "us." "Whatever Melville's life was," Mumford writes, "his art in *Moby-Dick* exhibits that integration and synthesis which we seek. . . . The day of Herman Melville's vision is now in the beginning. It hangs like a cloud over the horizon at dawn; and as the sun rises, it will become more radiant, and more a part of the living day" (368). Mumford reads Melville apocalyptically; the sun's radiance is linked to Ahab's sun-worship, and the radiant cloud evokes the New Jerusalem. The problem of modernity is that the modern self is "dissevered" into a "positive, practical, scientific, externalized self, bent on conquest and knowledge," and an "imaginative, ideal half, bent on the transposition of conflict into art, and power into humanity" (193). In the Melvillean apocalypse the quest for power will be sublimated, the sins of materialistic culture synthesized away, and a humanized quest for power will embrace Ahab's spirit. "Some day the physical powers of man may be commensurate with his utmost spirit, and he will meet Leviathan on even terms" (190). Meaning and life emerge in the struggle with Leviathan; Mumford's apocalypse is the humanization of the quest for power yet also that quest's *empowering* and final rationalization: the synthesized man who turns the power of material culture toward proper ends will be capable of anything.

Mumford's argument contains the seed of its own ruin: "Herman Melville portrayed a human purpose, concentrated to almost maniacal intensity, in Moby-Dick; and in Pierre and The Confidence Man, he showed the black aftermath, when the purpose was not sustained and carried out in art" (363). Mumford embraces Ahab's worldview: history is the narrative of a quest; humanizing that quest leads to an *eschatos.* Mumford can't completely ignore the dark ruins of *Pierre* and *The Confidence-Man,* but he does attempt to dismiss them, arguing that they display the consequences of an insufficiently humanized teleology, an improperly directed quest for power. Mumford attacks a teleology gone bad but embraces a new, synthetic *telos.* The realities of material civilization are brutal and cruel, but a shining city is embedded in the artistic vision of that material civilization, in a repetition of the main idea of Mumford's *The Golden Day* (1926).

But even at this early point Mumford nearly admits that *Pierre* and *The Confidence-Man* pose an intractable problem, by positing a shattered world post-*eschatos.*

Like Melville, Mumford positions himself on romanticism's margins: technology is dehumanizing, but if it is turned away from strictly materialistic ends it offers a positive *telos;* Mumford blends romanticism and American optimism in a manner indebted to Whitman, Thoreau, and especially Emerson. He attempts to reconcile Melville with Whitman's and Emerson's teleology in *The Golden Day,* establishing the line of thinking usually attributed to F. O. Matthiessen: Leo Marx, Matthiessen's most famous student, argues in "Lewis Mumford: Prophet of Organicism" that Matthiessen's debt to Mumford has been greatly underestimated. But while the dominant tradition of American studies, which Mumford helped establish, continued to reconcile Melville with Whitman and Emerson, Mumford himself moved in a different direction.

Mumford published *Herman Melville* in 1929. His next book, *The Brown Decades* (1931), was a meditation on post–Civil War architecture, focusing on Chicago and skyscrapers. For Mumford, the decades following the Civil War were a low point for written culture but important for architecture. In this volume he tamed his earlier assaults on the period's culture and architecture and attempted to find some redeeming, synthetic value in modern architecture.

Before *The Brown Decades,* and straight on the heels of *Herman Melville,* Mumford published an article in *Scribner's* titled "The Drama of the Machines." This essay explored the psychological and practical origins of the machine and judged the machine by practical *and* ethical standards (Mumford, *Technics and Civilization* xi). The connection to Melville is clear: the problems of modernity Melville raised, and the problem of the gap between Melville and Emerson, demanded a more thorough investigation of industrialism, capitalism, and modern art.

"The Drama of the Machines" eventually led to *Technics and Civilization* (1934), Mumford's first masterpiece. It is a classic of the history of technology, still widely admired, and a critical document in the formation of a "humanist philosophy of technology," in Carl Mitcham's terminology; Mitcham, a philosopher of technology, partially credits Mumford with formalizing that tradition, while David Nye deliberately modeled his *Con-*

suming Power upon *Technics and Civilization* (251). *Technics and Civilization* is distinct within that tradition by not being *only* a general critique of "technology" or "the machine," a tradition running from Carlyle through Langdon Winner's *The Whale and the Reactor* (1986) and beyond. It makes general claims, but they are rooted in deep historical research.

Technics and Civilization begins with a discussion of the relationship between time and technology. For Mumford, the clock is foundational to modernity: "it dissociated time from human events and helped create the belief in an independent world of mathematically measurable sequences: the special world of science" (15). Under Bergson's influence, Mumford argues that modernity's time is a time of mathematical points, a spatialized time that can be viewed as a whole or analyzed at any particular point, as opposed to irreducibly cumulative organic time (16). Mumford links the development of spatialized time to cartography and wars of exploration, attributing developments in the technologies of war to the "itch to *use* space and time" (22). In moves that have become familiar but were not at the time, Mumford makes a three-way connection between the development of technics, Protestantism, and capitalism, with the trio helping to develop a "mechanical world-picture" (46). Within the mechanical world-picture, industrialism and militarization are one: "The spread of conscription and volunteer military forces throughout the Western World after the French Revolution made army and factory . . . interchangeable terms" (84). For Mumford the development of a mechanical world-picture and spatialized time produces useful power machines as a late, secondary development, preceded by the regimentation of the world and of humanity.

With modernity, mechanical concepts and entities have replaced organic ones at every level. Spatialized time replaces organic time, mechanical relationships replace organic ones, and machines disrupt every aspect of life. In "Lewis Mumford: Prophet of Organicism," Leo Marx describes Mumford's thought as focused on the conflict between "the Organic" and "the Machine." The crisis of modernity is the mechanization of world and time. Though rooted in the ancient world, this crisis is closely tied to the industrial, military, and political developments of the West, starting in the seventeenth century. "The regularization of time, the increase in mechanical power, the multiplication of goods, the contraction of time and space, the standardization of performance and product, the transfer of skill to automata, and the increase of collective interdependence," writes Mumford, "are the chief characteristics of our machine civilization" (*Technics and Civilization* 281).

I will pass over the historical and theoretical details of Mumford's argument and go directly to his solution. How to deal with modernity, the leveling and deadening of time, space, and life itself? His answer, as in *Herman Melville,* is synthesis, or assimilation: "Until we have absorbed the lessons of objectivity, impersonality, neutrality, the lessons of the mechanical realm, we cannot go further in our development toward the more richly organic, the more profoundly human" (*Technics and Civilization* 363). We must cope with the machine by learning it fully and using it properly: the excesses of the machine age are a necessary stage in human development. Life is internally teleological: "the most rigorous scientific description of the physical basis of life indicates it to be internally teleological" (370). Although Mumford refers to biological teleology, his use of the term in a historical work is telling. He assaults most characteristics of contemporary mechanical civilization while aspiring to a "dynamic equilibrium" in which the nature of progress is questioned without being fully rejected: "the notion of progress in a single line without goal or limit seems perhaps the most parochial notion of a very parochial century. Limits in thought and actions" (429). To push this point—which implicitly includes his frequent jeremiads against monumental architecture—one might say that Mumford loudly and increasingly opposed works of what Nye calls the technological sublime and eventually the electrical sublime. Mumford calls for equilibrium to be achieved regionally, industrially, agriculturally, and communally and admits to speaking in a "prophetic form" in order to advocate the "rebuilding of the individual personality and the collective group, and the reorientation of all forms of thought and social activity towards life" (433). The machine's endless acceleration must be suspended in a dynamic equilibrium, a secular version of the New Jerusalem. Like Stephen Gould decades later, Mumford opposes progress and teleology only to turn and embrace them. History and life itself once again have a *telos;* as in Revelation, the end days are preceded by accelerating errors and cruelties, but history will end in a luminous suspension that evokes Emerson and Whitman, especially humanity's ascension of the staircase to godhead in "Song of Myself." Significantly, Mumford's first book, *The Story of Utopias* (1922), embraces the utopian/eschatological mode. As in his readings of *Moby-Dick* and Melville's life, Mumford asserts confidently that history will be justified, that the story of the West will have its proper ending as it has a proper origin: that ending will be "they all lived happily ever after."

Then came the war and the bomb, while Melville's venom still circulated in Mumford's veins. Melville's influence on such major works as *Technics and Civilization* (1934) and *The Culture of Cities* (1938) is not obvious. It is even less obvious in Mumford's works of the 1940s and 1950s, which even Mumford acknowledged as rushed and mediocre (Miller 451). But Mumford came to analyze the cold war through Melvillean lenses, and his early work in Melville criticism bore fruit in the 1960s and 1970s.

Mumford's two-volume *The Myth of the Machine,* comprising *Technics and Human Development* (1967) and *The Pentagon of Power* (1970), argues that "our present over-commitment to technics is in part due to a radical misinterpretation of the whole course of human development" (*Technics and Human Development* 4). From Marx to contemporary anthropology, intellectuals have given "material instruments of production the central place and directive function in human development." Man is, Mumford agrees, a tool-making animal, but not *principally* a tool-making animal: "Tool-technics . . . is but a fragment of biotechnics: man's total equipment for life" (7). Mumford emphasizes the centrality of language, make-believe, and the unconscious in human existence. From this beginning, he examines the megamachine, the primeval machine that, he argues, is the model for other machines: "the Machine Age . . . had its origin, not in the so-called Industrial Revolution of the eighteenth century, but at the very outset in the organization of an archetypal machine composed of human parts" (11).[1] Mumford argues that this machine built the pyramids, as well as the Egyptian, Greek, and Babylonian war machines; he reads Exodus as the Jewish escape from the megamachine (recall the oppressive brick-making that Pharaoh imposes upon them, a brick-making that Melville displaces to London in *Israel Potter*).[2] The megamachine was quiescent for centuries, but the total regimentation of humanity, supplemented by ever more machinery, has reappeared in our own era. Mumford gives an account of medieval technics, familiar to readers of *Technics and Civilization,* which emphasizes that the Dark Ages were anything but dark, arguing that our present lines of technical development originated in the medieval monastery;[3] these lines of development, originally benign, led to the return of megatechnics, including such symptoms as the U.S. and Soviet space programs, totalitarianism, and secret systems of quasi-mystical knowledge, Haraway's C^3I.

For Mumford the exploration of the "New World" involved two components, Western imperialism and a parallel excavation of ancient history: "As geographical exploration loosed the spatial bonds to a particular soil and culture, so these new temporal explorations loosed the bonds to the immediate present . . . the human mind began to move about freely in both past and future, picking and choosing, anticipating and projecting" (*Pentagon* 13). This double movement attempted "to escape time and cumulative effects of time (tradition and history) by exchanging it for unoccupied space" (13–14). This exchange of time for space resulted in reversion to the worst features of Egyptian and Babylonian civilization. Mumford's argument invites skepticism, but the relationship of Western colonialism and racism to a particular understanding of Egyptian civilization *has* been well documented by Scott Trafton. Mumford argues that the massive occupation of space and conquest of time achieved by the pyramids has its modern equivalent in nuclear weapons and space flight, which exist "to reduce the human organism itself, its habitat, and its mode of existence, and its life-purpose to just those minimal dimensions that will bring it under total external control" (306). With modest rephrasing, this sentence would fit into Heidegger's "The Question Concerning Technology": humanity is reduced to standing-reserve.

The megamachine presents humanity with the twin dangers of nuclear annihilation and total regimentation: "the universal imposition of the Megamachine . . . as the ultimate instrument of pure 'intelligence,' whereby every other manifestation of human potentialities will be suppressed. . . . Already the blueprints for that final structure are available: they have even been advertised as man's highest destiny" (Mumford, *Pentagon* 303). The end of history is marketed to us: space, cyberspace, endless growth. The megamachine is an instrument of an inhuman intelligence and the end of all human concerns; hence the impression of many readers, including David Nye, that Mumford is a determinist who believes in the autonomy of large technological systems (*Power* 254). Mumford offers no specific solutions to the megamachine, but he does offer a hope: the original pyramid age in Egypt ended, he asserts, in a popular uprising (*Pentagon* 303). The megamachine may never end, it may be consumed in nuclear fire, or it may end with a "newly incarnated personality" (423).

On what basis does Mumford believe that the megamachine, which is literally although invisibly a machine, arose in ancient Egypt and Babylonia? Leo Marx argues that Mumford's belief in the megamachine as a literal machine is intuitive, not based in sound history. Marx argues that the basis for Mumford's claim lies in his overall rhetorical strategy:

> After Hiroshima and the intensification of the nuclear arms race he had become increasingly alarmed about the potentially catastrophic uses of America's technological power. He no longer could summon the hope he had attached to the latest technologies. . . . [As] the United States was getting enmeshed in Vietnam, he evidently decided to focus on the impending culmination of the ancient conflict between organic and mechanical technics. If . . . that conflict is the crux of modern history, the American "pentagon of power"—an updated, nuclear-armed version of the Egyptian pyramid-building system—is its potentially cataclysmic end-product. Hence the importance he retrospectively attaches to the ancient megamachine, with its manifestly totalitarian, death-oriented character, as the precursor of the vast superpower technological systems. . . . Not only does he locate the megamachine in the consciousness of the pyramid-builders, but he would have us believe (without presenting any evidence to indicate how, or whether, it was transmitted from epoch to epoch, mind to mind) that the same concept subsequently was present to the minds of the inventors of all complex forms of machinery. ("Mumford" 177–78)

Although Marx ignores some limited support Mumford provides for his thesis, he is substantially correct. Whether we follow Mumford's intuition or not, we must recognize it as an intuition serving a rhetorical purpose: to show that the conflict between the organic and the mechanical is *the* great historical narrative.

Marx argues that Mumford abandons optimism for essentially political reasons. But the intellectual seeds had been planted far earlier than the cold war, as is manifest in *Herman Melville* and *Technics and Civilization;* Mumford's interest in the relationship between time and technology is crucial to understanding this change. His analysis of modernity was always concerned with time; following Bergson, and laying the groundwork for future historians and philosophers of technology, Mumford was concerned with the spatialization and mechanization of time. Until *The Myth of the Machine,* though, his critique of the mechanical world-picture was committed to teleology and a spatialized time that could be analyzed and understood as a whole. The story of modernity was the story of a fall from the wholeness of the medieval self into a mechanical world concerned only with progress, which would ultimately result in a reintegration of the self and the machine's assimilation. Time had been organic before the Fall; it became mechanical; it would be organic again after the restoration. After the restoration, having integrated the machine, humanity would rise to a higher, more stable state. Mumford was a fly caught in teleology's web: however he struggled, he remained enmeshed. The machine erupts into the tranquil garden, struggles with the organic, and then a newer, better form of the organic is generated: when Marx analyzes Mumford, the positive ending he sees in the early Mumford is also the luminous eschatological ending of his own *The Machine in the Garden.*

Traces of this vision persist through *The Myth of the Machine,* which sometimes reads like a teleological, eschatological assault on teleology and eschatology (hence making it both more and less deterministic than Mumford's earlier work), but this account of history, moving from garden to Fall to New Jerusalem, is troubled by Mumford's changing concept of time. The megamachine is no longer strictly modern but receives roots at the "beginning of history" in Mumford's late works. The mechanical world-picture has become primordial, even mythical, while we, as cogs, have become interchangeable with those of Egypt and Sumer. The megamachine permeates time; the pyramid's shadow covers all, for Mumford as for Melville, making "organic" time seem impossibly distant.

"But for no holy purpose was the pyramid founded," Melville wrote in his journal (78). The lesson, even if it was belated, was no longer lost on Mumford: time has *always* been spatialized, mechanized, regimented; history always belonged to power.

Melville and the Roots of Mumford's Necropolis

Most of Mumford's books touch on Melville: he is important in *The Story of Utopias* (1922), appears seven times in *The Condition of Man* (1944) and five times in *The Conduct of Life* (1951), is mentioned in *The City in History* (1961) and *The Culture of Cities* (1938), and is frequently discussed in Mumford's autobiography, *Sketches from Life* (1982). Melville was, in short, always on Mumford's mind. In his correspondence, Mumford engaged in critical discussion of Melville with Van Wyck Brooks and David Liebovitz and habitually related his own life to Melville's. Clearly, Melville was important to Mumford. Most importantly, Mumford's ongoing brooding over Melville was formative to *The Myth of the Machine.* In particular, Mumford's concept of the megamachine is deeply indebted to his long engagement with Melville.

In *The City in History* (1961), Mumford compares the evils of ancient Roman cities and contemporary Western ones, focusing especially on technical and architectural achievements that serve elites. For instance, the useless ingenuities of Roman indoor plumbing, more advanced than anything until the late nineteenth century, were available to the powerful, while the masses died of cholera and typhus (216–17). He attacks the West for returning to some characteristics of Roman life: high rents, declining living conditions, high tenements, "mass contests and exhibitions . . . the multiplication of bathrooms and the over-expenditure on broadly paved motor roads." He considers these "symptoms of the end. . . . Necropolis is near" (242). Curiously, despite Mumford's fear of the Necropolis-as-end, related to what Nye refers to as Mumford's "'death-world' of pure technique," Mumford argues that the Necropolis *precedes* the living city: "the city of the dead is the forerunner . . . of every living city. Urban life spans the historic space between the earliest burial ground for dawn man and the final cemetery, the Necropolis, in which one civilization after another has met its end" (Mumford, *City in History*

7; Nye, *Sublime* 23). The end is in the beginning, which is death. Writing in *The Pentagon of Power,* in the caption under a photograph of a massive graveyard that foregrounds a city squeezed against the horizon, Mumford argues that there are three stages to a city's death: it becomes Parasitopolis, the city of parasites and elites; then Patholopolis, "the city of mental, moral, and bodily disorders"; and finally Necropolis (plate 24). The flaws of modern cities don't only come from contemporary problems; they are founded with the seeds of Necropolis already planted. In the fullness of time, death blossoms. Every city, every civilization, carries its end (*telos*) in its beginning (*arche*). This *telos* is not mere death but a monumental celebration of death—that is, in part, the technological sublime; Nye discusses Mumford's concept of the death-world in context with the sublimity of the atomic bomb and Apollo XI. The city's being is the spatialization of death-time: time and space are converted into a monument to death that sprawls into past and future: Necropolis is not impotent ruins but a (sublime) *polis* of death. In one age its monuments were pyramids, great walls, useless highways; now they are spaceships, hydrogen bombs, skyscrapers, and more useless highways.

Mumford's Necropolis is foundational to his concept of megatechnics. Leo Marx argues that Mumford always embraced "organic values." These values, though, are terribly bruised by the time of *The City in History,* because that book undercuts the notion of a legitimate organic past, a home one can return to. Civilizations cyclically rise in Mumford's account (in some respects he follows Toynbee and anticipates Braudel), but they rise *from* Necropolis, and instead of falling completely, they leave Necropolis behind; the Necropolis dominates both past and future. Mumford, like some nightmare avatar of Bergson, articulates an inversion of Bergson's "duration," in which the cumulative, irreducible nature of time is the accumulation of death's power; there are moments in Wallerstein's analysis of the *duration* of the capitalist world-system that are reminiscent of this aspect of Mumford's work.

The genealogy of Mumford's thought becomes more clear. In *Herman Melville* he embraced Ahab as exemplary: his teleological drive was vital, if in need of humanization; it was an *antidote* to mechanization. In *Technics and Civilization* the threat is clarified: time itself is mechanized; we must relearn organic time. Over the following decades, clouded though they are by Mumford's numerous minor books, something else arose in Mumford's thought. The mechanization of time, the transformation of world into automaton, was not a *modern* problem susceptible to the antibodies of a new "synthesis," for the Necropolis was ancient, and grew only more insistent over time; the Necropolis, as the city's womb and *telos,* becomes a mechanistic tyranny that owns and supervises all time: the megamachine.

Even in *Herman Melville* the seeds of this thought appear, where Mumford writes his account of Melville's journey to Egypt. Mumford claims to be the first person to have made use of this journal, which he paraphrases at great length. Selections from Melville's text and Mumford's paraphrase follow.

Melville's Text	**Mumford's Text**
Nothing in Nature gives such an idea of vastness. . . . Pain in chest. Exhaustion. Must hurry. None but the phlegmatic go deliberately. Old man with the spirits of youth—long looked for this chance—tried the ascent, half way—fainted—brought down. Tried to go into the interior—fainted—brought out—leaned against the pyramid by the entrance—pale as death. Nothing so pathetic. Too much for him; oppressed by the massiveness & mystery of the pyramids. I myself too. A feeling of awe & terror came over me. Dread of the Arabs. Offering to lead me into a side-hole. The Dust. Long arched way,—then down as in a coal shaft. . . . I shudder at idea of	Well, it was almost too much for Melville: it was not the sense of height but the sense of immensity that was stirred: with all other architecture, however vast, the eye is gradually inured to the sense of magnitude by passing from part to part: but here there was no storey or stage: it was all or nothing, not height or breadth or length or depth but unspeakable vastness. . . . The great Pyramid refused to be studied or adequately comprehended. . . . A feeling of awe and terror gradually came over Melville: the Arabs were no longer angels, but seemed, in their soft, imperturbable way, somehow malign. Stooping and doubling in the interior, as in a coal shaft, Melville shuddered at the ancient

ancient Egyptians. It was in these pyramids that was conceived the idea of Jehovah. Terrible mixture of the cunning and awful. Moses learned in all the lore of the Egyptians. The idea of Jehovah was born here. . . . Entrance of pyramids like shoot for coal or timber. Horrible place for assassination. (*Journals* 75)

Second Melville Passage

It refuses to be studied or adequately comprehended. It still looms in my imagination, dim & indefinite. . . . A dead calm of masonry. . . . Man seems to have had as little to do with it as Nature. It was that supernatural creature, the priest. They must needs have been terrible inventors, those Egyptian wise men. And one seems to see that as out of the crude forms of the natural earth they could evoke by art the transcendent mass & symmetry & unity of the pyramid so out of the rude elements of the insignificant thoughts that are in all men, they could rear the transcendent conception of a God. But for no holy purpose was the pyramid founded. (*Journals* 78)

Egyptians: they had a mixture of the cunning and the awful. Moses learned his lore from the Egyptians: the awful idea of Jehovah was born there. They must needs have been terrible inventors, those ancient wise men: as out of the crude forms of the natural earth they could evoke by art the Pyramids, so, out of the dull elements of the insignificant thoughts that are in all men, they could by analogous art rear the transcendent conception of God. Indeed, the Egyptians had outwitted mortality. The Pyramids were conceived out of an energy as mighty as Nature's: nought but an earthquake or a geological revolution could smother it up. That was something like an answer to the White Whale—albeit such a distant answer. The pyramidical energy as well as the pyramidical scorn, were both lacking in Melville now, high though they had towered in *Moby-Dick*. (*Herman Melville* 271–72)

Mumford remains close to the source material, sometimes keeping Melville's wording, but he blends two passages from Melville's journal with a layer of interpretation, forming a text expressing his understanding of Melville in a blend of his own words and Melville's. I quoted at length both to demonstrate the degree to which Mumford attempts fidelity to the original and to show how far from it his rendition veers.

Mumford acknowledges how extraordinary these journal entries are by reproducing them so closely. No other section of the biography remains so close to its source material. Nor did Mumford strictly copy it: he labored to transform it. Mumford preserves Melville's association between the dread of the pyramids and of technology, what Nye would call the technological sublime. Mumford's deepening gloom over the prospects of technological civilization is already implicit: he brings together and compacts Melville's lines about the coal shaft, the creation of Jehovah, and the Egyptians as inventors. *The Myth of the Machine,* written almost forty years later, would claim that pyramid builders invented both the megamachine and the sun god—but Mumford had already derived a version of this claim from Melville in this passage. But Mumford rejects the extremity of Melville's horror at the Egyptian wise men. Their construction of pyramid and Jehovah are no longer unholy and terrible, but admirable. Melville's horrors become Mumford's "pyramidical energy."

In rendering the pyramid builders as unholy, Melville comments on the American use of Egyptian iconography: Egypt represented both American power and the horrors of slavery. Melville's disgust at both is already clear in *Mardi,* wherein he describes a satirical monument to America that has the freedom/slavery dichotomy literally inscribed upon it. *Israel Potter* assaults American monuments, literal and figurative, from Benjamin Franklin to the Bunker Hill Monument. In *Subversive Genealogy,* Paul Rogin writes that Daniel Webster's address at the Bunker Hill Monument's completion compared its might and silence to those of a pyramid (229). Israel, despite being an American war hero, is abandoned to near slavery in the Egypt of London; when he returns after forty years, he finds himself memorialized on a tomblike monument: its transcendence is like death. But Mumford psychologizes Melville's pyramid-dread, arguing that Melville has lost his ambition and that this loss, not the monument itself, horrifies him.

Mumford transforms Melville's horror of the pyramid into a narrative of the triumph of the human will. The pyramid perversely becomes a triumph of the *organic,* the human. Whereas Israel's sojourn in Britain-as-Egypt and his return to America-as-Egypt is, in Rogin's words, a "biography of failure," Mumford's biography of Melville is triumphalist (Rogin 228). Yet for Melville, the teleological will of the pyramid builders is monstrous: the transcendental pyramid is murder, nightmare, Necropolis.

Mumford, too, eventually saw the pyramid as the achievement of an *inhuman* will, of the Necropolis and the megamachine. As his understanding of the pyramid changed, he returned, subtly but powerfully, to writing about Melville and an Ahab now grown terrible in Mumford's eyes. Mumford used *Moby-Dick* to analyze the cold war in a 1959 article for *Atlantic Monthly:* "Those who believe that any country has the right to make such a decision [use a nuclear weapon] share the madness of Captain Ahab in 'Moby-Dick.' For them Russia is the White Whale that must be hunted down and grappled with. Like Ahab in that mad pursuit, they will listen to no reminders of love . . . they will sink their own ship and drown their crew. To such unbalanced men, to such demoralized efforts, to such dehumanized purposes, the Nuclear Powers have entrusted our lives" (*My Works and Days* 460). Mumford now reads *Moby-Dick* as a critique of transcendental ambition rather than as a monument to it; no longer an artifact of the "golden day," it is constitutive of America's being: Ahab commands the ship of state *now.* Pyramid builders are heroes no more. In *The Pentagon of Power,* Mumford continues to link Ahab with the madness of American megatechnics. "In Ahab," he writes, "Melville gave expression both to the megatechnic 'Khans' of the global Pentagon and to the counter-forces they had brought into being" (376). Ahab is not merely *like* the megatechnic khans of the global pentagon; they are given expression through him. Ahab *is* the heart of the Pentagon of Power, the *telos* of history. Consider the following lines from *Technics and Human Development:* "No king could move safely or effectively without the support of such organized 'higher knowledge' [astronomy, astrology, etc.], any more than the Pentagon can move today without consulting its specialized scientists, technical experts, games theorists and computers—a new hierarchy supposedly less fallible than the entrail-diviners, but, to judge by their gross miscalculations, not notably so" (199). While Ahab needs secret knowledge to maintain his power—he is the supreme scientist of whaling, the lone priest of magnetism—he is not simply a "modern" man of the Pentagon, enslaving science to power. Ahab belongs to both the old and new megatechnics: he is the American captain of industry but also

Pharaoh with his mighty "Egyptian" chest and Parsi servant. "Modern" and "ancient" are confused: Starbuck and Ahab act on superstition, but Queequeg is reasonable and Fedallah belongs to a technocratic-capitalist elite.

Ahab is attended by a sun-worshipper; the reward for first spying the whale is a doubloon symbolizing the sun; Ahab believes that whales themselves are sun-worshippers (497). Ahab destroys the quadrant, suppressing one technology in favor of another: he is more powerful as the sole master of magnetism than as one of many masters of the quadrant; the secrecy of the technology is more important than its utility. Destroying the quadrant, Ahab curses "all things that cast man's eyes aloft to that heaven" (501). Ahab, surrounded by sun-worshippers, has cast aside the tools to use the sun. Has he defied the sun, or made greater use of it? Is he extending or rejecting the spatialization of time associated with astronomy and sun gods? Fedallah displays "sneering triumph" and "fatalistic despair" in response to Ahab's action, indicating that from his viewpoint Ahab's power has grown, along with the certainty of his doom; his relationships to sun, crew, and whale are optimal, yet insufficient for his monomaniac purpose. C. L. R. James argues that this passage shows that Ahab elevates man above all, a reading in accord with Mumford's earlier humanistic understanding of Ahab's voyage (55). This is, however, not the elevation of mankind as such but of a mechanized mankind arrayed under Ahab qua living pyramid.

Mumford does not discuss Ahab's complex relationship with the sun and sun-worship, but his analysis of sun-worship in modern and ancient life in *The Myth of the Machine* is indebted to Melville. Kingship, spatialized time, and the megamachine are bound to the sun, but so are the scientist and the new megamachine (*Technics and Human Development* 199). Within two centuries of Leonardo da Vinci and Agricola, Mumford argues, "the ideological fabric that supported the ancient megamachine had been reconstructed. . . . Power, speed, motion, standardization, mass production, quantification, regimentation, precision, uniformity, astronomical regularity, control, above all control. . . . Only one thing was needed to assemble and polarize all the new components of the megamachine: the birth of the Sun God. And in the sixteenth century, with Kepler, Tycho Brahe, and Copernicus officiating as accoucheurs, the new Sun God was born" (*Technics and Human Development* 294). Ahab himself is a site of the megamachine's reconstruction. Like a city beginning and ending with Necropolis, Ahab simultaneously embodies the megamachine's movement toward an apocalyptic ending, its primordial roots, and the too-human desire to be free of it. The ancient and modern cohabit in Ahab's person, as in the megamachine.

Mumford astutely claims that the Renaissance's excavation of the past did more for human development than any particular technical invention: "By unburying statues, monuments, buildings, cities, by reading old books and inscriptions, by re-entering a long-abandoned world of ideas, these new explorers in time became aware of fresh potentialities in their own existence" (*Pentagon* 13). We progress by regressing; the megamachine is never *new* but always re-created. By bringing "savages" into his inner sanctum, Ahab asserts control over mankind and its future; he unearths and masters the past, as he masters the secrets of the deep (C. L. R. James 55).

Mumford argues that the related institutions of kingship and sun-worship arose from Paleolithic hunters waging war on farmers, and explicitly connects the Paleolithic hunter to *Moby-Dick,* in which he finds "the psychal and social parallels of the paleolithic hunt. . . . Leadership and loyalty, those keys to military success and large-scale organization, flourished in this milieu. . . . [E]xhilarating self-confidence, venturesome command, and, not least, a certain savage readiness to take life, were the essential prerequisites for the greatest early achievement in technics: the collective human machine" (*Technics and Human Development* 117). *Moby-Dick*'s whale hunt unites the ancient requirements for the megamachine with the innovations of advanced technics. The crew even contains members of "aboriginal" cultures, mighty hunters suitable for absorption into either Paleolithic or modern megamachines: Queequeg, Tashtego, Dagoo, and Ahab fill the shoes of the chieftain Mumford describes. The *Pequod*'s voyage is also the primordial conquest of Egypt or Sumer, which resonates with its name: the Pequot tribe was destroyed by genocidal warfare. Ahab is both a Paleolithic hunting chief ("cannibal old me") and a scientifically minded whaler; the modern totalitarian state that is created or foreshadowed in *Moby-Dick* is also Egypt, Sumer, and the Incan Empire (544).

Even Queequeg, who recalls the rich among his people using the poor as couches, has megatechnic potential: if we don't simply treat it as a joke, what a level of domination that implies! The *Pequod,* despite its modern technology, depends on Indian-invented "druggs," devices that slow down a harpooned whale. The megamachine can be built using old or new technologies; since it spatializes time, it draws freely on the new and the old (386). Edgerton's *The Shock of the Old,* a contemporary technological history in an explicitly Mumfordian vein, argues that the most extensive and effective deployment of horses in warfare was by Nazi Germany; old technologies *always* intermingle with new ones (35). One of *Moby-Dick*'s last images is of Tashtego obeying Ahab's final command by nailing a banner to the mast while drowning. Ahab's will, like that of the sun god, dominates Tashtego even in his "death-grasp" (572). The cannibal hunters are not less vulnerable to becoming automatons than the more "civilized" of the crew; if anything, they are more vulnerable.

At the end of *Technics and Human Development,* Mumford reveals how deeply rooted the megamachine is in *Moby-Dick:* "From the sixteenth century on the secret of the megamachine was slowly re-discovered. In a series of empirical fumblings and improvisations, with little sense of the ultimate end toward which society was moving, that great mechanical Leviathan was fished up out of the depths of history. The expansion of the megamachine—its kingdom, its power, its glory—became progressively the chief end, or at least the fixed obsession, of Western Man" (293–94). Melville's automatons are both symptom and prophecy. They are the megamachine's cogs: Ahab can afford to jest about building literal mechanical men because he *already has* a working megamachine, built from the *Pequod*'s crew. In Ahab we have the mechanizing man, the sun king or Pharaoh; in the crew we have the mechanized men who have been appearing in Melville's fiction since *Typee.* What was once Mumford's story of mechanization and modernity has become the inevitable narrative of *all* (transcendental) history. Not coincidentally, this unity between the distant past and the hypermodern is central to Melville's *The Confidence-Man,* in which modernity becomes a collection of con games.

Resisting the Megamachine

The final chapter of *The Confidence-Man* begins with an old man studying scripture by the lone "solar lamp" still burning in the men's cabin of the steamboat *Fidèle.* A "perverse man" tried to extinguish the light, but the steward forbade him, reminding him that "to show one's self anxious to produce darkness" among strangers was "not becoming" (1099). The chapter recounts a conversation between the old man and the Cosmopolitan, one of the confidence-man's many incarnations. They discuss the Bible as "good news"—using passages not from the gospels but from the apocryphal book of Sirach; Melville the Hebraist is at work again. The passages warn against trust and "fair words," understood by someone who speaks from the darkness, interrupting the conversation, as a description of a confidence man. The Cosmopolitan and the old man discuss Sirach's apocryphal status: "to the right [and left] is certain truth . . . but all I hold in my hand here is apocrypha." The old man urges the Cosmopolitan to ignore Sirach's warnings, "for it's apocrypha." The voice calls from the darkness for the third time: "What's that about the Apocalypse?" (1102).

In *Satirical Apocalypse,* Jonathan Cook traces webs of biblical typology in *The Confidence-Man* on three levels, "relative to the Bible as a whole, the New Testament alone, and the Book of Revelation"; the novel moves from Mosaic "law" to Christian "grace," from "Christ's first advent in the first chapter to his Second Advent in the Last," and is an "enactment of the Apocalypse, with the Confidence Man conflating true messiah and false prophet, Christ and Antichrist" (58–59). Cook argues that the old man's conversation with the Cosmopolitan seems to elaborate an opposition between the old man "illumined with faith" and the "potentially damned sleepers . . . some of whom rudely advise him to go to bed"; however, the old man's obsession with security devices later in the chapter makes his own faith questionable (75). In the novel's last scene, the Cosmopolitan extinguishes the lamp, at which "the waning light expired, and with it the waning flames of the horned altar, and the waning halo round the robed man's brow; while in the darkness which ensued, the cosmopolitan kindly led the old man away. Something further may follow of this Masquerade" (1112). While this last scene symbolizes "the completion of a fictive Apocalypse," argues Cook, it also suggests continuance into a "post-apocalyptic world [which] is also post-Christian" (80). Decades earlier, Mumford similarly saw the novel as being about a world bereft of human purpose; its post-Christian nature is assumed.

Cook sees *The Confidence-Man* qua apocalypse as a predecessor to

Henry Adams's vision in *The Education of Henry Adams* of "an apocalyptic finale to the progressive-minded, outwardly prosperous nineteenth century" (215) and, following R. W. B. Lewis, calls it an ancestor to "apocalyptic framework narratives" by West, Ellison, Barth, and Pynchon (215).

Let us recall that this apocalyptic narrative, written in 1857, is set on a modern steamboat; by enabling Western nations to project sea power (Melville's topic in *Typee* and *Omoo*) into the African and Asian interiors, steamboats had already utterly revolutionized war in Asia and Africa (Headrick, *Tools* 18). This same ability to project power shortly transformed the American interior, enabling the North to win the Civil War. The mechanization of war at sea is later the subject of Melville's Civil War poem "A Utilitarian View of the Monitor's Fight": "Beyond the strife of fleets heroic; / Deadlier, closer, calm 'mid storm; / No passion; all went on by crank, / Pivot, and screw, / And calculations of caloric" (*Poems* 81). War is shifting toward calculation and certainty, driven by knowledge, not passion.

The modern war machine's internal teleology is a subject of Melville's apocalyptic narrative. When the voice cries out "What's that about the Apocalypse?" it responds to the old man's assertion that the Old and New Testaments contain certain truth, as opposed to the Apocrypha. The voice welds the concepts of Apocalypse and epistemological certainty: certainty, truth, and *confidence* in them *are* eschatology. If truth and certainty, confidence and faith, create only apocalyptic time (being-toward-death), what remains? "Something further may follow of this masquerade," *The Confidence-Man* ends. The only time that does not cease at the end is based on the masquerade, on betrayal and darkness: the darkness of Pierre's betrayal of his mother and fiancée, the darkness of the Tombs in which he and his shadowy sister kill themselves with a bottle of poison that drops like "a run-out sand-glass"; the darkness of Ishmael's betrayal of his people and their epistemology; the darkness of Queequeg's betrayal of *his* people and *their* epistemology; the darkness of Israel Potter's literal blindness at the end of his "biography of failure"; the darkness of Bartleby buried in the pyramid; the darkness of Babo's rebellion in *Benito Cereno*—Babo, who writes a script and plays a role worthy of Shakespeare, violently overthrowing all truth and certainty in the process (*Pierre* 420).

Out of Melville's renegade heroes, only two live to continue their treachery: Ishmael and the confidence-man. One after another, his traitor-heroes are slated for death. Those who rebel most openly against the megamachine must die: Babo, Bartleby, Pierre, Queequeg. The rebels die; the traitors, who are unfaithful to *all* powers above them, live. "Owning no allegiance but to the King of the Cannibals; and ready at any moment to rebel against him," Ishmael describes himself (270). The confidence-man's treachery runs still deeper.

Ishmael and the confidence-man realize that there is no lost time to return to, no garden, no organic principle. They see the pyramid spatializing time, which generates truth, God, and apocalypse, organizing all things and holding all power; and they see the masquerade as the system of deceptions and lies that betrays the pyramid. The pyramid owns time, which is, like Ahab, a locomotive with a destination. And the masquerade? Its promise—its *only* promise—is that "something further may follow." The pyramid looms over history; the masquerade reviles it. Both embrace and use technology: Ishmael is obsessed with the tools and techniques of whaling, and the confidence-man is at home aboard the *Fidèle,* not in an agricultural village. The pyramid is concerned with technology's destination: the finished pyramid, the completed cathedral, the laden ship, in short, with the sublime object. The masquerade deals with *process:* the gutting of a whale as sexual ecstasy in *Moby-Dick,* the convolutions of modern patent medicine in *The Confidence-Man.*

Many of Melville's critics see him as critiquing not only Western imperialism and metaphysics but also the relationship between them. William Spanos's "Pierre's Silence," a compact sequel to his sprawling *Errant Art of Moby-Dick,* addresses Melville's mockery of Western thought from Plato to Goethe: "the 'mapping' and 'colonization' of America inaugurated by the Puritans' 'founding' of the 'unmapped' 'New World' wilderness . . . [was] accomplished by the middle of the nineteenth century. . . . [T]hese affiliated key terms . . . suggest that they refer literally *both* to geographical space *and* . . . to a Western thinking that, at least since the Romans and increasingly thereafter, is informed by a spatial metaphorics that represents the truth of being (knowledge) as a 'territory' . . . to be won and dominated" (375). By elevating or praising a kind of "nomadic thought" that Spanos links with Deleuze, Melville "anticipates the postmodernist diagnosis of modernity as the 'end' of philosophy" (378).

I admire Spanos's argument, but it fails to critique itself: his reading itself invokes teleological history by asserting that at some moment Western thought "fell" into spatializing and that since then it has become increasingly spatialized. Time and space have been dominated; an organic grasp of being has been lost—but in this postmodern moment, we have the opportunity and need to rethink thinking: "he anticipates the decentered and errant thought of the new Europeans and thus becomes a truly American exceptionalist" ("Silence" 380). Despite their many differences, Spanos's reading of Melville is akin to Mumford's early reading: "The day of Herman Melville's vision is now in the beginning. It hangs like a cloud over the horizon at dawn; and as the sun rises, it will become more radiant, and more a part of the living day" (*Herman Melville* 368). Contra Spanos and Mumford, though, the man who was appalled by the pyramid had escaped from nothing; the thing he abhorred dated back not to Rome but to Egypt, and for Melville, *nothing* preceded Egypt's monumentalism, not even the "idyll" of the Typees, much like the resurrected Mummy in Poe's "A Few Words with a Mummy," who declares America's obsession with origins to be baseless: there was, Poe's mummy asserts, nothing at all before Egypt.

Melville did not have a problem *only* with Western metaphysics or "thinking," but with power as well; for him, time and power elide as aspects of the pyramid. Technological progress and humanity's mechanization are neither causes nor symptoms of teleological Western metaphysics: humanity has always been under the pyramid's mechanizing hand. Nothing, premodern or postmodern, can oppose the pyramid in history, for the pyramid *owns* history. Knowing that, the confidence-man has a piece of useful, at-hand knowledge, as empirical and versatile as Ishmael's knowledge of whaling: teleological thought becomes a tool, a machine for leading an old man into the darkness. The confidence-man is in no danger of suddenly *holding power;* he operates at the pyramid's edges, not its summit—but he can certainly survive it and manipulate it.

The earlier Mumford, despite his unsophistication, understood the relationship between technology, modernity, and Melville in a teleological/apocalyptic mode akin to how contemporary critics understand the same relationship. The later Mumford, although not primarily a literary critic, developed a much different understanding of Melville in conjunction with his increasingly sophisticated and dark understanding of technology and history, one from which contemporary criticism can benefit. My lingering question is: What can a more technologically sophisticated understanding of Melville, one attending to the relationship between technology and teleology, and which is more akin to the late than the early Mumford, be able to *do,* and why has this potential branch of Melville studies not been pursued?

The failure of literary critics to see Mumford's literary criticism as an ongoing project, rather than one beginning with *The Golden Day* and ending with *Herman Melville,* has marked Melville studies and American studies as a whole. Mumford has often been regarded as an Emersonian. This understandable categorization has deflected attention from Mumford's later work; he is often remembered only for the eager pieties of *The Golden Day:* "The sunlight had in Emerson and Whitman penetrated to every spot, and in its presence, the dark corners became more intense. If one explored the white summits of the glacier with Emerson, one might also fall into the abyss with Melville" (142). Among students of Mumford, though, there is some consensus that his early optimism fell into pessimism and darkness.[4] This darkness is linked to his changing understanding of the world, particularly the organic/mechanical divide, but also chronicles his shift from Emerson to Melville, and from a brighter to a darker Melville; the darkness that Mumford once exiled into *Pierre* and *The Confidence-Man* later *permeates* Melville.

Mumford's reading of Melville has received some critical attention, but mainly by way of understanding Melville's impact on Mumford's life, not his work. In "Tragedy, Responsibility, and the Intellectual," Richard Fox argues that Mumford derived his "tragic sense of life" from Melville (326–28), while Rosalind Williams writes that Mumford justified an affair using Melville: "as Melville had, Mumford felt he had to break free from past habits and received rules" (46).[5] Casey Blake argues that Mumford deliberately based his ethics on Melville's, which allowed him to emphasize "human limits" and the "tragic sense of life," to resist the "shabbiness" of American liberalism, and to seek a secular equivalent to the insights of religion (291). I have, in turn, detailed the debt Mumford's concept of megatechnics owes to Melville: Melville is central to Mumford's understanding of technology and time as well as ethics.

Those few Melvilleans who work with Mumford usually focus solely on *The Golden Day* and *Herman Melville.* Spanos, for example, argues that "the biographical critics of the 1920s—Raymond Weaver, Lewis Mumford [etc.]" were elitists who "attributed the vulgar materialism of the age to Puritanism" (*Errant* 16). He criticizes Mumford for "impositions [upon *Moby-Dick*] of larger, spatial categories to justify a preconceived ideological agenda" and for reading the novel "from the end" (58, 73). These criticisms carry some weight against the early Mumford (although Spanos does not escape these problems himself), but they are startling against the late Mumford, who deployed Melville precisely against the megamachine's *spatializing* tyranny.

Clare Spark's account of Mumford's role in Melville studies in *Hunting Captain Ahab* warrants discussion: "Disillusion with the idea of progress supposedly explains Melville's sudden acceptability in the twentieth century; it was Melville's all-too-graphic disintegration, though, that frightened his critics. His apparent corrective flights to corporatism were promoted by Nietzchean [*sic*] radicals such as Van Wyck Brooks or Lewis Mumford, defining themselves against a mechanistic and alien mass culture" (249–50). Setting aside the error of calling Brooks and Mumford "Nietzchean radicals"—Spark evidently confuses Brooks and Mumford with Raymond Weaver[6]—her reading of Mumford's understanding of Melville's "disintegration" is essentially correct if we attend only to *The Golden Day* and *Herman Melville:* Mumford praises the human power of *Moby-Dick,* virtually reviles *Pierre* and *The Confidence-Man,* then praises Melville's return to the "values of life"—Spark's corporatism. Mumford's later works treat Melville far differently, though, as Spark herself should have realized when she quoted a letter from Mumford to Henry Murray in which Mumford acknowledges his dissatisfaction with his own *Herman Melville.*[7] In a section of this letter that Spark doesn't quote, Mumford acknowledges the superficiality of *Herman Melville* and the value of Murray's work on *Pierre,* writing that, for his superficiality, "like Stubb, I probably deserve a kick in the rump from Ahab! But you couldn't have written anything more appropriately stimulating . . . when I am dealing with the

Nature of Man and with what, under heaven, may be done about it" (*My Works and Days* 293). Mumford did not withdraw in terror from Melville's disintegration (especially that of *Pierre*), as Spark argues, but put it to work: this disintegration was relevant to his ongoing project. Spark and Spanos note real flaws in Mumford's early criticism, but only in order to write off his whole career.

Melville critics and Mumford critics habitually focus on *The Golden Day* and *Herman Melville* to articulate the relationship between the two. Whether they are arguing that Mumford's work belongs to a particular movement—call it "the Melville revival"—or they are interested in ways that Melville influenced him, there is no sense that his ongoing work was formed by a continually shifting response to Melville or that his later work could matter to Melville studies.

In *Technics and Civilization,* Mumford argued, anticipating the apostles of the information age and following the work of Patrick Geddes, that mechanization could be transcended technologically, specifically through the decentralized use of electric "neotechnics"; he laid the basis for Nye's analysis of the "electrical sublime," as well as anticipating the exuberant varieties of posthumanist thought. In *The Myth of the Machine,* though, this belief was gone. How, then, is the megamachine to be dealt with? The megamachine, through which "mechanical regularity and mechanical perfection entered into every human activity, from the observation of the heavens to the winding of clocks, from the drilling of soldiers to the drilling of seeds," must be defied at impossible odds, certainly materially but essentially within the human mind: "Each one of us . . . may play a part in extricating himself from the power system by asserting his primacy as a person in quiet acts of mental or physical withdrawal—in gestures of non-conformity, in abstentions, restrictions, inhibitions, which will liberate him from the domination of the pentagon of power" (*Pentagon* 430, 433). Statements like this frustrate most of Mumford's readers: after hundreds of pages detailing the horrors of megatechnics, Mumford offers only a watered-down version of Thoreau's passive resistance. He should have remembered the late Melville better: Bartleby and Pierre resist the megamachine and perish, unlike Ishmael, who betrays it, and the confidence-man, who ridicules it, partially by drily asserting endless faith *in* it. Mumford ignores an obvious question: If we can wish the megamachine away, why hasn't it ever happened before? Mumford's eschatology is rooted in the individual, Emersonian will after all.

A similar frustrating moment arises in Heidegger's "The Question Concerning Technology":

> [T]he frenziedness of technology may entrench itself everywhere to such an extent that someday, throughout everything technological, the essence of technology may come to presence in the coming-to-pass of truth.
>
> Because the essence of technology is nothing technological, essential reflection upon technology and decisive confrontation with it must happen in a realm that is, on the one hand, akin to the essence of technology and, on the other, fundamentally different from it.
>
> Such a realm is art. (35)

Heidegger offers art as the answer to technology without specifying what form that art must take, while Mumford offers only the "regenerated human personality." Mumford asserts that "the gates of the technocratic prison will open automatically, despite their rusty ancient hinges, as soon as we choose to walk out" (*Pentagon* 435). Behold the pyramid, looming over all, spatializing and enslaving! Don't worry about it: wish it away, and it will be gone. Foucault, more wisely if less courageously, does not even attempt to close *Discipline and Punish* with a general solution to the mechanization of humanity, instead ending on a vague note of sorrow. Mumford's solution to megatechnics, despite its overt silliness, is not essentially different from a dream of achieving a new world by rethinking thinking. It is just another eschatology, which at least has the merit of not denying its own silliness.

Mumford does not *quite* leap straight from the megamachine's horrors into the belief that we can wish it away. First he toys with Byzantinizing the megamachine: "The Roman Empire in the East won a new lease on life . . . by coming to terms with Christianity. If the Power System is to continue in existence as a working partner in a more organic complex dedicated to the renewal of life, it will only be if its dynamic leaders, and those larger groups that they influence, have undergone a profound change of heart and mind . . . as great as that which for so long arrested the decay of the Eastern empire" (*Pentagon* 432). He toys with but then deprecates the Byzantinized megamachine, which would fuse organic and mechanical values, human and inhuman; having accepted, following Melville, that the megamachine *is* transcendence, he now toys with the treachery, chaotic interpenetrations, and blurred categories of the late Melville. What a confidence game, to imagine Ahab, the president, or a CEO betraying the megamachine! Mumford nearly embraces a cyborg-megamachine, betrayed from within. When Melville lets all categories slip and interpenetrate he envisions a cyborg world, again anticipating Donna Haraway (and her many followers): "By the late twentieth century, our time, a mythic time, we are all chimeras, theorized and fabricated hybrids of machine and organism; in short, we are cyborgs. . . . In the traditions of 'Western' science and politics—the tradition of racist, male-dominant capitalism; the tradition of progress; the tradition of the appropriation of nature as resource for the productions of culture; the tradition of reproduction of the self from the reflections of the other—the relation between organism and machine has been a border war" (*Simians* 151). Mumford was never an optimist *or* a Luddite about the technological future. He could seem like either, but his oscillation between the two positions indicates a struggle to find another position, although he didn't succeed even in *The Pentagon of Power.* In imagining a Byzantinized megamachine, following through on Melville's thinking about mechanized humanity and the pyramids, Mumford almost—but not quite—leapfrogs Haraway by envisioning not a cyborg individual but a cyborg world with a long history as such—a possibility Haraway dodges by eschatologically placing the cyborg in our time. Haraway's great error is to be, finally, a Western exceptionalist: the apocalyptic struggle between Michael and the Dragon is *ours.* We are the fulcrum on which history turns. Melville's vision, which Mumford comes achingly close to embracing, is otherwise: the battle is always already lost, and eternal defeat is the condition of our being—yet, the victor is eternally tricked and betrayed. Far back in *Herman Melville,* Mumford praised Melville for understanding that it was greater to surrender than to conquer. This is another lesson he might have learned better. Where else but in defeat and destruction, in the *failure* to progress, is there an answer to teleology?

Queequeg's Obstetrics: After the *Eschatos*

There is something deeply nihilistic about *Moby-Dick:* despite the love between Ishmael and Queequeg, despite the powerful homosocial bonds among the crew, despite Ishmael's hands-on, "spiralizing" epistemology, the novel continually proclaims "the universal cannibalism of the sea." When the cook, Fleece, is forced by Stubb to preach to sharks, he first addresses them as "belubbed fellow-critturs" and then "fellow-critturs" before giving this benediction: "Cussed fellow-critturs! Kick up de damndest row as every you can; fill your dam' bellies 'till dey bust—and den die" (295). The movement from hollow blessing to heartfelt curse feels inevitable. Man and shark are alike, carving into the whale: "were you to turn the whole affair upside down, it would still be pretty much the same thing . . . a shocking sharkish business enough for all parties" (293). The salvation of shark is as improbable as that of man. Stubb finally reduces Christian eschatology to a cooking lesson: "You must go home and be born over again; you don't know how to cook a whale-steak yet" (296).

Several chapters later, Tashtego, the "Gay-head Indian" harpooner, is baling oil from a whale's head—and plummets in. As he struggles within, the head comes loose from the ship. As it falls into the ocean, "my brave Queequeg" dives after it, naked, boarding-sword in hand. Queequeg soon emerges with Tashtego: "upon first thrusting in for him, a leg was presented; but well knowing that was not as it ought to be and might occasion great trouble;—he had thrust back the leg, and by a dexterous heave and toss, had wrought a somerset upon the Indian; so that with the next trial, he came forth in the good old way—head foremost . . . . [T]hus, through the courage and great skill in obstetrics of Queequeg, the deliverance, or rather, delivery of Tashtego, was successfully accomplished" (343–44). Delivery replaces deliverance; the complexities of biological birth replace the certain truth of eschatology. In one idiom, the Western *logos* has been decentered. Melville writes that Tashtego's death would have been a "precious smothering . . . coffined, hearsed, and tombed in the secret inner chamber and sanctum santorum of the whale." Only one sweeter death is imaginable: to perish embalmed in honey. "How many, think ye, have likewise fallen into Plato's honey head, and sweetly perished there" (344). Tashtego's delivery rescues him from a death that would be like metaphysics. One might say that the organic transcends or replaces the mechanical here, in the kind of transformative moment envisioned by the early Mumford, Wilson, Spanos, and so forth. But the text is complex: the drownings of Tashtego and the bee hunter would have been organic, but Tashtego is delivered into a rather different fate, as literally the last hand of the *Pequod* to sink. Ahab's final command is: "What ho, Tashtego! let me hear thy hammer" (571). So Tashtego hammers a flag to the mast as the ship sinks, even with his head underwater:

> a red arm and a hammer hovered backwardly uplifted in the open air, in the act of nailing the flag faster and yet faster to the subsiding spar. A sky-hawk that tauntingly had followed the main-truck downwards from its natural home among the stars, pecking at the flag, and incommoding Tashtego there; this bird now chanced to intercept its broad fluttering wing between the hammer and the wood; and simultaneously feeling that etherial thrill, the submerged savage beneath, in his death-gasp, kept his hammer frozen there; and so the bird of heaven, with archangelic shrieks, and his imperial beak thrust upwards, and his whole captive form folded in the flag of Ahab, went down with his ship. (572)

The "savage" Tashtego, a "natural" man, is delivered by Queequeg in what seems to be a return to organic processes, out of an industrial process that is explicitly aligned with monumentalism and Western metaphysics. But Tashtego then becomes the most mechanical of Ahab's machines; even while drowning he wreaks a final act of destruction on the organic by pulling the hawk into the abyss. Yet the hawk in his pride, "imperial beak thrust upwards," echoes Ahab's quest. Queequeg's delivery has brought no deliverance; it was a messy affair in which Queequeg is feminized as a midwife and yet cuts his way into a metaphorical female body; sex, violence, and delivery are tangled, while the inside of the whale's head and the honey-tree, organic objects both, represent the abstract death of metaphysics. The "savages" Tashtego and Queequeg are by no means liberated from the machine, from the problem of living technologically, nor are Plato or metaphysics "liberated" from the sweetness of organic death.

Haraway intends to explain the "postmodern" moment with the category of "cyborg," but Tashtego, Queequeg, Plato, and the pyramid builders are already cyborgs, already theorized under the sway of power, which is more primordial than metaphysics; they are already spatialized, analyzed, mechanized. Queequeg's war, a war within himself as well as a literal war, *is* Haraway's border war between organism and machine, with the two becoming interchangeable; as Katherine Hayles writes in a completely different context, "we have always been posthuman" (*Posthuman* 291). Queequeg, a prince who has claimed to use his subjects as furniture, a would-be Czar Peter emerging from a world (according to *Typee, Omoo,* and *Mardi*) already dominated by monuments and teleological time, a naturalist among the superstitious, a violent midwife, is never innocent: he is Bartleby and the pyramid, the power system and resistance to it, eschatological and organic time. He is the living union of ways of living that we ordinarily regard as irreconcilable, because of technological difference—a seemingly absolute breach that, examined by contemporary historians of technology, is as porous as the seemingly solid barrier between Queequeg and Ishmael.

In *Technology in World Civilization,* Arnold Pacey, who seldom addresses literature, discusses *Redburn*'s accurate portrayal of the complex relationship between European and Indian technologies. The narrator encounters an Indian ship and crew in Liverpool; one crewman argues that Indian ships are superior to European ships, although in northern climates their coconut-husk rigging is problematic. Confirming and extending the crewman's claim of Indian superiority, Pacey notes that "it is impossible not to be struck by the achievements of the [Indian] shipbuilding industry, which produced skilled carpenters and a model of large-scale organization. . . . Given an independent and more prosperous India, it is difficult not to believe that a response to British industrialization might well have taken the form of the spread of skill and innovation from the shipyards into other industries" (129). Pacey argues that Indian shipbuilding techniques in the nineteenth century were as "advanced" as English ones and that the transfer of tools and techniques between cultures was two-sided. Analyzing the early years of the European "age of exploration," Pacey argues that Europeans are best seen as "Mongols of the Sea"—sophisticated in the tools and especially the techniques of war, but otherwise dependent on "native" technologies (68). He argues that the fundamental European advantage was organizational, not material. Indian firearms were often better made than European firearms, but the European variety was more standardized, as was their management (discipline) (131). Similarly, Wallerstein argues that in many ways the economic (and thus, following Braudel, technological in the sense of the technologies of everyday life) position of ordinary people in India was better than that of equivalent Europeans prior to the integration of India into the world-system (*Mercantilism* 158–59).

Especially when analyzing the West and Western imperialism, the role of physical machines and tools, whether in industry or in war, has been greatly exaggerated, as Mumford argued. True, by the time the interior of Africa was invaded, the West had achieved, in D. R. Headrick's words, the "unleashing of overwhelming force at minimal costs," but the organizational advantage was earlier and more critical (*Tools* 10). Like Melville and the Mumford of *The Myth of the Machine,* Pacey argues that the West's advantage in physical technologies *followed* its organizational advantage (the megamachine). Many characteristics of Western imperialism emerge from a combination of Western organizational techniques and "primitive" physical technologies, with the rice plantations of South Carolina serving as a perfect example (*World* 101).

Tools and techniques together constitute technology: the former is the machine in the world, the latter the machine in the self. This essential complexity makes comparing technological systems difficult, as Mumford recognizes in *Technics and Human Development,* where he argues that technology has been persistently misunderstood as being a matter of tools, when containers were really more important (4). Analyzing navigation, a technology-as-technique intensely relevant to Melville and Mumford, Pacey discusses the tremendous navigational capabilities of "primitive" peoples: "On the Pacific Ocean, for instance, people could travel by canoe . . . undertaking voyages lasting several days out of sight of land. . . . People of the Caroline Islands have continued to practice traditional navigation and have intrigued and puzzled mathematicians with their skills" (*Meaning* 113–14). Elsewhere Pacey argues that the relative technological development of the Maya has been terribly misunderstood, because despite the complexity and success of their farming techniques, they used few tools (*World* 59). In *The Evolution of Technology,* George

Basalla argues that "far from fulfilling universal needs, they [technologies] derive their importance within a specific cultural context or value system" (12). Technology changes continuously, incrementally, in response to perceived needs in a specific time and place. For instance, the wheel, well known in the ancient Middle East, was abandoned there for centuries. Current analysis, writes Basalla, suggests that this abandonment was not regression; given the dominant conditions of the Middle East for several centuries, pack camels were more economical than wheeled vehicles (11). An amusing example of the totemic power of teleological progress (along with widespread ignorance of the history of technology) can be found in Bernard Lewis's *What Went Wrong?*—a neo-conservative analysis of historical causes for the inferiority of the Middle East. "Some have sought the causes of this painful asymmetry," writes Lewis, in "the disuse of wheeled vehicles in the pre-modern Middle East, variously explained as a cause or a symptom of what went wrong" (157). If we define the "right" way as including the use of wheeled vehicles, then proper human progress must include wheeled vehicles. If a culture doesn't use them, or abandons them, it "went wrong." Historians of technology have documented that the wheel was "abandoned" in the Middle East because it was not competitive in local conditions; to ask why it was "abandoned" is like asking why the U.S. Army "abandoned" the use of horses (a contingent and incomplete abandonment based on petroleum prices). In teleological time—Lewis's time—when history is known and mastered, there is no room for such talk.

To speak of technological "progress" is problematic; contrary to the dominant teleological model of history, shared by those who embrace the West and those who would see it "re-thought," both physical and organizational technologies emerge in response to particular sets of physical and social conditions. Technology is constitutive of Being, and power/machine technology is continuous with other technologies. To unthink or rethink Western metaphysics, teleology, "The End of History," and the *eschatos* requires a movement from the concept of progress to that of change, to a concept of evolution stripped of the stairway that Walt Whitman uses to imagine it in *Song of Myself:* "I am an acme of things accomplished, and I an encloser of things to be. / My feet strike an apex of apices of the stairs, / On every step bunches of ages, and larger bunches between the steps, / and still I mount and mount / . . . / Before

I was born out of my mother generations guided me, / . . . / Monstrous sauroids transported it in their mouths and deposited it with care" (46–47). This is teleological evolution, coming from a definite origin and proceeding toward a definite end. *This* "evolution" is fundamentally ideological, unnecessarily so, as the Marxist geneticist R. C. Lewontin has argued in *Biology as Ideology,* in which he attacks biological determinism and the notion that there is a fundamental separation between organisms and their environments (Maturana and Varela take this belief particularly far, by turning each living thing, essentially, into a monad): he argues that "Organisms do not experience environments. They create them" (109). To take the notion one step further (anticipating my conclusion), one might say that all life is technological; *bios,* by definition, engages in *technē.*

In "On Replacing the Idea of Progress with an Operational Notion of Directionality," Stephen Gould claims that, in general usage, "evolution" *means* progress, and that progress has been tacked on to the concept of evolution for transparent psychological reasons.

> Our geological confinement to a moment at the very end of recorded time must engender suspicions that we are a lucky accident, an afterthought, rather than the goal of all creation. Progress . . . dispels this chilling thought—for if life moves inexorably forward, however fitfully, towards its ultimate embodiment in human consciousness, then the restriction of *Home sapiens* to a final moment poses no challenge to the general hope; for all that came before may now be interpreted as part of a process scheduled to yield our form from the start. We may then continue to pervade time through a long chain of imperfect surrogates, mounting their steady course towards our exalted state. (650)

Driven by this desire to discover progress, biologists and geologists make a logical error, argues Gould, by equating "progress" with increasing variance; that is, the diversity of life and the complexity of *some* forms of life increase over time, but calling this movement "progress" is an error: "we usually seek the link of progress with adaptation in a subset of morphological novelties qualifying as 'general adaptations' or biomechanical improvements in overall function. I believe a logical error underlies this standard view. . . . [E]ven these general improvements arise for particular reasons in definite environments. . . . They do not usually evolve 'for' the general use that underlies their role" (661). In evolution, particular developments in response to particular conditions *seem* like "general" improvements, linear progress, but complexity is not exaltedness or survivability. As with biology, so with technology, and so also with power. Skyscrapers are a particular adaptation to a particular set of conditions, but their mechanical complexity does not make them "superior" in an absolute sense. Contemporary farming with bioengineered seeds is arguably more complex than Mayan agriculture and better adapted to contemporary perceived needs. There has been change, even directional change—but where is the "better" in that? Like David Nye, I "do not assume that more energy is better, that more energy equals more civilization" (*Power* 1). Faith in progress assumes that specific adaptations are general adaptations, which is the logical error Gould finds in much biological thought. Similarly, the "pyramid system" of ancient Egypt, although less complex than "the pyramid system" of the contemporary United States, is not necessarily inferior in a general sense (with both being adapted to their own specific conditions, not general ones), although there has been directional change from the former to the later.

"Something further may follow of this Masquerade," Melville writes, ending *The Confidence-Man,* a novel of a man/men/God(s) who is/are supremely and fluidly adapted to the precise conditions in which he/they finds himself/themselves. Ishmael and the confidence-man have come to see a time that is neither "mechanical" nor "organic," neither progressive nor cyclic. Time is change, not progress or deliverance; technology changes, but it has neither origin nor *telos;* we are creatures who use tools and techniques, which (we) happen to adapt and complicate. So, too, with the megamachine: it is an adaptation, or set of adaptations, the turn of instrumentality upon humanity itself. Lewis Mumford's great success, developing out of his reading of Melville, was to rebel thoroughly against "progress" as constitutive of humanity, by understanding the adaptive nature and essential continuity of technology. His error was to insist on the possibility of progress, of a saving *telos,* even while denying it.

4
Faulkner, Dead Time, and the Southern Machine

Faulkner, Modernity, and Modernism

Faulkner criticism is diverse: critics argue that Faulkner's primary concern is race (Eric Sundquist), ontology (Jean-Paul Sartre), the fine details of psychology in a Freudian or pseudo-Lacanian mode (John Irwin and Doreen Fowler), or the history of the American South and its defeat. Faulkner is read fiercely politically (Sundquist) and fiercely apolitically (Cleanth Brooks), as an optimist and a pessimist, as a reactionary and a radical. Much of Faulkner's importance doubtless derives from the plausibility of this wealth of contradictory positions. Many rich fields have been sown in Faulkner criticism; I intend to reap no harvest from most of them, but by way of introduction I will glean from several to make a simple statement, at the risk of belaboring the obvious: although Faulkner was once dismissed as a regionalist and a nostalgic romantic, the waves of critics who have pushed him to the peaks of the canon focus on his relationship with modernity. That is, the diversity of Faulkner criticism testifies that Faulkner's work is concerned with those things *we* care about most—those that we care about in an intensely contemporary way. Is this a tautology? *Of course* critics address those writers who speak to contemporary concerns! What else could we do?

But my point is not merely tautological. Certainly, Faulkner speaks to contemporary concerns. What distinguishes him is that he seemingly speaks to *every* contemporary concern. Reading Doreen Fowler's closely argued *The Return of the Repressed* (1997), one can hardly avoid the eerie impression that Faulkner clairvoyantly mastered Lacan, and proleptically mastered Lacanian criticism. Reading Noel Polk's *Children of the Dark House* (1996), we might be convinced that Faulkner was a better Freudian than Freud, despite the absence of evidence that Faulkner was deeply familiar with Freud's work (32). Faulkner's primary and highly political concern with race is clear in Sundquist's *A House Divided* (1983), while his primary focus on gender is transparent in *Children of the Dark House.* In R. Rio-Jelliffe's *Obscurity's Myriad Components* (2001), a future-oriented, optimistic Faulkner deeply influenced by Henri Bergson emerges as clearly as the doom-obsessed Faulkner, for whom time is "decapitated" and empty, of Sartre's classic essay "On *The Sound and the Fury.*" In Philip Weinstein's *Faulkner's Subject* (1992), Faulkner's work is equally concerned with several of our current obsessions: the sections of the book are titled "Race," "Gender," "Subjectivity," and "Culture."

More even than the other authors who dominate the headings of *American Literary Scholarship,* Faulkner's work remains all things to all people—or at least an object of every kind of criticism to every kind of critic. Authors who become embedded in the canon must have a degree of plasticity, but Faulkner's is Protean. One can attribute this plasticity to the stylistic convolutions of Faulkner's best-loved works, and many have done so. Faulkner's language is not playfully obscure, though; it is not *merely* (post)modernist. His is a language that, being skeptical of language, always tries to push through language. Rio-Jelliffe details Faulkner's "profound distrust" of language, which honeycombs his essays, speeches, and interviews (26–27). Although attributing a character's wisdom to an author is problematic, Addie Bundren's chthonic, enraged, and rhetorically brilliant dismissal of language in *As I Lay Dying* is of a piece with Faulkner's own statements. The word, despite Faulkner's mastery of it, is untrustworthy, and secondary to the act: "I would lie by him in the dark, hearing the dark land talking of God's love and His beauty and His sin; hearing the dark voicelessness in which the words are the deeds, and the other words that are not deeds, that are just the gaps in people's lacks, coming down like the cries of geese out of the wild darkness in the old terrible nights, fumbling at the deeds like orphans" (117). In Faulkner, the word insistently condemns the word. Krister Friday, following Sundquist, argues that the real danger of miscegenation in his work is that it threatens to erase whiteness itself, by rendering the difference between whiteness and blackness unclear; miscegenation challenges "the genealogical and ideological ambitions of white patriarchs" *and* their very identities (51, 41). Faulkner's *language,* in fact, is miscegenated, both literally and metaphorically. When the sadomasochist Addie Bundren gets pleasure from whipping children, she finds true meaning: "When the switch fell I could feel it upon my flesh; when it welted and ridged it was my blood that ran, and I would think with each blow of the switch: Now you are aware of me! Now I am something in your secret and selfish life, who have marked your blood with my own for ever and ever" (114). Only in a language that produces damaged flesh, only in the voicelessness in which words are deeds, only in a destructive language that is no language, is there meaning. We might recall the brutal words recorded in *Go Down, Moses,* where the "words that are deeds," the history of McCaslin incest and miscegenation, appear in a financial ledger (200). When Ike McCaslin reads this text, a semblance of an ordinary sentence emerges after pages of shattered syntax: "The old frail pages seemed to turn of their own accord even while he thought *His own daughter*" (200). At the moment of crisis, when language names an unforgivable deed, an automatism emerges (in Ike? The pages? Language itself?). *The pages seemed to turn of their own accord.* So too with Addie Bundren; after establishing the unspeakable connection between herself and the children, the next sentence reads: "And so I took Anse" (114). She flees from the unspeakable deed into Anse's empty words, without a clear motivation: the bloody meaning falls to automatism, which haunts all of Faulkner's work.

Language's inadequacy in the face of modernity is a stereotypical subject for modernism; this is T. S. Eliot's wasteland. John T. Matthews argues that a major source of *As I Lay Dying* is the background of the "dynamic relation between modernization and modernism" in the South. The racist modernism of the Fugitives, the authors of *I'll Take My Stand* (1930), who included Allen Tate and Robert Penn Warren, was, by Matthews's reading (and by consensus), a modernist response, rooted in Eliot and Pound, to commercial and industrial modernization (69–70). Despite modernism's tendency toward "autonomous texts," Matthews argues, bits and pieces of social reality creep into Faulkner's novel, which becomes a turning point in his career; Faulkner "reequips" by abandoning "idle metafiction" and "exorcising the effete poeticism of Quentin Compson and Darl Bundren" and "prepares for an experimentalism deeply implicated in the search for truth about the South" (93). Faulkner's fiction is not simply a meditation on the helplessness of language and the endless confusion/miscegenation between word and deed. Faulkner keeps "the dialectic between modernization and modernism critically charged" by resisting "with the force of decomposition the impulse toward reintegration and commodification" (93). Faulkner does not utterly eschew modernism, mechanization, or even the commodification of art; after all, he willingly made his living for years writing in Hollywood. He keeps tension between modernism and modernization—not unlike the tension Gavin Stevens sees between Joe Christmas's white and black blood in *Light in August* (731).

I return now to the problem of Faulkner's unique plasticity, which we might explain through Matthews's modernization/modernism divide. Many have argued that Faulkner fundamentally opposed modernization; a few, that he embraced it. There is also disagreement over his exact relationship with modernism. This diversity of readings resonates with Matthews: modernism and modernity are *at stake* for Faulkner. Like race and gender, they are unsolved problems in his work. Dynamic tension in Faulkner's *form* cascades through those issues we associate with (our) modernity.

This is not to say that I embrace all sides of all questions in Faulkner criticism. In fact, I side with those (like Sundquist) who argue for the relative importance of race and politics, and with those (like Rio-Jelliffe) who see Bergson as being centrally important. Bergson plays a part in my argument: that Faulkner sees automatism not in modernization as such but in ways of thinking and being that underlie and precede both modernization and modernism. To make this argument in detail, I will attend to Sartre's essay on *The Sound and the Fury* and discuss Bergson's automatism before I proceed to readings of Faulkner's novels in relationship to modernization and mechanization.

Many major Faulkner critics agree that Faulkner responds powerfully, even appallingly, to modernity, rejecting or attacking it. In *William Faulkner: The Yoknapatawpha Country* (1963), Cleanth Brooks argues that Faulkner is a regionalist whom readers will automatically associate with the South, as they associate Frost with New England and Yeats with Ireland. These three places "have in common a basically agricultural economy, a life of farms, villages, and small towns, an old-fashioned set of values, and a still vital religion" (1). Brooks argues that all three authors are morally and artistically superior, rather than merely sociologically wiser, because they write about provincials (1–9). The title of Brooks's first chapter, in a book that celebrates Faulkner's work, is "Faulkner the Provincial." Brooks believes in the moral superiority of "provincials." Faulkner's work, like that of Frost and Yeats, as part of a local tradition, "embodies a criticism of the prevailing commercial and urban culture, a criticism made from the standpoint of a provincial and traditional culture" (1–2). Brooks's implicit hope is that the capacity to rebuild *something* in the wasteland of modernity will emanate from the good, traditional (white) people of northern Mississippi.

Faulkner's great art, according to Brooks, is *pastoral*. When discussing *Light in August* (1932), Brooks argues that Joe Christmas (the "negro" murderer), Joanna Burden (the victim), and Hightower (the fallen minister) are destroyed by isolation and that Lena (the pregnant woman who opens and closes the novel) "leads a charmed life" because of her affiliation with the community (54–55): "The plight of the isolated individual [is] a dominant theme of contemporary literature. But by developing this theme in a rural setting in which a powerful sense of community still exists, Faulkner has given us a kind of pastoral—that is, he has let us see our modern and complex problems mirrored in a simpler and more primitive world" (55). *Light in August* is a pastoral (for Brooks) because it sets the agony of modernity against the soft, comic luminance of Lena and Byron Bunch: Lena's story shows what modernity has lost, while Christmas's story illustrates the horrors of the modern condition. Similarly, *The Hamlet* is "a transparent allegory of modernity" and a "sardonic Horatio Alger story" in which the rise of the Snopes family represents the social and economic changes of modernization (172, 4). Thomas Sutpen's "innocence and failure to learn" in *Absalom, Absalom!* characterizes modernity; Sutpen, although an uneducated Virginian who owned or supervised slaves since his teens, is characterized as a "rationalist" and "Yankee" (306). Shreve, who narrates/invents much of the novel's latter half, becomes a stand-in for the hypothetical "modern" reader, who is "pretty well emancipated from the ties of family, race, or section" (313). For Brooks, Faulkner is important because he conducts a frontal assault on modernity.

Malcolm Cowley's introduction to *The Portable Faulkner* (1946) makes a similar case, although more compactly and subtly. According to Cowley, the young Faulkner "brooded" on the South; his fiction served as a "legend of all of the Deep South" (vii–viii). The rise of the Snopes family is a parable of modernity: "the Sartorises were defeated in advance by a traditional code that kept them from using the weapons of the enemy. . . . [T]he Snopeses had to serve the mechanized civilization of the North, which was morally impotent in itself, but which . . . ended by corrupting the Southern nation" (xxi). The Snopeses—who are, despite critics' bile, little more than petty usurers, excepting the race-baiting Clarence Snopes—serve the North's mechanized evil, which is their great sin. The vicious rapist and murderer Popeye of *Sanctuary* represents "the mechanical civilization that has invaded and conquered the South. He is always described in mechanical terms" (xxii). Note that because Popeye is consistently described mechanically, he *must* therefore represent the North; as in Brooks, the reality of the South as the site of an *authentic* pastoral reality is unquestioned.

It is unsurprising that two major critics from the South doing early work on Faulkner would discuss his work in such terms; Faulkner's concern with modernity becomes another way of saying that he was concerned with crimes against the South by the North. But earlier than either Cowley or Brooks, Sartre's position was similar.

Sartre's 1939 essay "On *The Sound and the Fury:* Time in the Work of Faulkner" does not take the novel as an "autonomous" modern text; Sartre assumes that it responds to the world. After noting that *The Sound and the Fury* doesn't follow the rules of the classical novel, Sartre claims that a critic's first duty is to define "the novelist's metaphysics"—in Faulkner's case, a "metaphysics of time" (84–85). Sartre argues that in Faulkner the present "is essentially catastrophic. It is the event which creeps upon us like a thief, huge, unthinkable—. . . then disappears. Beyond this present time there is nothing, since the future does not exist" (85). In his 1938 essay "William Faulkner's *Sartoris*" Sartre makes a similar complaint: "Suddenly, from the depths of this drama, like a bolt form the blue, appears the Act. At least, an act! something *happening,* a message! But Faulkner disappoints us again; he rarely describes acts" (80). Faulkner's world, asserts Sartre, is denuded of action; time is "decapitated . . . deprived [of] its future, that is, its dimension of deeds and freedom" (90).

So far, Sartre hardly resembles Brooks and Cowley. But at the end of his second essay, Sartre justifies Faulkner's metaphysics: "Faulkner's despair seems to me to precede his metaphysics. For him, as for all of us, the future is closed. Everything we see and experience impels us to say, 'This can't last.' And yet change is not even conceivable, except in the form of a cataclysm. We are living in a time of impossible revolutions, and Faulkner uses his extraordinary art to describe our suffocation and a world dying of old age" (93). Sartre, like Cowley and Brooks, asserts that Faulkner's art responds to the contemporary scene. But, whereas for Cowley and Brooks Faulkner contrasts the pastoral South to modernity's ruins, Sartre argues that Faulkner shows only the wasteland.

Again, I flirt with tautology: it's no surprise that an antifascist French philosopher writing in 1939 understood Faulkner's response to modernity differently than two southern reactionaries understood it in 1946 and 1963. Brooks, appropriately, objects to Sartre's reading of *The Sound and the Fury,* making the understandable claim that Sartre has confused Quentin's understanding of time with Faulkner's (329).

Sartre, despite geographical and intellectual distance from Faulkner, is essentially correct: Faulkner's "pastoral" vision *is* a vision of the wasteland, of decapitated time; the Brooks/Cowley fantasy of a pastoral South oppressed by the rapacious, industrial North is continually undercut by Faulkner, who portrays a South always already modern, always already technological. The Brooks/Cowley fantasy—akin to Leo Marx's narrative of the machine's sudden entry into the garden—is false, and *Faulkner knows it.* Faulkner's wasteland is not a product of industry, despite having a relationship to it, nor does it result (as Sartre implies) from depression and impending war: it is an enduring metaphysical condition, tightly coupled to Bergson's philosophy. I will next discuss Bergson, adding my thoughts to the substantial literature on Bergson's influence on Faulkner, before turning to specific texts, beginning with *Light in August*.

Faulkner and Bergson

Faulkner expressed interest in Bergson through his life. Most famously, he urged his young lover Joan Williams to read Bergson's *Creative Evolution* (1907), saying that "it helped me" (Blotner 511). In an interview with Loïc Bouvard, he endorsed both Bergson's concept of God and Bergson's "theory of the fluidity of time" (Blotner 563). Peter Puchek argues that Faulkner's use of epiphanies was deeply rooted in his reading of Bergson: "To Faulkner as to Bergson, an epiphany involves recognizing the cycle or some aspect either of it or of one's place in it. Whether the person undergoing it realizes it or not, the experience devolves from the interconnectedness of past, present, and future" (33). It is noteworthy, however, that Puchek bases his reading of Bergson only on the early *Time and Free Will* (1889). This problem pervades the criticism of authors influenced by Bergson; despite the shorthand concept of "Bergson's fluidity of time" to which critics habitually refer, Bergson's thought, argues John Mularkey in *Bergson and Philosophy,* was "non-systematic" and continually changing (4–5); Bergson's concept of time in *Time and Free Will* is not the same as in *Creative Evolution,* the work Faulkner explicitly endorses. In "The Later Faulkner, Bergson, and God," Mick Gidley, after noting Faulkner's endorsement of Bergson's concept of God, evaluates the different Bergsonian concepts of God that Faulkner might have meant, including the mystical God of Bergson's final book, *Two Sources of Morality and Religion* (1932), and the God of *Creative Evolution;* Gidley argues that the latter is "God as activity, as force, as the original source of the [Bergsonian] *élan vital*" (381). Such a concept of God seems to be in radical disagreement with the "decapitation" of time and lack of freedom that Sartre finds in Faulkner, but a more detailed discussion of *Creative Evolution* will clarify the fundamental compatibility between Faulkner's Bergson and Sartre's Faulkner.

Many critics deny that Bergson greatly influenced Faulkner, starting with Cleanth Brooks; Sarah Bell lists a number of other skeptics in her 1990 dissertation, "William Faulkner's Creative Evolution," including Dale Parker, Paul Douglass, and Michel Gresset (7–8). This skepticism responds to the thinness of the evidence: Bell makes use of the same Faulkner quotes (referring to Bergson) that I do, because only a handful of comments are on record. Despite his endorsement of Bergson, Faulkner didn't own any of Bergson's books at the time of his death (Douglass, *Bergson* 119). There is no direct evidence that Faulkner had read Bergson extensively, although Douglass argues that the influence of Bergson on Faulkner could have been partially transmitted via the works of T. S. Eliot (120).

Despite the thin evidence, I agree that Bergson's thought "articulated for Faulkner something he had within him all along" (Bell 5). Bell argues that discussions of Bergson and Faulkner have focused excessively on time in isolation: "Bergson's main concerns, especially in *Creative Evolution,* stem from his concept that motion is life and stasis is death—a concept pervasive in the Faulkner canon" (8). Bell oversimplifies Bergson, but productively so: especially in *Creative Evolution,* freedom, time, and the nature of evolution and life itself are intermingled and inseparable, which brings me to an aspect of Bergson's thought critical to illuminating Faulkner: automatism.

A commonplace of Faulkner criticism concerned with Bergson is that Bergson attacks "clock time" or "mechanical time"; we are told that Bergson advocates his concept of duration, *durée,* in opposition to clock time. This is a simplification. In fact, the nuances and reality of "clock time" were intensely important to Bergson: *Duration and Simultaneity* (1921) was meant to qualify Einstein's relativity by claiming that the relativity of time, unlike that of space, was only apparent. Under Bergson's interpretation of Einstein, a traveler moving near the speed of light would, upon returning to earth, have recorded the same time passed as someone remaining on earth, whereas in relativity as normally understood, the traveler would record less time elapsed. The *unity* of time was so important to Bergson that he counterintuitively argued that relativity *strengthened* its unity (*Simultaneity* 96). Bergson does not *oppose* measured or mechanical time; in fact, he asserts its inevitability. His essential argument, detailed in *Creative Evolution,* is that reason operates—must operate—through mechanical, spatialized time: "Our intellect has been cast in the mold of action. . . . [W]e begin by proposing an end; we make a plan, then we go on to the detail of the mechanism which will bring it to pass. This latter operation is possible only if we know what we can reckon on. We must therefore have managed to extract resemblances from nature, which enable us to anticipate the future. Thus we must, consciously or unconsciously, have made use of the law of causality" (44). Thinking causally, the human mind imposes form on the universe. Life is "a tendency to act on inert matter," argues Bergson (96). Life builds, shapes, acts. To do so it must calculate *as if* acting upon a supine universe. "Life is mobility itself," but that mobility shapes (128). Bergson sees mechanical time as vital for an intellect that exists for action, not speculation. The problem lies in the fact that he regards mechanical time as a vital and necessary illusion. Science must, argues Bergson, treat the universe mechanically; philosophy must not (93). In mathematical reasoning, which is the active intellect itself, "certain aspects of the present are calculable as functions of the immediate past. Nothing of the sort in the domain of life. . . . As for the idea that the living body might be treated by some superhuman calculator in the same mathematical way as our solar system, this has gradually arisen from a metaphysic which has taken a more precise form since the physical discoveries of Galileo, but which . . . *was always the natural metaphysic of the human mind*" (20; emphasis added). Inert systems can be fully calculated from a set of data; life cannot, but life must treat life as inert in order to act upon it. There is nothing wrong with the spatializing, mechanizing metaphysic within its proper domain, but philosophy must push for an understanding of real duration, an understanding of time unfolding continuously: any given instant is *not* merely a result of the instant before it, and repetition is impossible. "Real duration . . . gnaws on things, and leaves on them the mark of its tooth. If everything is in time, everything changes inwardly, and the same concrete reality never recurs. Repetition is possible only in the abstract. . . . We do not *think* real time. But we *live* it" (46).

Life is structured to treat the world as inert; the task of philosophy is to "do violence to the mind, go counter to the natural bent of the intellect," to assert the counterintuitive—that is, countermathematical—nature of lived time. Philosophy must show that we are not automatons, although we are structured to treat all things as such:

> [Through] the organized world we do indeed find one great effort; but most often this effort turns short, sometimes paralyzed by contrary forces, sometimes diverted from what it should do by what it does, absorbed by the form it is engaged in taking, hypnotized by it as by a mirror. . . . [I]t is at the mercy of the materiality which it has had to assume. It is what each of us may experience in himself. Our freedom, in the very movements by which it is affirmed, creates the growing habits that will stifle it if it fails to renew itself by a constant effort: it is dogged by automatism. The most living thought becomes frigid in the formula that expresses it. The word turns against the idea. (127)

The next paragraph begins, "The letter kills the spirit." Saint Paul's suspicion of the literal word is linked to Bergson's suspicion of the automatism that haunts life, continually foiling it. Though our being urges toward action as an expression of freedom, "We are at ease only in the discontinuous, in the immobile, in the dead" (165). The paradoxical purpose of life is to "create with matter, which is necessity itself, an instrument of freedom, to make a machine which should triumph over mechanism, and to use the determinism of nature to pass through the meshes of the net which this determinism had spread." But, Bergson writes, "everywhere except in man, consciousness has let itself be caught in the net whose meshes it tried to pass through; it has remained the captive of the mechanisms it had set up. . . . But man not only maintains his machine, he succeeds in using it as he pleases" (264). Life *is* rebellion against automatism, death, and disorder, but to impose order upon the world, it treats the world as inert, while its own ways and habits, language and reason, generate an inner automatism. Bergson is usually understood as an optimist, a believer in progress. This claim has some truth: Bergson believes in evolutionary change as progress—but how contingently, and hemmed in by how many qualifications! The evolutionary force of life, despite its drive toward freedom, is dogged and hemmed in by automatism at every turn: it is a contingent freedom made of mechanical materials, thinking mechanically, imposing a mechanical vision on the world, while being inwardly mechanized. Although life endures in one kind of time, it thinks in another—a mechanized, spatialized time that inevitably views the world as an automaton.

The complexity of and interrelationships among Bergson's ideas about evolution, time, and automatism, as discussed in *Creative Evolution,* Bergson's only book that Faulkner explicitly endorsed (and must therefore have read), are critical to a proper discussion of Faulkner's time, as I will show, beginning with a reading of *Light in August.*

Light in August as Shattered Pastoral

Light in August begins with Lena Grove watching a wagon creep toward her "like something moving forever and without progress across an urn," an obvious reference to Keats. Most of the novel tells the story of Joe Christmas, whose father may be of mixed race, who lives among whites and blacks without feeling at home anywhere, who lives, works, has an affair with Joanna Burden, kills her, and is finally hunted, castrated, and killed for his crime. But his story is set against Lena's. She is pregnant at the beginning and gives birth near the end; she is searching for Lucas Burch, who abandoned her—alone at first, then finally with Byron Bunch, who loves her, in tow. Lena comes from a simple rural background, a "log house of three rooms and a hall, without screens . . . the naked floor worn smooth as old silver by naked feet" (401). She speaks placidly, gently, in an uneducated country idiom. Delivering her child seems to be the spiritual deliverance of Gail Hightower, the fallen minister; her quiet life exists in radical contrast to the deadly uproar of Christmas's.

Generations of critics have seen Lena's story as essentially pastoral and have seen Lena as representing nature, femininity, or traditional life. Her name is Grove, she is associated with Greek urns, and she is an earthy, tranquil mother. Cleanth Brooks calls *Light in August* a "bloody pastoral," in which Lena represents a traditional culture rooted in nature, while Joe Christmas represents the alienation of modernity (54). Alfred Kazin's earlier essay "The Stillness of *Light in August*" argues that Lena provides "provincial foundations" for Christmas's story. The "stillness" of the essay's title is "rooted in the peaceful and timeless world which Lena Grove personifies and in which she has her being. It is the stillness of the personal darkness inside which Joe Christmas lives" (154). Kazin's position is not merely sentimental: he sees Lena as belonging to a peaceful and timeless world, while acknowledging that the relationship between that world and Christmas's war-world is not strictly oppositional: the two are inwardly connected. Nonetheless, Kazin's premise is revealing: Lena belongs to the timeless, the rural, presumably to the endless cycle of nature; Christmas belongs to violence, the city, the mechanical civilization that violates nature.

This line of thought does not end with Kazin and Brooks; Stephen Hahn's essay "What Leaf-Fring'd Legend Haunts about Thy Shape?" asserts that Lena is an "emanation of the landscape and a synecdoche for it" (31), while Harold Hungerford's "Past and Present in *Light in August*" comments on the dual "timelessness" of Lena and the urn (185, 198). Peter Puchek, following Judith Sensibar, argues that Lena presents an antimodern alternative of "simple faith and delight in the world." Starting with Brooks's belief that Lena "is nature," Puchek argues that Lena, as a kind of pagan goddess, generates epiphanies in those around her (29, 32).

Lena becomes a synecdoche for a whole world of values and possibilities outside modernity: cyclic time, not linear time; paganism, not Calvinism; nature, not the machine. Unquestionably, she plays a vital role in the novel, and this role has something to do with nature and traditional culture—but most criticism has missed Faulkner's harsh countersignals; we tend to seek and find an "original nature" when nothing of the kind exists.

In the novel's opening paragraph, Lena thinks about home, and her distance from it. "*I am now further from Doane's Mill than I have been since I was twelve years old*" (401). She has spent all of her life in the shadow of a timber town, which is hardly timeless:

> [The men] worked in the mill or for it. . . . It had been there seven years and in seven years more it would destroy all the timber within its reach. Then some of the machinery and most of the men who ran it and existed because of it and for it would be loaded onto freight

> cars and moved away. But some of the machinery would be left, since new pieces could always be bought on the installment plan—gaunt, staring, motionless wheels rising from mounds of brick rubble and ragged weeds with a quality profoundly astonishing, and gutted boilers lifting their rusting and unsmoking stacks with an air stubborn, baffled and bemused upon a stumpocked scene of profound and peaceful desolation, unplowed, untilled, gutting slowly into red and choked ravines beneath the long quiet rains of autumn and the galloping fury of vernal equinoxes. (402)

The mill from which Lena emerges is ephemeral, not timeless: a clock runs on it, and on the machinery within it. With timber and people gone, the soil washes into the sea and the remaining machinery mutely rusts: Lena emerges not from a timeless traditional culture but from an industrial wasteland with apocalyptic overtones. The first wheels described in the novel are the motionless wheels in the sawmill's wreckage; the wagon wheels are, as it were, in their shadow: "a succession of creakwheeled and limpeared avatars, like something moving forever and without progress across an urn" (404). The "creakwheels," which seem motionless even in motion, evoke the truly motionless wheels in the sawmill's ruins. At the chapter's end, before Lena sees smoke from Joanna Burden's burning house, the wagon is described again: "The wagon goes on, slow, timeless. The red and unhurried miles unroll beneath the steady feet of the mules, beneath the creaking and clanking wheels" (420). The "timeless" wagon is *ironic,* for the whole economy of Lena's "natural" upbringing and surroundings is based upon a destructive, dangerous, and profoundly temporary extractive industry that has a totalitarian, regimenting power over its workers, who exist "for it."

In "Faulkner and the Claims of the Natural World," Lawrence Buell writes that his reading of *Light in August* was transformed by reading it ecologically. Buell glosses the passage about Doane's Mill as "a concise history of the cut-and-get-out phase of the timber industry in the Deep South: a half-century of intensive exploitation and chronic wastefulness . . . that Faulkner probably was well aware was nearly played out." The novel was published when "Mississippi's first forest finally ran out and lumber production hit a fifty-year low" (2). If Lena is a synecdoche for nature, it is an endangered, half-broken nature, already damaged before the "New South" threatened the Old. Brooks's representative of provincial values emerges from industry—southern industry at that. The supposed timelessness of the roads and wagons that evoke Lena's timelessness ring hollow beside the fleeting timber industry, which certainly provided the financial basis for the roads and wagons.[1] The characters change when we notice the timber industry and its ticking clock, as Buell argues: Lucas Bunch's placelessness, for instance, comes from the timber industry (3). Timbering required a highly mobile workforce, willing to work dangerous, demanding jobs in return for wages; it is not, therefore, easily distinguished from the industries of the "mechanized" North. The American South, like the Caribbean, had belonged to Wallerstein's capitalist "world-system" long before "northern" industry arrived. "Industrialization" and "modernity" have long since arrived in the "Old South," albeit in a different form than the critics might expect.

What does this have to do with Bergson? Reading Faulkner with technology *and* Bergson in mind exposes the *illusion* of timelessness in Faulkner's work. When something seems timeless in Faulkner (think of Sartre's "decapitated time") the real issue is automatism, which pervades Faulkner's universe; one might think of the determinism of Wallerstein's analysis of world history, in which history becomes purely the story of near-autonomous systems, with individuals receding almost infinitely.

Lena emerges from a timbering community, in a Mississippi dominated by the destructive, extractive cotton and timber industries: the very roads are built to serve these businesses, and will shift with them. The landscape is fluid: the trees are stripped, and soil washes down to the sea, a point greatly elaborated in *Go Down, Moses.* The people who populate Faulkner's fiction may deny or resist change, but when the land itself becomes nothing but change itself, the appearance of timelessness is pure fantasy: Lena's timelessness, if it exists, is akin to the backward-looking obsessions of the Compsons and Sartorises. Which is not to say that *Lena* believes in timelessness. Her focus is always on motion and change. She enters the novel with the comic thought, "I have come from Alabama: a fur piece" (401). She is amazed at her swift movement; she relishes tinned sardines. As the furniture salesman at the end realizes, when she resumes her wandering she is indifferent about actually catching Lucas Birch. The furniture salesman reckons "this was the first time she had ever been further away from home than she could walk back before sundown in her life. And that she had got along all right this far. . . . [She would] travel a little further and see as much as she could, since I reckon she knew that when she settled down this time, it would likely be for the rest of her life" (774). Lena is in motion, encountering something different daily, and thriving on the experience. But, argues the salesman, once she stops she'll never move again: automatism threatens, and she wants to avoid it while she can. Lena is no earth goddess, although she may be a hobo queen: the ending, with Byron and Lena gladly facing the apparently endless road, their love unconsummated, resonates with the ending of Charlie Chaplin's *Modern Times* (1936).

Reading the ending with Bergson in mind reveals another complication. The salesman describes the baby breast-feeding in the truck: "That had been eating breakfast now for about ten miles" (774). Lena's final sentence, closing the novel, is, "Here we aint been coming from Alabama but two months, and now it's already Tennessee" (774). Lena and the salesman comically replace time with space, which in Bergson is the inevitable hallmark of instrumental, rational thought. It's funny and charming, but it doesn't bode well for their ability to resist automatism.

This threat is a lighthearted shadow, like the moment in *Modern Times* when Chaplin is processed, unharmed, all the way through an assembly line—it's funny, but has teeth. We dare not forget that Lena and Byron have moved to the edges of their world, without means or protection; like Chaplin and his companion, they teeter at the brink of starvation. Only nomadism keeps automatism at bay (which is one connection of many between Deleuze and Bergson). In *Light in August* and *Modern Times* the individual's victory is temporary, contingent on good health and youth, and does nothing against the forces of mechanization and automatism. In Lena and Byron's case, we know that automatism will come sooner, not later: they have a baby to provide for.

Lena and Byron's story is the twilight surrounding Faulkner's "Heart of Darkness"; the story of Joe Christmas, Joanna Burden, and their automatism is midnight. Christmas sees himself as manufactured—which he is, being sculpted by his grandfather Hines and his stepfather, McEachern; his artificiality is linked to racial ambiguity. "He watched his body grow white out of the darkness like a kodak print emerging from the liquid" (478). A refrain punctuates the book: "*Something is going to happen to me*" (486). Things are done to and through Christmas, but never really by him. As the five-year-old Christmas witnesses the orphanage dietician and doctor having sex, he compulsively eats toothpaste: "By taste and not seeing he contemplated the cool invisible worm as it coiled onto his finger and smeared sharp, automatonlike and sweet, into his mouth" (488). When approached by Hines, the dietician experiences herself as "a puppet in some burlesque of rapine and despair. . . . [S]he appeared to be in deepest thought, as if the puppet . . . had gone astray within itself" (495). When McEachern adopts Christmas he examines him like "a secondhand plow" (503), searching for flaws. Later, when Christmas goes to meet the prostitute Bobby, her eyes are like "button eyes of a toy animal: a quality beyond hardness, without being hard" (526). When she tells Christmas about menstruation, he kills a sheep in a volitionless, robotic ritual (535).

In *Light in August* human action is fully known, fully calculated: when McEachern tries to hunt down Joe at a dance, he immediately finds him, as if by chance; after striking and possibly killing his adoptive father, Joe immediately finds his father's horse in the darkness, without having any reason to know where it is (547, 551). Automatic knowledge pervades the novel. As Joe gallops away "the horse and rider—had a strange, dreamy effect, like a moving picture in slow motion"; Joe is reduced to a sequence of images, which is precisely what describes mechanical time for Bergson, who argues that "the mechanism of our ordinary knowledge is of the cinematographical kind" (*Creative* 306). When Bobby rejects Christmas and he flees permanently, "he entered the street which was to run for fifteen years." Time is spatialized: Joe's route and destination are always already known; the street has a *telos*. The novel's metaphysics are the dark side of Bergson's.

Religion, too, is automatic in *Light in August*. After having already been in an affair with Christmas for some time, the aging Joanna Burden feels the unwelcome stirrings of religious faith.

> It was something out of the darkness, the earth, the dying summer itself: something threatful and terrible to her because instinct as-

> sured her that it would not harm her; that it would overtake and betray her completely, but she would not be harmed: that on the contrary, she would be saved. . . . What was terrible was that she did not want to be saved. "I'm not ready to pray yet," she said aloud, quietly, rigid, soundless, her eyes wide open, while the moon poured and poured into the window, filling the room with something cold and irrevocable and wild with regret. "Dont make me have to pray yet. Dear God, let me be damned a little longer, a little while." She seemed to see her whole past life, the starved years, like a gray tunnel, at the far and irrevocable end of which, as unfading as a reproach, her naked breast of three short years ago ached as though in agony. (593–94)

Salvation is mechanized: one can observe and regret it, but not resist it. The past and current Joannas are terribly conflated, as if the latter inevitably resulted from the former. At a minimum, the structure of Joanna's heritage and faith automates her. She mechanically commands Christmas to pray with her, and he kills her equally mechanically. He prepares to enter her room for the last time: "The dark was filled with the voices, myriad, out of all time that he had known, as though all the past was a flat pattern. And going on: tomorrow night, all the tomorrows, to be a part of the flat pattern, going on. . . . all that had ever been was the same as all that was to be. . . . then it was time" (606). Time is flattened—"decapitated," as Sartre argues. It is fully mechanized, with no hope of "lived time," *durée,* behind it. In Faulkner, as in Melville, the danger of mechanization is not something new but something old. It belongs no more to the evils of northern modernity than to the southern past.

No *telos* looms in Faulkner's work, for the end of history, the perfect spatialization of time, has already arrived. Later in the book, when we move into Hightower's story, we learn that, living without clocks, Hightower is "dissociated from mechanical time. Yet for that reason he had never lost it . . . as though out of his subconscious he produces without volition the few crystallizations of stated instances by which his dead life in the actual world had been governed and ordered once" (669–70). Mechanical time, contra many critics, doesn't exist in the clocks themselves, nor is it generated by them: it precedes them. The distillation of life into instants from which the remainder of a life can be calculated is the shadowy essence of Bergson's mechanical time. Hines has always been an automaton, led as if by chance to kill Christmas's father, taking "the only short cut he could possibly have taken, choosing it in the dark . . . that would ever have caught up with them" (676). His wife's voice is like a phonograph, as is his own; their words are at hand long before being spoken (674, 676). When the narrative briefly attaches to Lucas Birch, he begins to understand the world as "shapes like chessmen," moved by an unseen player (722). Percy Grimm and Hightower feel "the player" too, as Percy kills the unresisting Christmas. After Christmas's murder, Hightower's thinking is like a wheel running in sand. "It spins now, fading, without progress, as though turned by that final flood . . . so that it can be now Now" (763). Hightower needs for now to be Now; he struggles toward something like Bergson's duration or living time, but without hope: his thought-wheel, like the rusted wheel in the abandoned sawmill, does not actually move.

Faulkner's automatism does not arrive with "modernity," with mechanization as such, which in any event has always already arrived. It arrives, as in Bergson, when time is turned into space, when the reality of change (e.g., the shifting landscape) is overwhelmed by a sense of all things already being foreseen. Lena's brief rise out of automatism—that inevitable automatism, which is the product of an inevitable way of being—is the bright contrast to Christmas's uninterrupted road.

Douglass discusses many of these issues in *Bergson, Eliot, and American Literature,* arguing that the key to the shared madness of Hines, Christmas, and Joanna is "its tunnel-vision. . . . Joanna is preparing for a foregone conclusion, the natural outcome of her bigoted background. For McEachern, too, 'bigotry and clairvoyance were practically one' " (161). Douglas argues that the issue is that Joe and Hightower have "given up free choice" (163). This is true but simplistic: what I emphasize is the extreme difficulty—presuming, following Bergson, the absolute necessity of spatialized time and instrumental reasoning—of choosing other than they do. Lena's rise out of automatism is contingent, incomplete, and temporary; its contingency makes it even more admirable.

Light in August details a South that implicitly rejects the reading of Faulkner, rooted in Brooks and Cowley, as essentially a modernist who rejects modernity in favor of the Old South's traditions. The modernism of *Light in August* exposes the always already mechanically compromised and always already temporally mechanized South. The South was no more innocent than the North in its transformation of the world into raw materials, and less innocent in the transformation of *people* into raw materials. The southern "bloody pastoral" is always a lie, which makes *Light in August* the greatest American anti-pastoral: it reveals that the machine never arrives in the garden, for it was always already there.

Faulkner's Cyborgs: *Absalom, Absalom!* and *Pylon*

Faulkner wrote *Pylon* (arguably his worst novel) in a lull in *Absalom, Absalom!* (probably his best). His life was chaotic during this period, marked by his daughter's birth in 1933, heavy drinking, excessive financial commitments, an attempt to establish a semi-conservationist hunting club, a deteriorating relationship with his wife, an affair, sporadic and much-loathed work in Hollywood, and an obsession with flying that indirectly led to his brother's death. While beginning *Absalom,* then entitled *Dark House* (also *Light in August*'s original title), in December 1933, he earned his pilot's license and was absorbed in flying and in the lives of pilots. His brother Dean also became a pilot, with intentions of earning a living flying; William and Dean even performed in air shows together. In November 1935, Dean died in the plane he had been purchasing from William. Faulkner finished *Absalom* in January 1936; *Pylon* was written mostly in November 1934, a caesura close to the middle of the composition of *Absalom* (Blotner 322–76).

Many judge *Pylon* as a failure in its own right, as do I, but it is an invaluable document for the study of *Absalom. Pylon* is an abrupt novel populated by underdeveloped characters who seem to belong more to Dashiell Hammett's fiction than Faulkner's. *Pylon* is rich with strange neologisms and dominated by a remarkable setting: an otherworldly version of New Orleans, simultaneously glittering and dank, antediluvian and ultramodern. It is ostensibly the story of a nameless reporter's obsession with an unconventional family of barnstormers: the husband, Shumann; his wife, Laverne; their son; and Laverne's lover, Jiggs. Nearly every man who sees Laverne, including the narrator, lusts after her, while her husband and lover exist in a kind of erotic suspension of their own. At novel's end the strange family scatters: the husband wrecks the plane, and Laverne leaves the boy with her husband's father and continues her adventures with Jiggs.

Those who have written on *Pylon* seem to speak with one voice: it is about T. S. Eliot's wasteland, the wreckage of modernity, and it refers frequently to Eliot's poem. Blotner writes: "Faulkner's anti-modernist sentiments, so clear in his description of the Bauhaus-style airport with its inhuman voices, were now further generalized. . . . [W]here airplanes are 'trim vicious fragile' machines, there is a kind of unresolved ambivalence, for he had been a hero worshipper since childhood, where his imagination was stirred by the very names of airmen. In his artistic development he had placed a higher and higher valuation on the best of the past and on harmony with organic nature" (340). Brooks ignores *Pylon* altogether. This might be explained by his focus on the novels set in Yoknapatawpha County, but this only begs the question: Why does he attend only to these novels? Brooks is invested in Faulkner as a regionalist and antimodernizer; even the ambivalence Blotner finds in *Pylon* is too much for Brooks to swallow.

Few critics have treated *Pylon* at length, and those who do tend to provide variations on Blotner's argument. William Brevda argues that *Pylon* attacks the futurist movement and writes that "machines in *Pylon* portend a dangerous evolution of man into machine and machine into man" (218). That is, machines and people interpenetrate dangerously. In "*Pylon:* Faulkner's Waste Land" (1985), Susie Johnson notes that most critics have seen the wasteland imagery of the novel as being only so much rehashed Eliot (287). She, however, argues that Faulkner extends Eliot: the kinship between New Orleans and New Valois makes the cruelty and emptiness of the latter all the more shocking; she finds that New Valois is a city erected "in defiance of nature" and that the novel strips the city of New Orleans's greenery (289–90). The modernist airport is accompanied by the mountains of junk it necessitates (292). Planes become instruments of exploitation, drawing crowds at the ultimate expense of human life (292). Exploitation is universal; Johnson argues that even the reporter becomes "a violator," like the rest of the city; the violators have "inherited the earth," much as in *Light in August* (294). Her analysis is unobjectionable yet incomplete: the universality of treachery and exploitation in *Pylon,* as in the crime novels it unsuccessfully emulates—*Pylon*'s indictment of an entire city seems like an echo of Hammett's *Red Harvest* (1929) or a foreshadowing of Chester Himes's *Blind Man with a Pistol* (1969)—implies a question: Is a different world possible? One brief answer, returning to Bergson's theory of the necessity of instrumental reasoning, is that the world *as such* is no wasteland, nor are its inhabitants *only* violators, but that their exploitative orientation toward the world as standing-reserve is inevitable. Automatism and the world-as-standing-reserve will always haunt us, because they are intrinsic to instrumental reasoning, which can no more be abandoned than, say, the use of hands.

Michael Zeitlin analyzes *Pylon* using Leo Marx and Walter Benjamin, arguing that we must contextualize *Pylon* within Faulkner's movement toward savage criticism of "contemporary reality" (230). Its strange, obsessive descriptions and neologisms are central to the novel's importance, "which is to record, transcribe, interpret, and so *manage* successfully the phenomena of a radically transfigured reality" (233). The novel describes an alien, weirdly dead city in which even electricity signifies death, the opposite of its usual meaning (Nye, *Sublime* 152, 192). Zeitlin ends by quoting Marx's argument that the machine's violation of the garden is the defining moment in American literature. Faulkner, Zeitlin writes, needed *Pylon* to exorcise *Absalom* of the corruption of modernity and mechanization:

> As the narrative absorbs and transfigures the city's myriad "garblement" . . . it acts out a loss of imaginative control over it, alien aspects of reality freely penetrating and finally overwhelming the mind.
>
> Of course, *Pylon* only dramatizes the failure Faulkner himself avoided: he emerged, as we know, from the nightmare of the contemporary scene—his estrangement having generated a powerful renewal of language—to bring *Absalom, Absalom!* (the nightmare of history) to a decisive completion (237).

Zeitlin finds *Pylon* important precisely because of its ambivalent embrace of modernity: *Pylon* is a purgative that purifies Faulkner's endangered aesthetic, freeing *Absalom* from the machine, sanctifying it. The virtue of Zeitlin's reading is that it addresses why Faulkner interrupted *Absalom* to write *Pylon,* and why the former so outstrips the latter. Its weaknesses are, first, that it seeks to restore our image of an antimodern Faulkner that *Pylon* destabilizes; and second, that it neglects the unavoidable relevance of Faulkner's biography. *Pylon* was written out of genuine obsession with airplanes and pilots: Faulkner had been in an air show shortly before *Absalom*'s publication—not just before *Pylon*'s. Surely *Pylon* answers *some* problem raised by the composition of *Absalom,* but Zeitlin's answers are too tranquilizing: in Zeitlin's version of the story, Faulkner must deal with Marx's story of the machine's entry into the garden, but then, by writing *Pylon,* he simply *transcends* it.

In my version of the *Pylon-Absalom* story, Faulkner becomes enmeshed in the ongoing intermingling of machine and organism. For critics have noted another side of *Pylon,* even if they haven't contextualized it with Faulkner's other works. Vivian Wagner, following John Duvall and John Matthews, demonstrates that in Faulkner's airplane stories, including *Pylon* and the related "Honor," "the bodies of barnstormers are technologized and roboticized to the point of being interchangeable with the bodies of the airplanes" (79). These cyborg bodies become highly eroticized and fluidly gendered, but only in and around planes: on the ground, Laverne is the object of every man's sometimes violent desire, but in the air she becomes partially masculinized and powerful—"someone who fucks" rather than "something to be fucked," in Wagner's memorable phrasing (93). Around the airplanes an alternative family forms, sustained by the machine: when they fall from the sky, they fall from "a technological utopia, in which men and women can desire each other equally, freely, and without social constraint, into a world in which gender distinctions signify violence, pain, and degradation" (93).

In *Pylon* a nameless voice states that pilots don't fly for money; they fly "because they have got to do it, like some women have got to be whores. They cant help themselves" (975). There is an automatism in the wild, liberated life in the air, among pilots seemingly half machine themselves. The pilots are both farther from mechanical life and deeper in it than others, which fuels the reporter's fascination: "he just waked . . . like so many people who, living always on the outside of the mechanical regimentation of hours, seem able at need to coincide with a given moment with a sort of unflagging instinctive facility. But the train would be ordered by mechanical postulation though. . . . [He] turned in this side of the window and the immemorial grapefruit halves which apparently each morning at the same moment at which the street lamps went out would be set, age- and timeproved for intactness and imperviousness like the peasant vases exhumed from Greek and Roman ruins" (918–19). Like the pilots, he is removed from mechanical time yet subject to it; the automatism of the daily grapefruit elides into a Keatsian Greek vase in which *Light in August*'s link between automatism and eternity is clarified. Automatism rules the city and threatens the pilots, who resist it precisely through their eroticized intermingling with machines, like the simultaneous embrace/resistance of the Mumfordian megamachine we find in Queequeg and Ahab.

My concern, however, has never been with *Pylon* itself but with *Pylon* embedded within *Absalom*. By turning to *Pylon* amidst *Absalom*, Faulkner wrestled with mechanization, automatism, and modernity. Contrary to Zeitlin's reading, though, *Pylon* demonstrates that we should not regard Faulkner, including *Absalom*, as *rejecting* modernity and mechanization, but rather as struggling with their ambiguously utopian and dystopian possibilities: rather than eliminating these struggles, *Pylon* renders them more lucid.

Absalom, Absalom! begins with Rosa Coldfield's outraged voice in a dark, suffocating room; she bores Quentin Compson, who has always known the story she tells of Thomas Sutpen's rise and fall, which reeks of sentimentality and lost paradise: "Out of a quiet thunderclap he would abrupt (man-horse-demon) upon a scene peaceful and decorous as a school-prize water color, faint sulphur-reek still in hair clothes and beard, with grouped behind him his band of wild niggers like beasts half tamed to walk upright like men, in attitudes wild and reposed, and manacled among them the French architect with his air grim, haggard, and tatterran" (4). Myths and lies pile up, collapsing of their own weight. The "wild niggers," who always seem a mixture of man and beast, are Haitian, we learn; Sutpen went to Haiti as a teenager, worked for a planter, suppressed a slave rebellion, received the planter's daughter in marriage, had a son; then abandoned wife, son, and newfound wealth upon discovering his wife's racial impurity. He moved to Mississippi, where he and his slaves seem unutterably barbarous to the people of Jackson, recently carved from wilderness itself, though he and the slaves came from an older, more powerful colony.

One of *Absalom*'s many distortions and lies is that, with the dates given, Sutpen could not have suppressed a slave rebellion in Haiti: Haiti was already independent, after a successful slave rebellion. Richard Godden argues that this "mistake" is too blatant to be an error, because "Faulkner wishes to foreground the continuous potential for revolution within the institution of slavery, he needs Haiti, the only successful black revolution. Given that he wishes to characterize the plantocracy as a class that suppresses revolution, he requires that his ur-planter suppress the Haitian revolution and go on doing so" (53). Godden argues that slaves in *Absalom* are figured as simultaneously threatening and volitionless: the "good nigger"/"bad nigger" dichotomy blends with that of the obedient and rampaging robot in science fiction. Black and miscegenated characters are automatons, forever on the brink of violence. Charles Bon, Thomas Sutpen's lost son who seemingly wants to marry his legitimate daughter, offers no resistance when Henry, the legitimate son, murders him. Charles's son by his octoroon wife/mistress, Charles Etienne Saint-Valery Bon, is raised by Judith and Clytie, Thomas's legitimate and illegitimate/mixed-race daughters, then leaves them only to return with a "coal black and ape-like woman" who "existed in that aghast and automaton-like state in which she had arrived" (166). She is wife and mother, ape and automaton, but also, like the biblical Sarah, the future's improbable mother. Her son is the "idiot" Jim Bond, the only Sutpen to survive the destruction of their home, of whom Shreve, Quentin's roommate and the co-creator of the latter half of the novel, says: "in time the Jim Bonds are going to conquer the western hemisphere. Of course it wont quite be in our time. . . . But it will still be Jim Bond; and so in a few thousand years, I who regard you will also have sprung from the loins of African kings" (302).

The ambiguity Godden addresses, the simultaneous revelation and suppression of "the simple and debilitating truth of slave production, that the master's body is made by the slave's work: a fact that casts ethnic interdependency as white dependency," is preserved throughout the novel (72). Jim Bond and his mother are automatons and conquerors, rendered idiotic and powerful by their silence: they evade the treachery of language and instrumental reasoning that destroys so many other characters, from Thomas Sutpen's obsession with reasoning out where he had gone astray to Quentin's father's knowledge that language is unreliable but irreplaceable. Godden argues that the moment when young Thomas Sutpen is turned away from a planter's door is a monad (in Benjamin's sense), a crystallization of time. "Sutpen and Rosa lead lives more or less committed to the plantocracy, yet each remains internally divided by a single moment in which recognition of the laboring presence of the slave 'shatters the continuum of [their] language.' That moment is forbidden and repercussive" (100). The monad reveals the structures of southern oppression; the "moment" must be continually repressed, yet it cannot be. Godden, myopically, focuses on Charles Bon, who owned slaves and never did a day's work before the war, as a manifestation of slave labor, instead of looking to his descendants' mute automatism.

Faulkner's work obsessively displays horror at and desire for the blurring of difference. Characters *desire* miscegenation literally and metaphorically; desire for unity counteracts pressures toward division, as critics from Dorreen Fowler to James Snead argue. The novel's end forcefully locates automatism in the safely black and beastlike bodies of Jim Bond and his mother. But this automatism, which is both a perpetual reference to and a denial of the Haitian revolution, *triumphs.* In *Pylon* the pilots are wholly mechanized, yet most authentically struggle for freedom. Similarly, Jim Bond is both the only authentic future and the foreclosure of all possible futures: his howl is the only surviving (anti)language, his automatism the only surviving response to automatism. Rosa captures this ambiguity when remembering her response to Clytie as Rosa tried to ascend the stairs to see Bon's body: "*hurling myself into that inscrutable coffee-colored face, that cold implacable mindless (no, not mindless: anything but mindless: his own clairvoyant will tempered to amoral evil's undeviating absolute by the black willing blood with which he had crossed it)*" (110). Is Clytie terrible *as* an automaton, an extension of Sutpen's will? Or because she *does* have volition, and is willingly allied to Sutpen? Either way, all of time is threatened by mindlessness and/or by Sutpen's evil, miscegenated will, which blur together.

Rosa Compson herself, despite seeing Sutpen as violating the "water color" of the Old South, continually shifts and overflows, desiring to become those she is divided from, while pushing them away. She desires and nearly attains Sutpen, although (because) her aunt impresses upon her the quasi-racial abyss separating her from the "ogre" Sutpen. In this context, her desire for him becomes a variation on the miscegenation that, following Sundquist, is for Faulkner the curse of slavery and the reason the South deserved to lose the war (123). But miscegenation is only part of what Rosa desires. Godden argues that Rosa lusts for her sister's house and bed, a lust tangled up with her ambiguous gender and sexuality: her desire for Bon and the house is also desire for Judith (92–96). "I became all of polymath loves androgynous advocate," Rosa says of her obsession with Bon and Judith's relationship: she wants to be male and female, Bon and Judith, to be and to emanate love itself (117). Rosa's raging polymath desire floods even racial barriers, despite her bigotry: her rage at Clytie is also desire. After Bon's death and Henry's departure, Rosa stays at the plantation. She claims utter difference from Judith and Clytie: "one woman whom, for all she was blood kin to me . . . I did not wish to understand, and another who was so foreign to me and to all that I was that we might have been not only of different races (which we were), not only of different sexes (which we were not), but of different species, speaking no language which the other understood, the very simple words with which we were forced to adjust our days to one another being even less inferential of thought and intention than the sounds which a beast and bird might make to each other" (123–24). The abysses dividing her from Clytie and Judith are unbridgeable, particularly by language; note that Rosa imagines herself and Clytie as mutually uncomprehending, rather than seeing Clytie as an idiot. Rosa discusses their time together as a strange evolution: "sex was some forgotten atrophy like the rudimentary gills we call the tonsils or the still-opposable thumbs for old climbing" (125). Their voiceless, volitionless, pleasureless lives are figured as evolutionary, prefiguring the evolutionary figure of Jim Bond: the future is the end of time. Two pages after asserting their unbridgeable difference, Rosa reverses herself: "It was as though we were one being, interchangeable and indiscriminate" (125). In their difference-as-oneness, they await Sutpen's return, while the memory of Bon's death falls into nothingness:

"a retroactive severance of the stream of event: a forever crystallized instant in imponderable time accomplished by three weak yet indomitable women" (127). Absolute difference and absolute oneness are confused, desire and automatism merge, the future becomes the crystallization and the destruction of time; evolution is the destruction of will and language, reversing Bergson, for whom it is the *struggle* against automatism.

Rosa desires Sutpen, Judith, Bon, Clytie, the land and house. Her impossible, tangled desires are indistinguishable from the lack of desire, this chaotic time indistinguishable from a spatialized time in which every event is crystallized and forever known. The novel begins: "From a little after two oclock until almost sundown of the long still hot weary dead September afternoon" (3). We open with the contrast between two o'clock, which is measured, mechanical time, and sundown, which is agricultural, organic time. Rosa yearns for the lost agricultural time (sundown) that allegedly prevailed before the arrival of the clock (two o'clock). The fact that she has been stuck in one crystallized moment for forty-three years seemingly confirms that she mourns for "lost time" and that her mourning for this lost world is pointless, effectless. Yet this time-stranded Rosa is uniquely capable of effective action.

Rosa is described as "sitting so bolt upright in the straight hard chair that was so tall for her that her legs hung straight and rigid as if she had iron shinbones and ankles" (3). She is characterized by a mechanical stiffness that alludes to her stubborn retention of the "lost time," organic time, yet also to the illusory nature of that organic time. The very advocate for organic time and the Old South is most mechanical, and, like *Pylon*'s barnstormers, lusts for the machine. Rosa speaks about Bon's face, which she has seen only in photographs: "But I never saw it. I do not even know of my own knowledge that Ellen ever saw it, that Judith ever loved it, that Henry slew it: so who will dispute me when I say, Why did I not invent, create it?—And I know this: if I were God I would invent out of this seething turmoil we call progress something (a machine perhaps) which would adorn the barren mirror altars of every plain girl who breathes with such as this—which is so little since we want so little—this pictured face" (118). Rosa's desire for Bon, whom she never saw, becomes the desire for desire—more specifically, the desire for a simulated, mechanized desire. Rosa doesn't simply want Bon, or Bon's image, or for every plain girl to have a similar image: she wants to be the God who makes the machine that abstractly and mechanically fulfills the desire for desire. This desire is, as in *Pylon,* a desire for a union of human and machine. Rosa desires not reproduction but mechanical reproduction. In her most transgressive moment, she envisions every young woman going through a mechanized puberty and an automated love: the very image of the good, natural, and organic (i.e., the virginal white woman) is violated not merely by human miscegenation but by mechanical miscegenation. Her desire leaps unbridgeable gaps to Judith, Clytie, Sutpen, Bon, and finally the machine; it originates in rejection, in this case in her seeming rejection of "progress" and mechanical time.

Rosa eroticizes her father's mechanizing Calvinism. Where her father disentangles himself from difference—for instance, by freeing two slaves and then charging their market value against their wages—Rosa is enmeshed in the dialectic of "difference from" and "oneness with"; where her father uses the church "exactly as he would have used a cotton gin in which he considered himself to have incurred either interest or responsibility" (38), taking exactly what he is entitled to, Rosa takes both less and more than she has earned, as with the supplies she collects over the years for the ostensible value of her father's store.

At the novel's end, Rosa shoves Clytie aside as she goes upstairs, toward Henry. Upstairs she sees Jim Bond and stumbles:

> "You, nigger! What's your name?"
> "Calls me Jim Bond."
> "Help me up! You aint any Sutpen! You dont have to leave me lying in the dirt!" (297)

Then, unsignaled, the novel slips through time, past Quentin's actual encounter with Henry (which he later remembers in his room), and goes immediately, without white space or italics, to Quentin and Rosa's return to her house: "[He] lifted her down; she was almost as light as Clytie had been; when she moved it was like a mechanical doll, so that he supported and led her through the gate and up the short walk and into the doll-sized house and turned on the light for her and looked at the fixed sleep-walking face" (297). The radical difference between the actively intelligent, bitter, obsessed Rosa and the idiotic, inactive, near-mute Jim Bond, who anticipates no future but embodies all futures, is erased. Seeing Bond and his idiocy/automatism, Rosa falls; having fallen, she claims a kind of kinship with him—at least he isn't a Sutpen. Then the novel skips the "important" part, the actual encounter with Henry, cutting to Rosa's return home as a "mechanical doll" with a "sleep-walking face." The difference between Bond and Rosa is erased, as her earlier differences from Clytie and Judith were erased: the automatism of the future is revealed as implicit in the past. Jim Bond retains his grandfather's knack, which made Thomas Sutpen so powerful and so hated: he uncovers the truth, even when he doesn't understand it. Just as Sutpen's fights with his slaves, and Judith's observation of those fights, obliterate the romanticism built around slavery and the cult of white womanhood, and as Sutpen's relationship with Clytie (who never called herself a slave) destabilizes the same barriers that he erects by denying his son, Charles Bon, Jim Bond exposes to Rosa the continuity between his automatism and her own.

That same automatism is in Sutpen, who seems so free. As soon as he has "erected that shell of a house," he stops moving: "for three years he had remained completely static, as if he were run by electricity and someone had come along and removed, dismantled the wiring or the dynamo" (31–32). What many critics see in *Pylon*—modernity's emptiness and automatism—*Absalom* locates in Mississippi's mythic past. Among the novel's deadly secrets is the identity of Sutpen's awful volitionlessness and automatism with Jim Bond's howl; this same automatism lurks in the "natural" men who preceded Sutpen into Mississippi (they hate him as an overly honest version of themselves) and in the young white men who "while young and supple and strong reacted to a single simple Yes and a single simple No as instantaneous and complete and unthinking as the snapping on and off of electricity" (218).

The identity of Bond's automatism with the plantocracy's (beginning with Sutpen) is significant. Historically, it responds to the lie that an American pastoral scene was violated by the machine's arrival: the machine was already there, at least as the industrial organization of the plantation system;[2] the role of industry in the South's defeat (satirically detailed in Bon's letter to Judith, written in Union-made stove polish) becomes, perhaps, the difference between the North's acknowledgment of its mechanization and the South's denial of *its* mechanization.

Absalom is no triumphant recovery from *Pylon*'s threatening automatism and modernity, but rather the recognition that this modernity and automatism stretch both into the distant past and forward into the intolerable future.

Snopesism and Automatism

A truism of Faulkner criticism is that the Snopes family—especially Flem Snopes, who is, more than a character, the void around whom *The Hamlet* (1940), *The Town* (1957), and *The Mansion* (1959) revolve—represents industrialism and mechanization, the alleged "values" of the North. Cowley and Brooks are again representative. Brooks writes that "the insidious horror of Snopesism is its lack of any kind of integrity—its pliability, its parasitic vitality. . . . Like finance-capitalism itself, Flem works inside the law," and that "Snopesism is the enemy not only of the old aristocratic order but also of the old folk society," a peril necessitating resistance from both the white aristocracy and the implicitly white folk society (222).

What is the story of the Snopes family? In "Barn Burning" (1938), young Sarty Snopes is torn by the knowledge that his father burns their landlords' barns; he has conflicting duties to his father and the landlords. When the family, headed by Ab the barn burner, arrives in the hamlet of Frenchman's Bend, another son (Sarty having disappeared), Flem, uses his father's barn-burning habit to blackmail Will Varner, their landlord, into giving him a job at his store. Will Varner is what passes for aristocracy in this isolated corner of the county, being "the chief man of the country. . . . [A] milder-mannered man never bled a mule or stuffed a ballot box. He owned most of the good land in the country and held mortgages on the rest. He owned the store and the cotton gin and the combined grist mill and blacksmith shop and it was considered . . . bad luck for a man of the neighborhood to do his trading or gin his cotton or grind his meal or shoe his stock anywhere else" (9). Varner is a political boss and monopolist who dominates the local industries and supply networks (which connect to global systems) that sustain cotton farming in this "natural," "pastoral" community. In *The Hamlet,* Flem improves the efficiency of Varner's store, marries his daughter (pregnant, although not by Flem), getting the Old Frenchman place as a dowry. He returns from a Texas honeymoon with dangerous, untamably wild ponies, which he barters away through a proxy. Presumably using that money, he seeds the Old Frenchman place with buried money, which attracts treasure hunters, including V. K. Ratliff and Henry Armstid, who buy the place at a markup. This marks the end of *The Hamlet;* in *The Town* Flem moves to the town of Jefferson, rising from being a small restaurateur to the power plant's supervisor, to eventually holding a job in a bank, which he obtains by ignoring his wife's affair with Major De Spain, the bank's part-owner. In *The Mansion* Flem awaits death at the hands of his kinsman Mink, recently released from prison, whom he doesn't help after Mink murders Jack Houston, the second-largest landowner in Frenchman's Bend.

Flem is nobody's hero: he twice impoverishes Henry Armstid and indirectly encourages his own wife's suicide. That does not explain the animosity he attracts, both from other characters and from critics. Armstid brutalizes his wife and deprives his children without receiving more than a passing glance; Will Varner remains generally well liked by other characters and even often by critics, despite being a local tyrant with far more power than Flem ever acquires. Yet Ratliff, who narrates much of the trilogy, dedicates himself to watching and resisting Flem while remaining on good terms with Armstid and Varner.

One reason for the animosity is Flem's coldness: he makes no friends and gets no pleasure from his chicanery, unlike Varner and Ratliff. Another explanation is that Flem acts as a mirror, revealing to others a version of themselves without trappings or dissembling. James Snead states in *Figures of Division* that critics have split, with most seeing Flem as representing the "changing economic order of the South," while others emphasize the similarity of Varner and Flem, making the case that Varner only hides his Snopesism (why Snopesism, not Varnerism?) behind a happy face. Snead articulates the reason for the critical split: "Flem knows the game, but as an outsider cannot and does not have any reason to hide its cost. He represents 'the commercial spirit in its purity,' but this pure attack brings out impurities that the hamlet has formerly preferred to carry forward" (159). Frenchman's Bend is racially uniform (and dangerous to "strange negroes") and, Snead argues, dedicated to a myth of equality, which the folksy/sharkish Will Varner perpetuates. This myth still convinces many critics. Carl Dimitri confidently asserts that Varner, despite his ownership of industries and enterprises, and his control of a congressional district, is premodern, as opposed to Flem, an avatar of instrumental reasoning (75). "Everyone" is happy with the myth that all the (white) people of the hamlet are equal, that nothing ever changes, that they are a pastoral community, not a producer of a raw material for a global industry. Flem Snopes owes nothing to this facade and sees no need to carry it on—thus he is hated.

Despite the Snopeses' outer whiteness, an undercurrent of blackness swirls around them. "I'll have word with the man that aims to begin to-morrow owning me body and soul," Ab declares in "Barn Burning" (*Stories* 9). For the *honest* white sharecropper, his condition verges on slavery. Snopesism holds no illusions. Godden argues that Ab is racially ambiguous and that "Barn Burning" was written "out of Faulkner's despair over modernization," with the story exploring "the limited patterns of resistance within the cropping contract" (129).[3] "Barn Burning" still reeks of despair—the barn burning itself seems automatic—but if Faulkner despairs at modernization, this modernization is indistinct from preceding states of being; if Ab's near-serfdom is modernization, then who, paraphrasing Ishmael, ain't modern? Ab's automatism may respond to the failure of all resistance to this *old* "modernity." Under Flem's sway, everything *should* change, yet nothing does: the Snopes family reveals that modernization's dark side is one with what the South has always been: a sophisticated, organized link in a global structure (a long-enduring world-system), that was highly innovative in its mixture of "aboriginal" agricultural technologies and "Western" organizational techniques; Pacey, following Peter Worsley, argues that plantation agriculture served as a model for factory labor: "modernity" migrated north, east, and west from the sugar plantations (*World* 100–101). Flem reveals the South to be everything its mythology denies. Factory laborer, slave, and sharecropper all belong to the same system; Varner's and Flem's managerial techniques are continuous with those of northern factories; the *South* exported scientific management to the *North*.

Many critics see Ratliff as opposing Flem's mechanizing worldview;

Corinne Dale argues that Ratliff is an organic alternative to Flem while she acknowledges an essential kinship between planters of the "Old South" and businessman of the "New South" (337, 323–24). But believing that Ratliff opposes mechanization is dangerous: a smiling face does not make his worldview different from Flem's. John Lutz, who sees continuity between Flem and Varner, argues that Ratliff, as a sewing-machine salesman and stakeholder in various businesses, is himself a capitalist who can be as "predatory and cold blooded" as Flem, because he aggressively sells unneeded machines to the poor (89). Arguing that Flem's ponies and the desire they evoke tell a story about commodity fetishism, Lutz writes: "Rather than being described as a moral community under assault by a single individual, the society of Frenchman's Bend might be better characterized as one in which an emerging market economy is substituting exchange value for personal worth while further eroding the conditions under which individuals can achieve autonomy by participating in a community" (74). Lutz is partially correct (although horses are not commodities in Faulkner's fiction; they are individuals); the threat to human autonomy in the novel is real, as Ab Snopes, for one, reveals—but Lutz fails to recognize that there was no time when there *was* autonomy. The slave economy blurs into the sharecropping economy, which blurs into the market economy. The destruction of autonomy is partially economic, yet automatism is *not* chronologically modern, but almost primordial. One reason to see the issue of automatism as continuous in the Snopes trilogy is that Flem, despite knowing that Mink hunts him, takes no effectual action. Despite Snopesism's apparent vitality, Flem ultimately surrenders to his fate, not unlike Quentin Compson. "What do you reckon Flem's reason was for setting there in that chair letting Mink snap them two shells at him until one of them went off and killed him," Ratliff wonders (*Snopes* 1060). The all-powerful man, seemingly autonomous, collapses into nothingness; the belief in and acceptance of destiny is automatism. Flem is a victim of the worldview that, in a scapegoating process, he is blamed for introducing.

Scattered moments in the trilogy give the lie to the concept of a machine suddenly disrupting the southern garden. As Varner and Ab talk at the beginning of *The Hamlet,* Varner sees Ab's yard (on Varner's land) as a "grassless desolation scarred with the ashes and charred stick-ends"; he sees two women pumping "with metronome-like regularity . . . turning slowly again as though riveted and synchronized to one another by a mechanical arm" (24). Varner fails to understand that *he himself* is the mechanical arm riveting and synchronizing the Snopes women; *he* is the personification of the economic system that mechanizes them: Flem emerges from this environment. The image of the metronome returns at the novel's end, with Henry Armstid digging hopelessly for treasure (348). He is there because of Flem's trickery, but also Ratliff's, and because of the whole system in which he exists: his one attempt to escape the automatism of his daily life ends with him as a metronome. Shortly after Ab and Varner's conversation we discover that Colonel Sartoris, the ultimate emblem of the Confederacy, built a railroad (32). The mechanization of the South is in the beginning, not in the end. Much of *The Town* is concerned with the transformations wrought by the automobile. While we get many details about these changes, they are amusingly superficial, mainly providing occasions for men to continue old grudges about women.

The Mansion ends shortly after Mink murders Flem. Mink, whose language echoes Faulkner's great novels of the 1930s, has been called a kind of epic hero (Brooks 220). Yet, unlike the epic hero, who, following Lukács, is characterized by belonging within the rounded totality of the world, Mink is a deeply novelistic hero, at odds with everyone and everything, the earth most of all (Lukács 32–33). He is utterly estranged from his dead wife and living daughters; his life is given meaning only by his quest to destroy Flem. Although a cotton farmer, he experiences no bucolic unity with the earth; rather, he is at war with it: "the dirt which any and every tenant farmer and sharecropper knew to be his sworn foe and mortal enemy—the hard implacable land which wore out his youth and his tools and his body itself. . . . [W]as it any wonder that a man would look at the inimical irreconcilable square of dirt to which he was bound and chained for the rest of his life, and say to it: *You got me, you'll wear me out because you are stronger than me since I'm jest bone and flesh. . . . But we can burn you. Every late February or March we can set fire to the surface of you*" (760). Mink speaks out of utter alienation and despair, in rage against gods (landlords) above and earth below. His bottomless bile in *The Mansion* reveals what *The Hamlet* insistently implies: the nostalgia and romanticism that yearn for the "traditional values" shattered by modernity are a mirage. Agriculture is alienation, Mink bitterly attests, or, as Bergson puts it so eloquently: "We are at ease only in the discontinuous, in the immobile, in the dead" (*Creative* 165). Instrumental reasoning is ugly and alienating but also primordial. Mink must forever turn his world to ashes to survive. Automatism and alienation pervade all time; the struggle against the Snopes family is an attempt to deny the truth; it is not a noble cause.

Many critics have seen Faulkner's work as portraying a world devastated by mechanization and modernity. There is truth in this widespread idea, but a truth that, returning to Sartre, is insufficiently metaphysical. Faulkner's concern with the danger posed by the "machine" to "nature" and regional culture is actually a concern with automatism, which haunts all life. However old the threat of automatism, it is relatively old, stretching back at least to the origins of American slavery and plantation culture. Automatism is not a northern imposition but is fully native and deeply rooted in racial ideology, as we see in *Light in August*. It is not simply manifested through particular technological devices and practices: it is manifested *and* resisted by these devices and practices, as in *Pylon*. *Absalom, Absalom!* combines the insights of both novels; in it, time has long been threatened and even overcome by automatism. Among the many concerns of the *Snopes* novels is the *problematized* link between mechanization/modernity and automatism; Flem Snopes is a scapegoat, reviled for decapitating a future always already decapitated.

Despite what has appeared to be Faulkner's forthright opposition to modernity, especially qua mechanization and capitalism, running through his work is a countermovement that recognizes the deception involved in setting up a "natural" ideal, rooted in the sophisticated slave culture of the antebellum South, against a "mechanization" that mirrors and interpenetrates it. Modernity, mechanization, and instrumental reasoning have a long history. The darkest component of this realization is that it participates in what Sartre sees as the future-annihilating aspect of Faulkner's work.

In an understanding of history that contrasts a good past to present horrors, we retain the reactionary hope for a return to the golden age. If, however, one agrees with modernity's darkest critics by arguing that "modernity" is nothing essentially new but rather an evolving facade for a permanent aspect of human life, then how does one see anything in the future other than the perpetuation of the present? In many works of high modernism, the end of history looms: the distinction of Faulkner's work, still best articulated by Sartre, is that history has already ended: the instrumental reasoning that Adorno and Horkheimer assail for brutally exploiting the world originated much earlier than they acknowledge, even equiprimordially with humanity itself, if we follow Bergson. From another viewpoint, Faulkner's critique of modernity is a variation of Bergson's concept of time and history, but stripped of Bergson's notion of life's overall forward progress: to rephrase Sartre, Faulkner's concept of time, history, and technology is Bergson's with the head lopped off. The extremity of Faulkner's despair in the face of modernity and its long history owes much to his always explosive and contradictory reaction to the reality of American racial oppression: he saw a rawer edge of instrumental reasoning, with its primeval roots more exposed, perhaps, than Bergson.

Faulkner's understanding of history, time, and technology resembles Melville's; in Faulkner, as in Melville (especially the late Mumford's Melville), instrumental reasoning only *seems* to be peculiar to our historical moment. The reality for Faulkner and Melville is that the struggle between freedom and automatism is old. Faulkner's thought, though, is darker than Melville's; while Faulkner's automatism may not be as old in some sense as Melville's, which dates to the pyramids and the creation of God, it is less easily resisted. The resistance put up by Lena Grove, for instance, is but a shadow of the resistance of Ishmael and the Confidence Man. In Faulkner, the confidence game itself is subverted by automatism, with V. K. Ratliff thinking that he resists Snopesism when he is really another incarnation of it.

Perversely, this increased darkness is a kind of progress; Faulkner connects automatism with racial oppression more clearly than Melville does. This is not an improvement in itself, but it offers an opening. It would take someone on the *inside* of the American system of racial oppression to show that, just as the brutality of instrumental, technological reasoning is old, an equally old hope also dwells within it. This is Ralph Ellison's accomplishment.

5
Ellison and the Technological Hero

Technology and race have never been isolated concepts; Michael Adas argues in *Machines as the Measure of Men* (1989) that they have been especially connected in Western empires, where technological difference signifies or even constructs racial difference. I begin with an observation from *Technology and the African-American Experience* (2004), which Bruce Sinclair's introduction presents as the crystallization of the unified study of race and technology. Among essays focused on race and *machine* technology, one stands out. In "Raising Fish with a Song," Barbara Garrity-Blake argues that the work songs sung by black sailor-laborers in the menhaden fishery in the early twentieth century were "more than an accompaniment to the work process: it was used by laborers as a necessary means of raising the heaviest sets of fish" (107). The work song, she argues, was necessary to the industry and can properly be called technological: "critical technologies do not necessarily come out of formalized learning or from the use of mechanical devices" (108). This claim resembles Mumford's statement that "Tool-technics . . . is but a fragment of biotechnics: man's total equipment for life" (*Technics and Human Development* 7). More importantly, it indirectly follows the work of Ralph Ellison, who articulates the relationship between race and technology: teleological conceptions of technology are used to create hierarchies, including racial ones, but anti-teleological conceptions of technology undermine hierarchies; the former frame time apocalyptically, while the latter imagine time in a new, desirable way.

I begin with two claims: first, race and technology are not independent; and second, machine technology is continuous with cultural techniques. What is acknowledged as technology is partially a matter of racial and social hierarchies; "white" and "black" technologies become technology proper and folk techniques, respectively. The remainder of this chapter is partially an elaboration of these two ideas.

Ellison's vision of technology and time is connected to his evolving understanding of what he calls "that vanished tribe . . . the American Negro"; it is not a fixed entity, but a snapshot of a turbulent stream, related to the flexible hypermodernity of the Negro, which he contrasts to ideological faith (Marxist and capitalist, black and white) in history as progress (*Juneteenth* ix). American racial oppression does not operate on premodern objects but on hypermodern ones.

Ellison's interests in time and technology are frequent objects of critical inquiry; however, there has been no systematic discussion of the relationship between the two in his thought. I am concerned with the centrality of this relationship in his art and politics, and with its roots in Melville, Mumford, Faulkner, and Raglan. His interest in the "timeless" archetype of the hero, based on his reading of Raglan, is a vital part of this relationship. Ellison's use of the hero's mythic time and the accelerated time of the modern, reified Negro are one; this connection lets his art demand and enact change, while refuting progress and teleology as totalitarian.

I begin with two sources of *Invisible Man,* the electrical engineering department at Tuskegee and Ellison's work with Angelo Herndon at *Negro Quarterly,* to demonstrate the political origins and purpose of Ellison's later artistic articulation of a theory of time and technology. That is followed by an extended analysis of Ellison's use of Mumford and Raglan, who laid the groundwork for Ellison's anti-teleological exploration of the relationships among time, race, and technology—an exploration that reveals the interdependency between racial oppression and technological domination: an anti-teleological understanding of time is necessary to both technological and racial liberation.

Tuskegee Electrified

The prologue and epilogue of *Invisible Man* exemplify Ellison at his best, allusively and elusively modernist, yet thoroughly vernacular. They are well-baited traps for the unwary fly, rich with treasures not easily opened. I begin perilously, then, with a passage that has snared many. The narrator is in his basement, contemplating light, invisibility, and the nature of history, which leads him to his confrontation with Monopolated Light and Power: "It allows me to feel my vital aliveness. I also fight them for taking so much of my money before I learned to protect myself. In my hole in the basement there are exactly 1,369 lights. I've wired the whole ceiling. . . . [N]ot with fluorescent bulbs, but with the older, more-expensive-to-operate kind" (7). The narrator is an individual fighting a megatechnic institution, using technological means. The number 1,369 demands interpretation yet refuses it. Is it a simple number, or a sequence of digits in a series? The order and symmetry imply the latter, but the comma interferes. It isn't quite a sequence of the powers of 3: $3^0 = 1$, $3^1 = 3$, $3^2 = 9$, giving us 139—where does the 6 come from? Nor is it a sequence of integer multiples of 3: 3 x 1, 3 x 2, 3 x 3, which would yield the sequence 369. These digits both allude and elude, hint at mathematical sequence and avoid it. The next member would break the number's symmetry, or give its equation a name: is the next integer 12 or 27 (136912 or 136927)? The number creaks portentously: another digit would resolve the question of whether it is a mere integer or a set generated by an equation. It is a preposterously large number of lights, enough for a very sizable building; I count twenty-two bulbs in my house, fifty years of profligacy past *Invisible Man*. This is both absurdity and numerology; his basement would be an oven, as even efficient bulbs expend more energy on heat than light, and he is using deliberately inefficient ones. His situation is impossible: the number, hinting at progress through a series of ascending digits, teeters at the breaking point where it must, seemingly, resolve its ambiguous status.

The bulbs are also a historical reference. I refer to Charles Pierce's article "How Electricity Is Taught at Tuskegee," a straightforward piece of boosterism (published originally in 1904 in *The Colored American Maga-*

zine) that presents a forward-looking, industrially oriented program following Booker T. Washington's educational ideals (Washington's *Working with the Hands* appeared in the same year). The article begins with the practical reasons for generating electricity on campus and a description of the machinery used. It discusses the program's international scope (an important aspect of Tuskegee in Washington's *Working with the Hands*), its academic aspects and requirements, and the program's practical focus (136–38). Then Pierce describes the *use* of the power: "There are at present thirty-four buildings lighted by electricity with a total of 1,717 lights. The division supplies lights to several places off the school grounds, among these being the residence of the late Col. Charles Thompson, Congressmen from the district, the Tuskegee railroad station, and a church. . . . There are 34,000 feet of primary line, 22,000 feet of secondary line, and 8,000 feet of street-light wiring" (138). There may have been exactly 1,717 lights at Tuskegee, although I find myself skeptical. Regardless, the number is appropriate: the digits *repeat,* in accordance with the Tuskegee promise to accept the existing political order, as long as educational and material development were possible within it. Ellison's four digits are ambiguous, yet poised at the brink of a crisis; Tuskegee's four digits are reliable.

Before proceeding further, it's important to remember that electricity generated at a black college was inevitably political, because the rhetoric of electrification and light, as David Nye recounts, was "embedded in a social Darwinist ideology of racial superiority. Only the most advanced societies had electrified machines and lighting. Darkness was a metaphor for the primitive" (*Electrifying* 36). Electricity was always already political, and electrification, which demonstrated one's stable, reliable place in "advanced" civilization, was a vital part of the Tuskegee project.

Pierce's article emphasizes the program's practicality, not its implicit politics: it provides valuable services while producing employable professionals. Following Washington's teachings, the electrical plant is thrifty, producing power at competitive rates despite the high cost and low quality of available coal (139). The invisible man's lights, however, are extravagantly wasteful: "An act of sabotage, you know. . . . A junk man I know, a man of vision, has supplied me with wire and sockets. Nothing, storm or flood, must get in the way of our need for light and ever more and brighter light" (7). The narrator gathers his materials, in all their chaotic diversity, from the junk heap, whereas the diversity that exists in the Tuskegee program is strictly pedagogical: "a variety of forms of wiring being selected in order to familiarize the student with the different methods" (138).

Whether or not Ellison is responding to Pierce, he might as well be. The narrator's basement is a Dostoyevskian counter-institution, an anti-Tuskegee, mirroring and parodying the Tuskegee project: his project is chaotic where Tuskegee's is ordered, based on deliberately antiquated technology where Tuskegee's is cutting-edge, compact where Tuskegee's is expansive, secretive where Tuskegee's is painfully and perilously open, in numerological crisis where even Tuskegee's numerology is steady, dependable. While Tuskegee husbands light and power, the narrator expends his wildly, having nearly as many lights as the whole campus.

In both Tuskegee and the anti-Tuskegee, black men are the source of power, light, and knowledge, which Ellison emphasizes in *Change the Joke and Slip the Yoke:* "his movement vertically downward (not into a 'sewer,' Freud notwithstanding, but into a coal cellar, a source of heat, light, power, and . . . self-perception) is a process of *rising* to an understanding of the human condition" (*Essays* 111). The difference between institution and anti-institution is a matter of how the power is applied: sluggishly and cautiously versus mercurially and profligately. It is also a matter of purpose: the institution and the anti-institution aspire for opposite kinds of leadership. The lights of Tuskegee generate the "progress of the Negro," while Ellison's narrator rejects progress, the "black rite of Horatio Alger" (Washington 238; Ellison, *Invisible* 111). Ellison describes his novel as attaining "timelessness through time"; his narrator "gets his restless mobility not so much from the blues or from sociology but because he appears in a literary form which has time and social change as its special province" (*Essays* 111). Change is opposed to progress; "timelessness through time" is opposed to linear history.

The invisible man repeatedly rejects progress, the "spiral of history," most strongly immediately before the epilogue: "I could only move ahead or stay here, underground. So I would stay here until I was chased out. . . . I could try to think things out in peace, or, if not in peace, in quiet. I would take up residence underground. The end was in the beginning" (571). He refuses progress, but his numerology (1,369) implies a crisis, whereas Tuskegee's (1,717) implies pure repetition. Paradoxically, boomeranging is change, and "progress" (uplift) is repetition. This paradoxical understanding is the "slightly different sense of time" that invisibility grants (8). For the Tuskegee ideology of uplift, progress is *real,* and the alternative is to be left behind history, as we see in Pierce's essay when he tells a story to "illustrate the popular conception" of the electrical engineering program: "We were at work . . . clearing up the dynamo for an evening run, when one of the delegates [of a Negro conference] was seen looking in at the door. . . . [I] asked him in. He said to me that he was afraid; and when I assured him that he would be perfectly safe, he went on to say that he had 'no business fooling around the dynamite machine,' because at his home three men had been 'killed by dynamite made from the dynamite machine' " (141). Similar stories follow. The delegate's ignorance and Pierce's relish at relating it resonate with the narrator's hatred for Trueblood, the incestuous sharecropper who reflects so poorly upon him. While Pierce and the narrator *know* they have the proper, progressive understanding of history and technology, Trueblood's relationship to the college's technological power is radically different from the stereotyped delegate's merely primitive attitude, and the "true" nature of time and technology in *Invisible Man* is far different from the narrator's initial understanding.

Trueblood is many things. Susan Blake argues that he, like Ellison's other "successful" characters, inhabits an underworld, in this case of his own unconscious (129). He is a folk character, a trickster. His life is an open battle between id and superego, to the narrator's consternation. He yearns for technological, electrical power, unlike Pierce's bumpkin, who trembles before the "dynamite machine." Trueblood *lusts* for the dynamo; we might ask if it symbolizes his incestuous desire or if his daughter symbolizes his desire for it. Dreaming, Trueblood finds himself in a white woman's room, where he sees a grandfather clock: "I hears it strikin' and the glass door is openin' and a white lady is steppin' out of it. . . . I wants to run, but the only door I see is the one in the clock she's standin' in—and anyway, I can't move and this here clock is keepin' up a heap racket. It's gittin' faster and faster all the time. . . . I gits it open and gits inside and it's hot and dark in there. I goes up a dark tunnel, up near where the machinery is making all that noise and heat. It's like the power plant they got up to the school. It's burnin' hot as iffen the house was caught on fire" (57–58). Trueblood runs in the tunnel "so good it's like flyin." He sees a bright light, which "gits brighter and brighter and I know I got to catch up with it or else . . . it burst like a great big electric light in my eyes and scalded me all over" (59). Incestuous, miscegenous, and technological desire intermingle; his climax is associated with the machine, not with either woman. Nye argues that the narrator's massive use of electric lights at the end of the novel signifies his desire "to become real to himself"; but Trueblood and the narrator seek (electrical) power—which is, of course, its own kind of reality (*Electrifying* 286). Trueblood's urge for technological power is inextricably related to a vision of time rooted in the clock. The stereotypical rustic recoils from mechanical time, but Trueblood plunges lustily into it and the power plant behind it, symbolically entering the clock's pedagogy; clocks teach middle-class values: discipline, self-reliance, "time is money" (Adas 226, 251). Trueblood is a folk (anti)hero, a farmer who knows he must "move without moving" to escape his situation (59). Nonetheless, he unambiguously desires the clock and the power plant beyond it. *The rustic is no rustic.* Trueblood's dream seemingly begs for a Frazerian or Freudian interpretation, save that Trueblood's orgasm is for the power plant and the clock; the incest is a smoke screen, a source of voyeuristic pleasure for the white men around him; his desire for technological power, *not* incest, is unspeakable. Trueblood lusts for Tuskegee's power system, from which he is excluded; the narrator essentially attains Trueblood's desire with his 1,369 lights.

Trueblood's gothic dream and the narrator's equally gothic fulfillment of that dream respond to Booker T. Washington's philosophy of industrial education; unlike Washington, they seek technological *power* while eschewing progress, especially moral progress. For Washington, a principal reason for education is that it generates moral progress, but we see a powerful counterexample in the person of Norton, who shares Trueblood's inclinations despite his "advanced" condition.

Norton explains that his fate is tied to the narrator's: "*You* are important because if you fail *I* have failed by one individual, one defective cog" (45). The narrator is mechanically subordinate to Norton's understanding of time and fate. Not coincidentally, the invisible man despises

Trueblood: "How all of us at the college hated the black-belt people, the 'peasants,' during those days! We were trying to lift them up and they, like Trueblood, did everything it seemed to pull us down" (47). The peasants reject the "black rite of Horatio Alger," which is celebrated with "voices mechanically raised" (111). Yet Trueblood sees the world mechanically, even while refuting "progress." Describing his wife attacking him, he says "I might as well been pleadin' with a switch engine" (64). When women come to help his daughter they examine him like a "new kinda cotton-pickin' machine," an accurate description of a man reduced to standing-reserve (65).

Norton and the narrator need Trueblood to be a simple savage against whom they define themselves as civilized: their moral constraints, technological sophistication, and mechanical time contrast with his primitive abandon, closeness to nature, and what the narrator later calls "slow c.p. (colored people's) time" (163). They need to envy and despise him as a primitive—but Trueblood is no less "advanced" than they.

Trueblood belongs to a long tradition of black Americans whose *technologies* have been claimed and reinscribed as white technologies, which allows African Americans to be marked as primitives. The rice plantations of South Carolina are a perfect example. Traditional histories, even sympathetic ones, have accepted the plantation system as constituted by enslaved black bodies and domineering white minds, as Judith Carney argues in "Landscapes of Technology Transfer" (42). This view is problematic: the intricate waterworks that were the foundation of the rice plantations were adopted wholesale from Africa, although they eventually became creolized under the influence of "American" technologies (42). Carney notes that "the shares of slaves brought directly from the West African rice coast grew . . . from 12 percent in the 1730s . . . to 64 percent between 1769 and 1774" (36). As the plantations became more complex, they grew increasingly dependent on *slave* engineering. No mere laborers, slaves provided most of the technology for rice plantations. Trueblood is no more primitive than they are, but his technological desire and prowess, like theirs, is forbidden and therefore forgotten.

Trueblood may have a "different sense of time," but it is not one that renders "mechanical time" incomprehensible or undesirable. He may be an automaton, but as such he yearns for power; as in Bergson, automatism is inescapable, but the struggle against it defines life. Trueblood is no embarrassing relic; he does not need to be uplifted through the "black rite of Horatio Alger," although he is desperate for change. He is connected to myth and ritual, but that does nothing to repress his historical-technological reality.

I turn now to Ellison's earlier, wartime interest in the idea of the technological hero.

The Hero and the *Negro Quarterly*

By 1941 Ellison's enthusiasm for the Communist Party was waning, following the party's backpedaling on civil rights; when the opportunity arose he left the Communist *New Masses* for the charismatic Angelo Herndon's new publication, *Negro Quarterly,* where he quickly became managing editor (Jackson 253–54, 263, 279). Herndon and Ellison grew increasingly distant from the party over the journal's year-and-a-half run; Herndon's split from it became final in 1942 (Griffiths 625). Larry Neal argues in "Ellison's Zoot Suit" that the magazine was the last attempt by the period's black intellectuals to fashion a revolutionary ideology "not totally dominated by the white Marxist Left" (90).

Griffiths argues that "*Invisible Man* remakes images from *The Negro Quarterly*" (619). He gives a detailed reading of Herndon's "Frederick Douglass: Negro Leadership and the War," published in the journal's fourth and final issue, in conjunction with the "Editorial Comment" from that issue (which he attributes to Ellison *and* Herndon; Neal and Jackson attribute it to Ellison) and Homer Barbee's speech from *Invisible Man*. The language of Herndon's assault on false black leadership, as opposed to Douglass's authentic leadership, resonates with Barbee's mythologizing of the Founder in *Invisible Man*. Herndon writes: "When such a Negro is promoted by others than the Negro people themselves as a 'Negro leader,' his mind is orientated in directions away from the real problems of the Negro. He knows neither whom he leads nor where he is leading. Thus his vision is like the moon in eclipse. While an eclipse is a momentary thing, this type of leader goes on forever and ever. . . . He suffers from a lack of spiritual sustenance which can only come from that body of life which illuminates clearly and distinctly the authentic experience of the Negro people" (312). Barbee's speech on the Founder mentions the moonless sky as he enacts, "minstrel-like, the lunar eclipse of black leadership" (Griffiths 620). Griffiths notes numerous other references to Herndon in the novel, arguing that Herndon enters into Ellison's merger of "Marx and Freud and Raglan" (620).

Neal, Jackson, and Griffiths discuss the "Editorial Comment" heading the final issue of *Negro Quarterly.* I will give my own version of their reading, with one major additional observation, which is the fact that *technology* is central to the question of black leadership, especially in its mythical aspect. The editorial, which, following Jackson and Neal, I attribute to Ellison,[1] begins with a list of possible Negro attitudes toward "their war-time experiences" (295). These are, first, wholehearted participation and criticism of those who "want to be Negro first and American second"; second, unqualified rejection of the "white man's war"; and third, "critical participation" (295–98). Critical participation, Ellison's position, accepts "the historical role of Negroes to be that of integrating the larger American nation and compelling it untiringly toward true freedom" (298). Antifascism abroad demands equal, unwavering antifascism at home. Ellison argues that Negro power must be centralized so that Negroes will not "always play the role of a sacrificial goat" (300). His call for centralized power leads into a discussion of leadership. Negro leaders, he argues, "must integrate themselves with the Negro masses; they must be constantly alert to new concepts, new techniques and new trends among other peoples and nations with an eye toward appropriating those which are valid when tested against the reality of Negro life. . . . When needed concepts, techniques or theories do not exist they must create them. Many new concepts will evolve when the people are closely studied in action. And it will be out of this process that true Negro leadership will come" (300–301). The new leadership must study and imitate the best techniques it finds in the masses and abroad, supplemented with its own improvisations. The leadership emerges from the people and takes them as its *ongoing* inspiration; its technocracy is continually instructed by them. Only thus should centralized leadership appear. The editorial's next paragraph has occasioned little critical commentary: "A second problem for Negro leadership to master is that of accurately defining the relation between the increasing innovations in technology and the Negro peoples' political and economic survival and advancement. During the war the mastery of hitherto unavailable techniques by Negroes is equivalent to the winning of a major military objective" (301). The leadership must not merely use technological advances but also recognize the connection between them and the people's survival. This position resembles Washington's emphasis on industrial education, but only if one doesn't attend to the following paragraph, which has drawn far more commentary: "A third major problem, . . . indispensable to the centralization and direction of power, is that of learning the meaning of the myths and symbols which abound among the Negro masses. For without this knowledge, leadership, no matter how correct its program, will fail. Much in Negro life remains a mystery: perhaps the zoot suit conceals profound political meaning; perhaps the symmetrical frenzy of the Lindy-hop conceals clues to great potential power—if only Negro leaders would solve this riddle" (301). This is a "definite statement of cultural nationalism" and an attempt to surpass Marxist social realism's "simplistic analysis of folk culture. . . . Ellison turns Marxism on its head, and makes the manipulation of cultural mechanisms the basis for black liberation" (Neal 93). Neal's argument is insightful but incomplete; he, like Jackson and Griffiths, gives short shrift to Ellison's second point. Ellison's three points should not be separated: the true Negro leader must integrate with the masses, define (and control) their relationship to technology, and learn to understand and manipulate their symbols and folklore.

The problem Ellison acknowledges with his three-way prescription is that these tools are available to "the charlatan and agent provocateur" as well as the authentic leader (302). The danger, turning to *Invisible Man,* is Rinehartism, an application of technological and mythical knowledge to purely selfish ends. Rinehart is a charlatan, a preacher, a criminal, and a "spiritual technologist," among his other roles (495). Ellison's prescription for a combined understanding of folklore and technology seems almost fascistic, a danger he addresses in the novel's satire of the Tuskegee system, itself both technologically sophisticated and rooted in folklore, as we see most profoundly in Barbee's speech.

To articulate Ellison and Herndon's response to the threats of internal and external fascism, I turn to the "Editorial Comment" from the second issue of *Negro Quarterly,*[2] where they argue that "history moves by bombing planes, and what now threatens Britain and India might . . . threaten our own shores. Some might object to our identifying the American Negroes as a nation. But if this war is to be a peoples' war, based upon the Four Freedoms, then along with the discarded techniques of imperialist domination must go all of the old imperialist definitions and classifications of minority and colonial peoples. All peoples must be allowed to define themselves!" (iv). History is driven not only by machines but also by peoples' aspirations. Herndon and Ellison's nationalism demands self-determination, never expansion; their synthesis of folklore and technology, although sharing techniques with fascism, is radically anti-totalitarian, through their simple acknowledgment of endlessly divergent nationalisms, which do not require unification; each people—through folk customs, technologies, and aspirations—should direct *their* leaders. The Ellisonian leader must continually work to understand and use these aspects of the people's life; he is directed by the people's actual, evolving practices, unlike the fascist leader, who determines these practices. Ellison and Herndon's nationalist synthesis of technology and mythology is empiricist where fascism and Communism are idealist; they are breaking from Marx and Hegel.

Ellison and Herndon were disappointed in their hope for an authentic leadership, as opposed to one handpicked by the government "to bargain away the rights of the Negro people" ("Editorial Comment" ii). This seems to have only made the question of black leadership more important for Ellison, as it became central to *Invisible Man.* Before continuing with leadership as such, I turn to Ellison's interest in the works of Lewis Mumford, who helped Ellison articulate his understanding of the technological leg of the leadership triad.

Ellison, Mumford, and Technology

Ellison's interest in Mumford is obvious early in *Invisible Man:* the bar where the narrator takes Norton, prostrated by his encounter with Trueblood, is named the Golden Day, in pointed reference to Mumford's *The Golden Day* (1926). In *Invisible Criticism* (1988), Alan Nadel discusses Ellison's complex response to Mumford; no other critic has treated Ellison's relationship with Mumford at length.

Mumford's *The Golden Day* is mentioned thirty-four times in *Invisible Man* (Nadel 85). Mumford's book, Nadel recognizes, celebrates an ostensible high point in American culture: Mumford sees a pinnacle of thought and spiritual triumph in Emerson, Thoreau, Whitman, Melville, and Hawthorne, a pinnacle wrecked by the Civil War and the ensuing desolation and corruption. Mumford sees the Civil War "as a turn for the worse," argues Nadel (88); most of Mumford's readers would agree. Even at his best Mumford is obtuse, in his inimitable paleo-leftist fashion, to racial issues, and in *The Golden Day* he is not at his best. Nadel's reading is accurate:

> [O]versimplification is at its core. It seeks to reduce the course of American literature to one dramatic action. . . . The book is, in fact, organized like a classic tragedy, in which we see enacted a drama whose hero is the individual and antagonist the machine. The "Golden Day," the period from 1830 to 1860 that historians often call the Era of Reform, was, according to Mumford, the period when the individual had the greatest hopes of triumphing. Alas . . . he did not. Industrialism, the machine, the Gilded Age triumphed; materialism, cynicism, shallowness replaced idealism, optimism, depth. Revealing this tragedy is the purpose of Mumford's book. (86)

Yet, this thinker who boils down complex history into a simplistic morality play was also founding American architectural criticism and technology studies, in such books as *Technics and Civilization.* One wonders if Nadel knew of Mumford's lifelong ambition to be a novelist and playwright (Mumford, *Sketches* 370). The language of *The Golden Day* is melodramatic but reads easily; its characters become principles and its principles become characters. *The Golden Day* is criticism as art. In its own time it was a spellbinding book, critical to the intellectual formation of figures from Van Wyck Brooks to F. O. Matthiessen; yet Mumford himself dismissed it in his later correspondence (Spiller 409). The older Mumford might have agreed with Nadel that it was "a fictive conception, an ode to a period that never existed" (92).

Nadel, perhaps accidentally, has located the source of the book's power. Mumford was *creating* an era, and with it the beginnings of the American canon as we know it. One of Mumford's projects was to create a new literary genealogy of tremendous repercussive, contradictory force. How to accommodate Melville *and* Emerson? This conflict, along with that between organism and machine, defines the book. Mumford's forceful claim of Emerson *and* Melville resembles Ellison's claim in "The World and the Jug" that he has created his own literary ancestry, exemplified by Hemingway and T. S. Eliot, *not* Richard Wright (*Essays* 185).

Nadel reluctantly acknowledges *The Golden Day*'s influence, including the debt Matthiessen owed to it, but—presumably because it is a drama, not proper criticism—he downplays its importance, arguing that it was a good target for Ellison because it was "one of the earliest and most typical" books of its type, "a typical whitewashing of American history, one that flows from exactly that social/historical consciousness that forced the black into invisibility" (94). Mumford's book is not distinctive, but representative.

Nonetheless, Nadel admits that Ellison isn't merely satirizing Mumford, arguing that *The Golden Day* "confers the right name for the wrong reasons" (98). Nadel argues that the complexity and "protean aspects of the period" gave it a unique, chaotic energy; Norton finds stimulation in the Golden Day, in the form of "riot, chaos, manic energy," but also irony (98, 101). Ellison's relationship with Mumford is critical but complex.

Nadel argues that the narrator's movement north, where he is caught in an explosion and "given an electric lobotomy," represents black migration from country to city, from South to North, from "the nineteenth to the twentieth" centuries (103). Strangely, the narrator moves from the Golden Day directly to his dehumanizing encounter with the hospital machine (industrialism), by Nadel's reading: Ellison thus reproduces *The Golden Day*'s central organic/mechanical conflict when the narrator leaves the literal Golden Day. Moving north, away from the ancestral home of prejudice and slavery, he encounters mechanical enslavement. This movement from southern quasi-slavery to northern mechanized slavery is Mumford's understanding of the Civil War as a conflict between two kinds of servitude; Nadel ignores this correspondence between the plots of *The Golden Day* and *Invisible Man* (*Golden Day* 136). The South of *Invisible Man* is not, however, innocent of mechanical domination (think of the electrified mat and the power plant), while the North retains old-fashioned racism. Both mechanical domination and slavery's consequences pervade the country; the meaning of the machine is always ambiguous, offering enslavement *and* rebirth in the college's power plant, Brockway's basement, the hospital machine, and, finally, the narrator's descent into the coal cellar. After his plummet, he loses himself underground and dreams of castration by various authority figures:

> "Still," I said, "there's your universe, and that drip-drop upon the water you hear is all the history you've made, all you're going to make. Now laugh, you scientists. Let's hear you laugh!"
>
> And high above me now the bridge seemed to move off to where I could not see, striding like a robot, an iron man, whose iron legs clanged doomfully as it moved. And then I struggled up, full of sorrow and pain, shouting, "No, no, we must stop him!" (570)

After this dream, wherein he defies the power of the "scientists," accuses their history of emptiness, and their technological power arises with its own volition, he awakens into the place and time of his own future technological power, the coal cellar. This passage is deeply ambivalent about science and technology, which are associated with his enemies' historical vision but also with his laughing response to that vision; the iron man is under nobody's control. Nadel is correct that oversimplification is at *The Golden Day*'s core, but Ellison does not simply satirize it; he digs under its simplistic drama to create a complex one that remains indebted to Mumford.

The phrase "The end was in the beginning," which ends the prologue and precedes the epilogue, reminds us of Ellison's affiliation with European modernism, but more directly of his use of Dostoyevsky's *Notes from Underground,* which provides the model for Ellison's structure, although Dostoyevsky's epilogue is more radically truncated than Ellison's (*Invisible Man* 571). Ellison adopts the circular hyperconsciousness of Dostoyevsky's narrator, which is already a political consciousness opposed to history-as-progress, as when the underground man mocks the "crystal edifice, forever indestructible" based on the Crystal Palace of the London Exhibition of 1851, often understood as a central moment in human progress (35).[3] Ellison has an impulse toward aesthetic modernism, but also toward a Dostoyevskian rebellion against progressive history; he outdoes Dostoyevsky by stripping Dostoyevsky's chaotic, underground world of the Christian *eschatos* leavening it. Unlike Dostoyevsky's narrator, the invisible man struggles not for anonymity but for leadership. His politics, unlike those of Dostoyevsky's underground man and Mumford's hypothetical protestor against mechanical civilization, intends a return to the world: "Please, a definition: A hibernation is a covert preparation for a more overt action" (*Invisible Man* 13). Dostoyevsky's underground man plunges outside history; Ellison's uses his synthesis of technology and myth to be both inside and outside history, which makes his art unique. Through his unique understanding of time, which simultaneously engages with myth and technology, Ellison is able to abandon history-as-progress and meaningfully address the necessity of change (rather than progress) in the real, historical world.

The narrator finds power in his mythic struggle with Monopolated Light and Power, from which he steals electricity. Despite his apocalyptic vision of the iron man, he has entered the "American tradition of tinkers. That makes me kin to Ford, Edison and Franklin. Call me, since I have a theory and a concept, 'a thinker-tinker'" (7). His technological orientation clarifies his politics, unlike Dostoyevsky's underground man; it is no accident that the inventors he names were also political-managerial figures. Making, thinking, and leading are not separated, nor is epistemology prior to technology, once he plunges outside history. One side effect of this change is to eliminate the hierarchical relationship between science and technology that dominates Western thought: technology is liberated from the scientists, who seek to control history.[4] By stepping outside history, he escapes the process that excludes him from progressive history, as, we might note, most black inventors and engineers have been.[5]

Restaging the Mumfordian organic/machine drama, the narrator rediscovers life fighting Monopolated Light and Power, although he fights *using* machines as well as against them—which is consistent with the Mumford of *Technics and Civilization,* who predicts the end of technological domination with the spread of "neotechnics"—ethereal electrical technologies. Nadel, focusing on *The Golden Day,* understands Mumford's organic/machine struggle as coming to a head around the Civil

War, but as I argued earlier, Mumford came to understand this struggle as permeating history, a late Mumfordian development that resonates with Ellison.

John Wright analyzes the relationship between Mumford's and Ellison's understandings of technology in "'Jack-the-Bear' Dreaming: Ellison's Spiritual Technologies," arguing that both see a fundamental connection between artistic *technique* and mechanical *technology.* Wright quotes a letter from Ellison to Nadel that Nadel cites in *Invisible Criticism.* While the quote is clearly central to understanding the Ellison-Mumford relationship, Nadel buries it in a footnote to a passage about Mumford's whitewashing of American history. In the letter, Ellison says that he admires Mumford and owns most of his books, but he specifically criticizes *The Golden Day* for "implying that the war which freed my grandparents from slavery was of no real consequence to the broader issues of American society and its culture. . . . I was quite willing for Mumford to play Aeschylus, Jeremiah, or even God, but not at the price of his converting the most tragic incident in American history into bombastic farce. For in doing so he denied my people the sacrificial role which they had played in the drama" (Nadel 158). Ellison, unlike Nadel, does not criticize Mumford for reducing history to drama. In fact, following Raglan, Ellison addresses history as *ritual* drama, which must, *qua* ritual, be meaningful. Ellison's claim to have read most of Mumford's books indicates a broad familiarity with Mumford's thought on technology and the city; his criticism of *The Golden Day* occurs within a context of interest and general agreement. Mumford's sin is his *specific* denial that the Civil War was a somewhat efficacious response to slavery. As Wright acknowledges, Ellison's admiration for Mumford includes a Mumfordian understanding of the machine's omnipresence and "the artist's moral obligation to envision aesthetic possibilities for the machine that will not reinforce the fragmenting, life-denying, dehumanizing conditions created by capitalist technology" ("'Jack-the-Bear'" 178).

In Ellison, as in Mumford, machine and organism are at war, most dramatically in the narrator's torment in the hospital machine. Yet unlike Mumford, Ellison has no "pastoral" sympathies: Trueblood does not exist in a Jeffersonian rural Eden—or rather, he pays the price for others' pastoral dreams; "nature" has limited appeal for him, despite the perils of the machine. For Mumford the question is always one of balance, of ends and means: How can technology be turned to human purposes and away from the monstrous technological system? For Ellison the important questions are concrete: How can people, especially black people, be liberated rather than enslaved by technology? How does one become a thinker-tinker rather than a victim? Again I turn to a passage Wright uses, this one from "Some Questions and Some Answers," an interview in which Ellison addresses the role of technology in Negro life. He finds its role ambiguous; whether technology is good or bad depends on the "human suffering" that goes into industrialization and the details of how its products are distributed. The role of technology in Negro life is irreducibly complex. Slaves "contributed much of the brute labor" necessary for industrialization, Ellison argues; to this end "they were exploited, their natural resources were ravaged, their institutions and their cultures were devastated." Despite this condemnation, Ellison echoes Mumford and Heidegger, arguing that *only* technology can "release [them] from the brutalizing effects of over three hundred years of racism and European domination." Like Bergson, Ellison knows that "men cannot unmake history"; the question is not whether old cultures can be restored but how oppressed peoples can transform their lives through technology. Nor is technology simply a matter of producing more goods, for "certain possibilities of culture are achievable only through the presence of industrial techniques." Finally, Ellison discuss the role of exploitation in technology while keeping its *cultural* potential in mind: "It is not industrial progress per se which damages peoples or cultures; it is the exploitation of peoples in order to keep the machines fed with raw materials. It seems to me that the whole world is moving toward some new cultural synthesis, and partially through the discipline imposed by technology. There is, I believe, a threat when industrialism is linked to a political doctrine which has as its goal the subjugation of the world" (*Essays* 293–94). As for Heidegger, Ellison's humanity is in danger from a technological system, but amidst the danger "a saving power grows," which is technology itself ("Question" 32). Heidegger, Mumford, and Ellison alike understand that "technology" or even "the technological system" is not an arrays of artifacts but rather sets of techniques, related to artistic techniques. The danger is that humanity will be turned into just another raw material, or "standing-reserve," in Heidegger's terminology.

Ellison, unlike Mumford and Heidegger, is not writing about the abstract fear that humanity will become fully mechanized; his concern is with people who have *already* become standing-reserve, for whom the "middle state" before the locomotive's arrival is *slavery.* Ellison knows better than to fear the *arrival* of domination; he knows from the beginning what Mumford had begun to understand in *The Pentagon of Power* (1970): "our" domination is a variation of the slavery that afflicted Babylon and Egypt, a slavery that was fundamentally technological (rooted in *techniques* of management and domination). This takes me back, briefly, to Melville.

Invisible Man begins with an epigraph from Melville's *Benito Cereno,* a tale about rebellious slaves who now rule over their former masters, and an American ship that arrives, uncomprehending, on the scene. The ex-slaves have numbers on their side, along with a true understanding of the situation; the American ship has superior arms and certainty of their own superiority. Ironically, the superior intelligence of Babo, the slaves' leader, is insufficient to secure victory: brute force and ideological certainty win the day. Babo shares Queequeg's Petrine dream: he needs to master a variety of Western technologies, especially navigation, but cannot do so sufficiently quickly, and so his rebellion perishes.

The epigraph from *Benito Cereno* that opens *Invisible Man* is the famous line " 'You are saved,' cried Captain Delano, more and more astonished and pained; 'you are saved: what has cast such a shadow upon you?' " The answer in Melville's text is "The Negro." Ellison doesn't complete the line, letting it hang in silence; in Nadel's argument, this reveals that "the book is a critique on American blindness masked as American optimism," which is associated with both Emerson and Mumford (105). Nonetheless, Ellison's text explores from the start the very organic/machine conflict that Mumford uses to displace the moral meaning of the Civil War from his national drama—although in all fairness we should note one reason Mumford loathed the Civil War was that "the Negro question" persisted after it; the Civil War didn't *work* (*Golden Day* 158). Ellison, in turn, displaces Mumford: the dramatic conflict between individual and machine exists but is drawn out, with both sides becoming ambiguous—for instance, do we side with Norton's individualism rather than the machine?

For Mumford and Ellison, Melville is critical for understanding the problem of evil in America, but while Mumford focuses on the Ahabian megamachine, Ellison is continually fascinated, both through the novel and in his nonfiction, with the relationships among technology, management, and the "problem" of America, while still contextualizing these issues racially; he absorbs Mumford's concerns into his own, as one part of the triad necessary for a new, authentic leadership. Part of Captain Delano's blindness in *Benito Cereno* is his inability to understand Babo as a thinking, technical being, a thinker-tinker; Ellison takes up that project where Melville left it off, borrowing Mumford's half-blind, half-brilliant analysis of technology in the process.

Automatism and Time in *Invisible Man*

What Mumford saw late and dimly shines through *Invisible Man:* the battle with the megamachine is always already lost yet forever unfinished. Ellison's understanding of the relationship between time and technology is conditioned by historical oppression, not relative historical privilege; therefore the *eschatos* (the arrival of domination), instead of being imminent, is buried in the deep past.

Ellison calls for a Negro leadership based on integration with the Negro masses, defining the Negro's relationship to technology and understanding Negro "myths and symbols." An oppression technological in both means and character requires a response rooted in technology, myth, and integration. Technology and myth are never contradictory, as we see most radically in Trueblood's character.

Norton, the narrator, and Trueblood belong to the same hierarchical system; Trueblood, unlike the narrator, understands his own position. His lust for technological power combined with his blues-tinged art make him a potent, complex rebel. He takes the role of the narrator's "yokel" against the "scientific boxer"; stepping inside Norton's sense of time (literally stepping into the clock of his dream) brings the crisis that leads to the events at the Golden Day. According to Ellison's "Editorial Comment," Trueblood has the characteristics necessary for black leadership *except for leadership itself.* The narrator does not, of course, recognize his potential, thereby dramatically failing a test of his own leadership.

The fact that the narrator and Norton, unlike Trueblood, don't *know* themselves drives events in the Golden Day. The ex-brain surgeon who speaks with Norton and the narrator mocks them, especially the narrator: "He registers with his senses but short-circuits his brain. . . . Behold! a walking zombie! Already he's learned to repress not only his emotions but his humanity. He's invisible, a walking personification of the Negative, the most perfect achievement of your dreams, sir! The mechanical man!" (94). The narrator, like Trueblood, is mechanized; unlike Trueblood, he doesn't understand or rebel against his situation. As a zombie, he lacks the incestuous, miscegenous, power-plant-dominating urges driving Babo and Trueblood. The vet conflates the "mechanical man" with the "zombie"; the creature of science fiction, the future's apostle, is synonymous with voodoo's "primitivism." History boomerangs; the threat of automatism permeates it, as in Bergson.[6]

In this chapter the narrator moves "automatically" (86). He asks if Norton will need him in the evening; Norton accidentally voices their true (Mumfordian) relationship: "I won't be needing the machine" (108). Despite Ellison's critique of Mumford, Norton is the typical Mumfordian industrialist, one who replaces one kind of slavery with another; for him, the narrator is akin to an automobile. He is obsessed with the narrator as his *destiny,* an already-known future that is another form of automatism; his destiny *is* the zombie or mechanical man, if we follow the vet's thinking.

While Trueblood's desires remain unfulfilled, Lucius Brockway, operating the machines beneath Liberty Paints, fulfills his equivalent desires for technological power: "They got all this machinery, but . . . *we the machines inside the machine*" (217). But despite Brockway's achievement, he lacks volition; he seems fulfilled by the simple *acknowledgment* of his power by the "Old Man" who owns the factory (216). Brockway plays his part as the machine inside the machine, cantankerous but ultimately obedient. He is deeply technological without forgetting his folk roots (his marketing slogans are versions of folk sayings—"if you're white, you're right"), but he lacks self-consciousness (218). He is not in any sense integrated with the Negro masses, or with any other mass, but reacts with enraged hostility to the very idea that the narrator may belong to a union.

After the narrator nearly dies in the explosion Brockway engineered, he is practically re-created inside a gothic machine. "I was pounded between crushing electrical pressures; pumped between live electrodes like an accordion between a player's hands" (232). He is trapped in a mechanical nightmare, a "glass and nickel box" (233), subjected to electroshock under the direction of "scientists" and "doctors." The machine is a newfangled alternative to a lobotomy. One doctor/scientist preaches to another: "do your praying to my little machine. I'll deliver the cure" (235). Within this stunning image of mechanical oppression the invisible man is massively disoriented: "Where did my body end and the crystal and white world begin? Thoughts evaded me" (238). He no longer knows who his mother was, even identifying the machine *as* his mother (240). A "scholarly looking man" writes him questions on a slate, including "Who was Buckeye the Rabbit?" The narrator, delighted, associates himself with that childhood character. After making this association, he is allowed to leave the machine. Ironically, those who lobotomized him want him to retain only his folk identity, yet this identity is mechanically created: he is Buckeye-as-cyborg. Outside the machine, the scientists discuss history and politics, discourses they control: "it is a mistake to assume that solutions—cures, that is—that apply in, uh, primitive instances, are, uh . . . equally effective when more advanced conditions are in question" (236). The student from Tuskegee can't and won't be dealt into progressive history. "I wasn't sure whether they were talking about me or somebody else. Some of it sounded like a discussion of history" (236). His case has been "developing some three hundred years" (237). Their control of history accompanies their control of the hospital machine; an effective black leadership requires that progressive history be challenged and technology be seized.

While the scientists have mastered history, inside the machine time and space have little meaning; the narrator is in an embryonic state. In this *other,* electrified, terrorized state he finds a new identity in myth, then is suddenly freed. He doesn't retreat into his identity as Buckeye in a childish response to horror; the identity flows from his mechanical rebirth. He experiences the new mythic identity as automatism, yet it boomerangs back as his own ultimate seizure of technological power.

The hospital machine has received voluminous commentary. Brian Reed argues that it is properly understood not as "a symbol of external forces working to modify his behavior" but as an internal process in which the narrator becomes mechanically indifferent (261–63). For Reed, one central issue is that the Brotherhood insists on a mechanical, inhuman notion of history. Reed ends with the march of the mechanical man, writing: "The image of history which he sought in the machine he now finds in the chaos of night. . . . It is the hope of order that they all, the narrator and his tormentors, see the machine out of their lives as the bridge becomes a robot and clangs over the horizon, never to return" (273). To expand on Reed: the hope of all chronology and history marches into the dark: the narrator replaces history-the-spiral with the boomerang, which, returning to the politics of *Negro Quarterly,* is the persistence of black cultures and technologies despite brutal oppression. The narrator struggles to resist the oppression of all history and progress, explicitly including Tuskegee's "black rite of Horatio Alger" in favor of the boomerang of myth, anti-teleological history which asserts that slavery and oppression do not ever make one fully inhuman but that humanity is perpetually in crisis. Tod Clifton, whose bearing and dolls are a shocking mixture of human and inhuman, models this abandonment by choosing "to fall outside of *history.* . . . [H]e knew that only in the Brotherhood could we make ourselves known, could we avoid being empty Sambo dolls. Such an obscene flouncing of everything human!" (434–35). The Brotherhood offers a place within humanity, that is, progressive history. Clifton knows what the narrator must still learn: with or without Brotherhood, precisely *history and humanity* mark him as the Sambo doll, a mechanical man.

Despite his naïveté, the narrator can't consistently pretend that "humanity" and "history" include him, even in the Brotherhood's eyes. "Maybe she wants to see me sweat coal tar, ink, shoe polish, graphite," the invisible man thinks after overhearing speculation that he isn't black enough. "What was I, a man or a natural resource?" (303). Periodically he understands that he is reified into a technological object, a Sambo doll himself. Unlike Clifton, he believes that only those who *reject* "humanity" and history-as-progress reify him, whereas Clifton understands that the enemy *is* humanism and history-as-progress. The narrator battles against an instinctive agreement with Clifton: preparing to give his first great speech for the Brotherhood, he feels an "electric tingling" along his spine, reminding us of the way electricity was used to dominate him at the beginning and in the hospital machine (339). Facing the microphone he "felt the hard, mechanical isolation of the hospital machine and I didn't like it" (341). He accurately associates the Brotherhood's historical vision with entombment in the machine.

Several critics have acknowledged the complex, subversive role of electricity in *Invisible Man.* Douglas Ford argues that Ellison advocates not merely mastering the "social, political and technological apparatuses of white America," and thereby reproducing them, but "cagey rewiring, forging an ability to disrupt established forms of power from within" (896–97). Contra Ford, though, being *within* isn't enough. Brockway and Bledsoe are both inside the system, and alter it, but politically they are worse than useless. What they lack is an understanding of the metaphysical underpinnings of the power system: they fail to rewire *time.* A leadership that simply seizes technological power without simultaneously absorbing the "power of myths and symbols which abound among the Negro masses" will necessarily fail (Ellison, "Editorial Comment" 1.4, 301). Ellison demands intense modernity (dedication to contemporary technologies) *and* an atemporal or primordial dedication to myth: the plunge outside history. What the narrator accomplishes in the ending-as-beginning is to plunge outside history *with* the Mumfordian power system, or perhaps to rewire the Mumfordian power system through Raglanian "myths and symbols." The core of the rewiring is not the electricity itself but the displacement of history-as-progress.

The source of the narrator's potential in the prologue and epilogue is his new understanding of the drama of American history—the struggle for freedom—through myth and technology. He now willfully acts the (mythic) role of the mechanical man (thinker-tinker) against progressive history. As in Bergson, thought and technology are undivided; the mind is threatened by mechanization precisely because it is mechanization itself; the narrator's freedom comes from his conscious acknowledgment of his mechanical identity. To acknowledge the unity of organic and machine is to master ritual and act, like Dostoyevsky's underground man, against history and historical thinking, but Ellison's version of Dostoyevsky's "sick man . . . wicked man" transforms sickness and wickedness into self-education, parodying Booker T. Washington's ethos of self-help (*Notes from Underground* 3).

Several critics have written on the shattering of teleological time in *Invisible Man.* Jim Neighbors argues that Clifton's plunge outside history terrifies the narrator because the concept of ahistorical life challenges his understanding of what it means to be human (235). The narrator initially believes in what he calls "that progress goo," which "a transcendental history requires"; the challenge to progress in turn "belies the stable and unified Aristotelian Self still lingering behind his name, one capable of writing a 'useable history' " (Neighbors 237). The collapse of historical, teleological understanding threatens *everything,* starting with his humanity. Yonka Krasteva, picking up on the narrator's claim that invisibility gives one a "slightly different sense of time," argues that the "belief in the interdependence between 'historical time' and human progress is rendered problematic" (*Invisible Man* 8; Krasteva 59). Neighbors and Krasteva are correct, with the caveat that this attack on teleological time is essentially political and deeply rooted in technology.

Marc Singer proposes that *Invisible Man*'s time is "palimpsestic, as the novel constantly provides echoes of past eras within the narrative present," and that Ellison, influenced by Alain Locke's *The New Negro,* thinks "African-Americans' prolonged feudal indenture and their drastic transition into industrial modernity have resulted in an accelerated sense of time" (390). Singer argues that several concepts of time are found wanting within the novel: Norton's mechanical time, Brockway's acceptance of mechanical time, the Brotherhood's teleological time, and Ras's arrow of time, which "simply points back" (393, 399, 401, 411). The broken chain that Brother Tarp gives to the narrator becomes profoundly important: "When the Golden Day veterans tell Norton that history moves in a circle, they undermine his linear and deterministic view of time, yet when Tarp bestows his chain, time's circularity itself has become an oppressive feature that must be resisted and escaped. This dramatic change reflects the Invisible Man's growing temporal consciousness: he must first learn to perceive time's circularity before he can discover its ill effects"

(Singer 404). Singer proposes the palimpsest as an alternative to the destructiveness of linear and cyclic time, with Brother Tarp and the subway zoot-suiters illustrating this different temporality (406). Yet, Singer's description of palimpsestic time's *meaning* is uninspiring: "He realizes he is a composite man comprised of his past experiences, a living palimpsest of his own history . . . [which] is also African-American history" (409). In other words, the narrator learns the importance of the past: far from plunging "outside history," this is a wise, humanistic understanding of it. Singer makes palimpsestic time into a sociological statement in a novel that rejects progressive history and sociology. This is not to say that Ellison is not concerned with the history of racism, but that he portrays the history of racism and the organic/mechanical divide as indistinguishable from conventional historical thought itself.

To attack racism at its roots, one must attack history-as-progress without denying the empirical reality of technological change. We might think of the rice fields of South Carolina, which have been imagined by historians as simultaneously the site of terrible black suffering and the triumph of the white managerial mind. When we delve into the history, though, the technological basis of this system is fundamentally African: the technology is appropriated, rather than belonging to Western "progress." Technology belongs, then, outside progressive history as well as within it—an issue central to Edgerton's *The Shock of the Old;* Edgerton devotes considerable effort to detailing the distinctive technologies of third-world slums, for instance. The slaves of South Carolina were thinker-tinkers.

Our narrator rejects mechanical time but is mechanically reborn. His struggles begin with Mumford's *The Golden Day,* wherein history's *meaning* is the organic/mechanical conflict. He emphatically rejects teleological history by the novel's end, without embracing cyclic history. Seeing his understanding of time as either powerfully anti-mechanical and anti-progress, as Krasteva and Neighbors do, or as intensely humanistic and centered around the impact or experience of history, as Singer does, ignores one of the novel's central features. The hibernating narrator is not an intellectual, mystic, or humanist but rather a thinker-tinker, surrounded by and obsessed with electrical machinery. Despite rejecting teleological history, he follows Trueblood's and Brockway's embrace of the machine. His new, violent sense of time as a boomerang is intimately connected to his obsession with the mechanically reproduced music of Louis Armstrong and his obsession with electricity and electrical devices. He is, true to Donna Haraway's understanding of the cyborg, a bastard child of his mechanical mother (the hospital machine); we can't escape the reality of a machine-human interface in the novel (Ford 888).

The prologue and epilogue aren't simply saturated with machinery, nor is the narrator merely obsessed with it. The novel ends with Jack-the-Bear "beneath the inferno, under the underworld, waiting for the hero's call" (Schafer 123). He is waiting in hibernation, "a covert preparation for a more overt action" (*Invisible Man* 13). The thinker-tinker is also the hero; the type of Edison and Franklin is also a type of King Arthur. As one might except, based on Ellison's early articulation of the three things necessary for an authentic Negro leadership, the two identities merge as aspects of leadership.

Ellison and Lord Raglan: The Hero in the Machine Age

Ellison's interest in Lord Raglan's *The Hero* (1936), written under the influence of James Frazer's *The Golden Bough* (1890–1915), is explicit and substantial; Ellison comments on it repeatedly in his essays, and it deeply influenced *Invisible Man*. This influence has not received the sustained analysis it deserves, despite being addressed tangentially by many critics: relevant works include Lawrence Clipper's "Folkloric and Mythic Elements in *Invisible Man*" (1970), William Schafer's "Ralph Ellison and the Birth of the Anti-Hero" (1974), Robert O'Meally's *The Craft of Ralph Ellison* (1980), Larry Neal's "Ellison's Zoot Suit" (1987), and Frederick Griffiths's "Ralph Ellison, Richard Wright, and the Case of Angelo Herndon" (2001). These critics, despite their many merits, deal superficially and conventionally with Raglan's text, without attending, for instance, to Ellison's interest in Raglan's ideas on leadership. I will explore the influence of Raglan's text on Ellison's views on teleology, time, and technology and show (following Neal, Griffiths, and Jackson) the impact of this use of Raglan on Ellison's politics.

In "That Same Pain, That Same Pleasure," his 1961 interview with Richard Stern, Ellison uses Raglan to discuss leadership: "When I started writing *Invisible Man* I was reading Lord Raglan's *The Hero,* in which he goes into figures of history and myth to account for the features which make for the mythic hero, and at the same time I got to thinking about the ambiguity of Negro leadership during that period. This was the late forties, and I kept trying to account for the fact that when the chips were down, Negro leaders did not represent the Negro community" (*Essays* 77). Ellison uses Raglan to interrogate the ongoing absence of an authentic black leadership. Raglan's text is, by convention (not close reading), concerned with the characteristics of the mythic hero; most famously, Raglan lists twenty-two stages in the hero's life, running from his mother's status as a royal virgin to the sepulcher erected on his tomb, then uses these stages to discuss the essential unity and non-historicity of hero myths.

O'Meally, in his brief acknowledgment of Ellison's use of Raglan, simplistically claims that *The Hero* is about "historical and mythical heroes" (78). Clipper simply discusses the famous twenty-two points as if there were nothing else to Raglan's complex text. Schafer proposes that *Invisible Man*'s structure is indebted to Raglan, then pulls a bait and switch, substituting Joseph Campbell for Raglan, as if the two are identical. Griffiths, reading characteristically more deeply, describes Ellison's use of a Raglanian device; the letter the narrator carries to seven potential employers may be based on Raglan, as well as on Angelo Herndon's experience: "Myth must enter the world of the novel through historical moments, 'the specific texture of a specific form of social reality.' . . . For Lord Raglan mythic devices like 'Bellerophontic letters' do not happen in history. Save that it happened to Herndon . . . through the throwback of an Alabama judge [who set Herndon loose with a 'job recommendation' recommending him to the Klan]" (618). Griffiths argues that Raglan influenced Ellison as much as Marx and Freud did (620). Raglan's claim that archetypal occurrences like "kill the bearer" letters don't happen in history is significant to *Invisible Man. The Hero*'s main theme is that "real history" has little role in constructing the hero's narrative (or anything else); Raglan sees history as irrelevant. By linking Raglan to Angelo Herndon and to Homer Barbee's speech, Griffiths raises a question: Does Ellison's use of Raglan have political significance, or is Raglan, as most critics imply, only a formalistic influence upon him? To answer this question, I turn to Ellison's multiple explanations of Raglan's influence on the novel, which revolve not around "timeless archetypes" but rather around the problem of leadership.

Take "The Art of Fiction" (1955), wherein the interviewers ask when Ellison began *Invisible Man.* Ellison answers: "on a farm in Vermont where I was reading *The Hero* by Lord Raglan and speculating on the nature of Negro leadership in the United States, I wrote the first paragraph of *Invisible Man,* and was soon involved in the struggle of creating the novel" (*Essays* 218). The novel develops directly from Ellison's application of Raglan to the problem of "Negro leadership"—that is, from his continuing thought along the lines of his final "Editorial Comment."

In his 1969 West Point address (printed in 1975 as "On Initiation Rites and Power"), Ellison again discussed Raglan:

> I was reading Lord Raglan's *The Hero,* which has to do with tradition, myth and drama. . . . I was concerned with the nature of leadership, and thus with the nature of the hero . . . when I was working out the concept of *Invisible Man* my people were involved in a terrific quarrel with the federal government over our not being allowed to participate in the war as combat personnel in the armed forces on an equal basis. . . . This quarrel led to my concern with the nature of Negro leadership, from a different and nonliterary direction. I was very much involved with the question of just why our Negro leadership was never able to enforce its will. (*Essays* 524–25)

Ellison invokes Raglan to explain the intensely modern political problem that dominated his attention at *Negro Quarterly:* Why don't "Negro leaders" serve their ostensible constituents? Following Raglan, he understands the hero as leader and lawgiver, and the politician as hero (we might think of Odysseus); true political leaders answer the hero's call to defend their community. The "Negro leadership" is unwilling or unable to perform a successful ritual on the community's behalf.

Most critics implicitly argue that Ellison simply mines Raglan for mythic archetypes. However, even Raglan's list of twenty-two common elements among hero myths focuses on the hero's role as leader and legislator. Ritual and politics blur; both assert authority *over* and *for* a community. Raglan summarizes the mythic hero's significance thus: "The myth describes the victories that the hero won over the forces inimical to his people, the laws and customs which he instituted for their benefit, and finally the apotheosis that enables him still to be their guardian and guide" (203). The hero as legislator is foregrounded: on Raglan's scale, the bumbling, speech-impeded Moses is more of a hero (nineteen points) than the monster-slaying Perseus (eighteen points). Raglan's hero-king, like Ellison's ideal Negro leader, is a political being who represents his people through ritual. Ritual does not substitute for politics; it *is* politics. Returning to Ellison's "Editorial Comment" from the final issue of *Negro Quarterly,* Ellison asserts that the Negro leader must simultaneously integrate with the Negro people, define their relationship to technology, and understand their myths and symbols: the simultaneous use of technology and myth is critical.

This critical point has been neglected in Ellison criticism. In "The Conscious Hero and the Rites of Man" (2004), John Wright acknowledges that "riffs on Lord Raglan's myth of heroic biography" guide "the ritual understructure of the novel" (222). Wright, though, argues that Rinehart is a "subversive antitype to Lord Raglan's hero of tradition," while the narrator is a "mock-heroic counterpart to Lord Raglan's hero of tradition" (224–25). Wright misses the significance of Lord Raglan's inclusion of the transparently mock-heroic Moses as a model hero. Lord Raglan's hero is a *ritual* hero and a leader, not necessarily a warrior. Ellison's mock-heroic epic is a development, not an inversion, of Raglan, in which the mock-heroic *is* nothing other than the heroic. Ellison is not satirizing Raglan but rather adopting him as part of a particular politics, a politics that Wright, in fact, analyzes:

> the zoot-suited trio in New York's subway underground provides a focal image for unmasking the character of leadership in the urban North. There, in symbolic tableau, Ellison's meditations on Raglan's heroic mythology and the problem of black leadership converge explicitly in a riddle of cultural creativity that his 1942–1943 *Negro Quarterly* editorials had proposed as a functional test in political decipherment for those who would be masters of social movements.

> Ellison's assertion then that the zoot suit . . . might conceal "profound political meaning" crucial to black leaders expands here, in the wake of the genuinely tragic death of Tod Clifton . . . into a metaphysical consolidation of all those notions of history, culture, consciousness, art, war and dominion that the ritual progress of the hero-narrator has cumulatively brought to the surface. (237)

Wright, although dealing with myth and, implicitly, the leader's integration with the masses, here ignores technology, the triad's third pillar. Without its connection to technology, myth seems like *mere* myth rather than part of a radical new politics. Consequently, Wright downplays the significance of the ritual hero as such: in a move typical of contemporary literature and criticism, the proper subject of all art becomes art, and the proper subject of criticism becomes criticism. For Wright, the hero is interesting not as hero but as artist: ritual becomes *artistic* ritual: "the problems of heroic leadership in *Invisible Man* through which Ellison focused his extrapolations from myth, folk tradition, history, and political philosophy ultimately move toward resolution through an assimilation of the myth of the birth of the hero to the myth of the birth of the artist" (244). Raglan's political hero is subordinated to the artist, Raglan to Ellison, the epic to the novel, and technology (the thinker-tinker) is forgotten. Instead of imagining a new, authentic leadership drawing on a polyphony of myth and technology, the novel is resolved in a modernist *telos* with the artist's birth. Though the hero myth is cyclic, according to most of Ellison's interpreters, its meaning, Wright argues, is linear: the myth of the artist owes something to the myth of the hero, and ascends from there. Wright's criticism takes part in the same salvific history that Ellison assaults.

Yet, Wright gives the best accounts of Ellison and myth *and* of Ellison and technology, in "'Jack the Bear' Dreaming: Ellison's Spiritual Technologies" (1993) and "Ellison's Experimental Attitude and the Technologies of Illumination" (2005). In the latter, Wright acknowledges that critics understate the "revolutionary technological modernity—of what he often posits as a triangular sense of African-American identity" (161). The only thing that Wright misses (likely as an artifact of article-length writing) is the simultaneity of the triad: myth, integration, and technology *together* form a new politics and Ellison's distinctive temporality (which Wright replaces with a new teleology). In Wright's formulation, technology's future orientation clashes with mythology's backward orientation. Ellison's great insight is that technology belongs not only to the present and future and that (following Raglan) myth does not belong only to the past; unlike Wright, he is not trying to *transcend* the epic hero. Ellison demands a technological, self-analytical mythic consciousness, rejecting salvation history. The self-analytical present contains both what is customarily pushed into the distant past and what is pushed into the looming future. *Arche* and *telos, protos* and *eschatos* run together in the ritual present.

We should beware of reading linear time and progress, specialties of the Brotherhood and the Tuskegee system, into *Invisible Man*. In the introduction we have the powerful image of a scientific boxer fighting a yokel, who triumphs by stepping inside "his opponent's sense of time" (8). The invisible man gives his absurd speech on humility as the secret of *progress* (17). Trueblood at his most cunning refers to progress: "You know, we gittin' to be a better-lookin' race of people" (54). As he gradually grows more discerning, the narrator mocks the "black rite of Horatio Alger" (111). Brother Jack at his worst teaches that "we stand at a terminal point in history" (307). When the invisible man, still mystified and naive, contemplates Clifton's death and the events preceding it, he is astonished that "he had chosen . . . to fall outside of history" (434). The introduction famously proposes the boomerang, not the arrow or spiral, as the proper model for time: "I have been boomeranged across my head so much that I now can see the darkness of lightness" (6). We are warned incessantly against progress, linearity, assimilation; things that had been destroyed, forgotten, or ignored boomerang back; Jonathan Arac argues that the spiral "gets reconfigured as a painful, even dangerous form of closure" (212). The narrator himself boomerangs: "I have come a long way and returned and boomeranged a long way from the point in society toward which I originally aspired" (573). "The end was in the beginning," the last full chapter concludes (571).

Ellison's temporality is indebted to Raglan's. The hero's time is not an arrow or spiral but rather *ritual* time. One aspect of ritual time is familiar. It is a cyclical concept of history, in which chronology is confused or nonexistent (Raglan 156); although Raglan begins the following passage with cyclical history, he ends very differently:

> The cyclic movement of the seasons and the heavenly bodies, together with the ritual system associated with them, "inevitably tended to produce a view of Time as a vast circle in which the pattern of the individual life and of the course of history was a recurring cyclic process." This view of time as a ritual circle seems to have been carried over into Christianity, since, according to Professor James, "in the Eucharistic sacrifice the redemptive work of Christ was celebrated, not as a mere commemoration of a historical event, for in the liturgy the past became the present, and the birth at Bethlehem and the death of Calvary were apprehended as ever-present realities independent of time and space."
>
> It is difficult for those who regard rites and ceremonies as desirable but not indispensable aids to the attainment of certain religious or social ends to understand the attitude of those to whom ritual means life. . . . Ritual is far more to millions today than history has ever been to anyone. (156)

The final sentence is striking: the importance of "history"—the arrow or spiral—remains marginal, despite all "progress," while ritual and its temporality endure. Raglan begins with the conventional concept of a primitive, cyclic temporality, while asserting that this premodern concept still endures. Then he describes Eucharistic time, wherein ritual enables the past to erupt into the present; yet this "past" is not really past, but outside ordinary time. He argues that this ritual, the past's eruption into the present, is life itself. Time is not cyclic; "Eucharistic time" is not a return to the past but an explosive emergence into the present. Hence Ellison's yokel's defeat of the scientific boxer: if the "other" time that the yokel enters is ritual time, he has entered into life and power. For Raglan, the hero's story has no historical basis: it *is* ritual, and is as such an alternative to chronological time. But why should Ellison draw on Raglan's temporality? Ellison demands that we recognize black hypermodernity; there is no question, as in Booker T. Washington, that the "race" needs to "rise" or "progress." Once we accept linear history, though, the oppressed are, at best, to be pitied: they require uplifting and/or discipline; as Adas details through *Machines as the Measure of Man,* they especially require technological discipline and assimilation or, in Wallerstein's terms, integration into the world-system; their potential technological identity is opposed to their folk identity. When Ellison combines folk and technological identities, he resists history-as-progress—the very structure of (Western) oppression. By appropriating Raglan's prioritization of myth over history, Ellison undermines history-as-progress without surrendering technology, which helps constitute the historical moment into which myth erupts. Ellison's Negro is distinctively modern *because of* folk beliefs, not despite them. Raglan describes the temporality of myth—the invisible man's temporality—thus: "[Myth] links the ritual of the present with the ritual of the past, . . . [and] actually identifies the present, in its ritual aspect, with a past conceived solely in terms of ritual" (127). Ritual time *invades* chronological time, re-identifying the present as past. The myth is a "narrative connected with a rite" (141). The rite's concern is *power,* with shaping and controlling the world on a community's behalf: the concern, in other words, of leadership.

Reading Raglan's ritual time as a powerful influence upon Ellison, we see that the narrator's movement underground is a removal into ritual time, which remains technological; his life becomes ritual, with his 1,369 lightbulbs, his reefer dreams, and his ritual near-slaughter of the man who insults him (4). Even his invisibility has a ritual aspect; hence he refers to himself as a "phantom" and "ectoplasm" as well as invisible (3, 4). Like a creature from a monster movie, he is only half real, but consequently more powerful. He is afflicted by the boomerang of history but also *is* the boomerang, the eruption of ritual world and time into "real" world and time.

This is not to say that Ellison is Raglan's *pupil,* but it is critical to understand Ellison's extensive *use* of Raglan to develop his vision of leadership, as originally articulated in *Negro Quarterly* before its development in *Invisible Man.* Ellison's demand that the Negro leader deploy both "myth and symbol" and technological modernity is problematic; how is that possible, when drawing on technology implies one sense of time and drawing on myth implies another?

The heart of Raglan's primary argument is encapsulated in the book's opening. He argues that for almost all people "the past is merely a prologue to the present, not merely without interest in so far as it is independent of the present, but simply inconceivable except in terms of the present. . . . [We] regard the story of our lives not as a crosscountry walk upon which we are still engaged, but as a path, cut deliberately by fate and ourselves, to the positions which we now occupy" (3). Raglan's thought is akin to, and possibly influenced by, the Bergson of *Creative Evolution:* we *organize* our understanding of life and the world to control our life and surroundings, and we mainly attempt to control the world through ritual, not through technology.

Raglan does not *merely* analyze similarities among hero myths; he examines them to prove the ahistoricity of all heroes from Moses to Robin Hood: his thesis "is that the traditional narrative . . . is based not upon historical facts on the one hand or imaginative fictions on the other, but upon dramatic ritual or ritual drama" (278). The ritual drama's god-hero is not primarily edifying or amusing, though he may be both; his purpose is to wield power: "The chief actor in a ritual drama pretends to be a god or hero . . . to exercise the power which that God or hero is believed to have exercised" (279). The hero's story is not bad or incomplete history; it is *unrelated* to ordinary chronology (145). In Frazer the myth's historical content is merely irrelevant; in Raglan it is relevant and important that myth has *no* historical content.

The ritual drama is an attempt, within ordinary time, to draw upon the god-hero's ahistorical power (248). It is characterized by the donning of ritual costumes and masks, particularly animal masks (252, 260). It focuses on royalty, but not real or historical royalty; the kings of myth are characterized by solitude, especially in combat; King Arthur's single combats and Jacob's wrestling match with God serve as perfect examples (270–71).

These characteristics appear in *Invisible Man:* the narrator assumes Rinehart's role and divine powers upon donning Rinehart's costume; Ras the destroyer appears in animal garb, wielding a spear. The narrator as god-hero dwells in solitude incommensurate with his divine state and undergoes ritual birth and castration; he witnesses the black *rite* of

Horatio Alger. Ellison's "different sense of time" fuses the temporalities of the mythic hero and modern technology (the locomotive's time). The authentic "Negro leader" embraces both temporalities and puts them to work, thus plunging outside history. The narrator's rejection of progress (always defined hierarchically) is not a rejection of *change,* which is how his temporality differs from the ritual god-hero's, which Raglan argues is changeless (246). The boomeranging of history is the enactment of the ritual: the ritual appearance of the god-hero reshapes and restores the world. Ritual time is opposed to "that progress goo" and also to Ras's merely reactionary time; the ritual hero *masters* the world—in Ellison's work, through the ritual use of technology.

What did *The Hero* teach Ellison about Negro leadership? It reveals a lack: the leadership was oriented toward the spiral of progress, not the boomerang of ritual; it was rooted in the exceptional, Bledsoeian individual rather than masked, invisible individual qua people's representative. The three pillars of authentic Negro leadership are augmented by invisibility—an invisibility that is one with an identity as ritual hero. The invisible leader, opposing the Tuskegee system that he mirrors and mocks, eschews individual progress, including technological progress, for technology as ritual.

The mythic hero abides in ritual time, in tension with the undeniable reality of historical and technological change. Rejecting "that progress goo" does not destroy the real change underlying that ideology. In "Indivisible Man," Ellison writes on the Negro and technology:

> Our experience in the acculturative process differed from the European's because he didn't have the necessity. This can be said about American culture in general: it *was* an extension of European culture. What is new about it is the presence of the African influence. . . . There was a modification of language necessary to communicate with the slaves and with people who came from other parts of Europe. All of these created a tension which in turn created what we all the vernacular style. Our technology was vernacular. And it grew so fast precisely because they had to throw off the assumptions of European technology and create one which was in keeping with conditions in the New World. (*Essays* 369)

The Negro *is* the power system's greatest victim, its living heart and potentially its greatest beneficiary. By the prologue and epilogue the narrator's technology is vernacular; it belongs to him, and he to it. He plays a part in a ritual drama under the control of outside forces until, under the influence of Rinehart "the spiritual technologist," he sheds automatism, seizing control of the ritual himself (495): "My entire body started to itch, as though I had just been removed from a plaster cast and was unused to the new freedom of movement. . . . I looked at the polished lenses of the glasses and laughed. I had been trying simply to turn them into a disguise but they had become a political instrument instead; for if Rinehart could use them in his work, no doubt I could use them in mine" (499). Rinehart's work is a vast con game, spanning religion, numbers running, and prostitution. Rinehart the rascal, like Bledsoe, who supervises the ritual invoking and commemorating the Founder's life and death, has ritual power; he plays a role in a ritual drama, which grants him a power that boomerangs into ordinary time. Bledsoe and Rinehart perform their rituals selfishly, refusing to *integrate* with the community. Bledsoe's manipulation of technology, myth and symbols is protofascist, while Rinehart's is merely criminal. Like *Juneteenth*'s Adam Sunraider, they are akin to Melville's Confidence Man. The mechanical man, played differently by the blues-singing Trueblood, the paranoid Brockway, and the naive invisible man, *suffers* as oppressed standing-reserve, and as a black American, simultaneously confirming, denying, and transforming the Mumfordian organic/mechanical divide, which contrasts with and becomes the gulf between master and slave; the specifics of the post–Civil War divide between organism and machine are another eruption, or boomeranging, of the rite of the mechanical man into ordinary time.

Unlike Mumford and Heidegger, Ellison writes about those who have been mechanized in advance of the technologies that supposedly threaten total mechanization. The apocalyptic moment is long past, as in Faulkner; mechanization looms over all history. As in Bergson, technology is related to automatism but is also part of any response to it. By entering into ritual time, the narrator struggles to impose a ritual adapted for American usage upon history; *thus* he is a thinker-tinker, a maker and saboteur of electrical systems, who wears the ritual mask of his era;

the details of the ritual are distinctive, but not its purpose, which is to empower the oppressed. This reading strengthens the novel's political thrust toward a new anti-totalitarian nationalism rooted in the chaos of American life, and yet which approaches the ritual-technological tools of fascism itself, avoiding them through a development of the third pillar of Ellison and Herndon's vision of leadership, continual learning from and consciousness of the masses.

I have one more item of evidence to offer for this reading of *Invisible Man:* my own version of a Raglanian schematization of the novel, using Raglan's twenty-two common points in the hero's life. Ellison synthesizes a Mumford-influenced understanding of automatization to his own understanding of slavery and oppression and attaches both of them to Raglan's schema; we can and should understand Ellison's hero *technologically.* (See table on pp. 197–99.)

The invisible man's total points (twenty to twenty-two) approach Oedipus's twenty-two, when one attends to the hero's mechanical aspects. In *Invisible Man,* Ellison adapts Mumford's organic/mechanical divide and Raglan's analysis of history and ritual (and the relative insignificance of history compared to ritual), using them both to develop his concept of the Negro leader, who must wield technology and myth, while integrated (invisibly) into the masses, in order to defy historical/mechanical thought—that is, the hierarchical story of human progress.

The Leader and the Machine

The narrator's self-consciousness as ritual actor and scapegoat grows with his self-consciousness as technological object and subject, under technological domination, yet uniquely able to exploit technological possibilities. Before knowing himself as the object and subject of a technological ritual, he is an utter failure as a leader. Only in self-awareness as a mechanical man is he free for himself and his people.

The prologue and epilogue of *Invisible Man* are largely meditations on leadership: problematic "Negro leaders," mirroring real ones, are contrasted to the narrator's alternative, Raglanian-technological conception of the leader. Early in the prologue the narrator claims his hole is bright enough to outshine Broadway and the Empire State Building. And yet "Those two spots are among the darkest of our whole civilization. . . .

	Raglan's Text	Commentary on *Invisible Man*
1	The hero's mother is a royal virgin.	The hospital machine, cold and inviolate, is his mother. (1)
2	His father is a king, and	His father is Brockway, master of the machines of Liberty Paints. (1)
3	Often a near relative of his mother, but	Given Brockway's involvement in the factory's operations and machinery, it seems likely that he was involved in the hospital machine's design. (1)
4	The circumstances of his conception are unusual, and	His conception begins with an outmatched physical struggle with his diminutive father. His gestation and birth from the machine are even more unusual. (1)
5	He is also reputed to be the son of a god.	He is sent by the godlike Bledsoe, whose own life story, as well as the Founder's, can be understood through Raglan. (1)
6	At birth an attempt is made, usually by his father or his maternal grandfather, to kill him, but	Brockway nearly kills him in the basement explosion; then he risks death in the hospital machine. (1)
7	He is spirited away, and	Mary spirits him away from the hospital and its machinery—more directly in the early drafts than in the published version. (1)
8	Reared by foster-parents in a far country.	He is raised by Mary, then by the Brotherhood, both of whom embrace "that progress goo." (1)

Continued on the next page

9	We are told nothing of his childhood, but	True for his literal childhood but not of his childhood with Mary and the Brotherhood (0–1).
10	On reaching manhood he returns or goes to his future kingdom	He immediately becomes a leader in the Brotherhood and community. (1)
11	After a victory over the king and/or a giant, dragon, or wild beast,	The moment of his ascension is his confrontation with the microphone, which evokes the hospital machine; here he accepts the Brotherhood's mechanical notion of historical progress. (1)
12	He marries a princess, often the daughter of his predecessor	His affairs with Brotherhood women. (1)
13	Becomes king.	See 10, and note the jealously that his individual power provokes. (1)
14	For a time reigns uneventfully, and	He concerns himself with small details, like magazine interviews; the membership expands. (1)
15	Prescribes laws, but	He absorbs and reissues the laws of the Brotherhood within the community. (1)
16	Later he loses favor with the gods and/or his subjects, and	He is displaced and rejected repeatedly by the Brotherhood's leadership. (1)
17	Is driven from the throne and city, after which	He wanders the city as Rinehart's doppelgänger; his ritual dethroning leads him to a new understanding of technology-as-ritual and ritual-as-technology. (1)

18	He meets with a mysterious death	His plummet into the coal cellar—and *into* technological power. (1)
19	Often at the top of a hill	Although he's in a cellar, the cellar involves, according to Ellison, a kind of rising (*Essays* 111). (0–1)
20	His children, if any, do not succeed him.	The Harlem branch of the Brotherhood disintegrates. (1)
21	His body is not buried, but nevertheless	Hibernating, not dead. (1)
22	He has one or more holy sepulchers.	A temple of light and electric power which is associated with *his* culture and folklore; electricity and religion were earlier connected in Rinehart's church. "Who knows but that, on the lower frequencies, I speak for you?" (1)

Which might sound like a hoax, or a contradiction, but that (by contradiction, I mean) is how the world moves: Not like an arrow, but a boomerang" (6).

The narrator, while describing his own technological-electrical sublime, rejects the classical example of that sublime, the lights of Broadway, as detailed in Nye's *American Technological Sublime* and *Electrifying America*. The narrator's understanding of world and time eschews both progress and Luddism. He asserts, much like Bergson, that "Life is to be lived, not controlled; and humanity is won by continuing to play in the face of certain defeat" (577). A new definition of humanity (some would see it as posthumanity) has replaced the old one, with the spiral's displacement by the boomerang. Automatism is inevitable; humanity is the ongoing struggle to be human despite automatism, even after disillusionment.

The language of light, which evokes Saint Paul, pervades the prologue: "Meanwhile I enjoy my life with the compliments of Monopolated Light

& Power. . . . Before that I lived in the darkness into which I was chased, but now I see. I've illuminated the blackness of my invisibility—and vice versa" (13). In the Pauline transvaluation of values, blindness becomes sight and sight becomes blindness. Invisibility becomes substance, visibility becomes insubstantiality, and automatization becomes freedom, most radically with Tod Clifton. In this upside-down, transvalued world, only the hibernating leader is a leader at all; to regard the narrator of the prologue and epilogue as leader requires the same kind of transvaluation as is necessary to regard a dead carpenter as king. The narrator's underground struggle (although not itself Christian) recalls the Christianity of the catacombs, in hiding from Rome's infinite power. Like Paul, who is opposed to the Roman state as it exists but cognizant of its potential if rewired, the invisible man cannot fully condemn the American state, because he, wrapped in light, sees it as it might become: "Diversity is the word. Let man keep his many parts and you'll have no tyrant states. Why, if they follow this conformity business they'll end up by forcing me, an invisible man, to become white. . . . America is woven of many strands; I would recognize them and let it so remain. It's 'winner take nothing' that is the great truth of our country or of any country. Life is to be lived, not controlled; and humanity is won by continuing to play in face of certain defeat" (577). The invisible man, the automaton, becomes the avatar and preacher of chaos, set against progress. His leadership is ambiguous and paradoxical because, in a dreamlike extension of one American ideal, he is a leader who promotes nothing but endless autonomy, an automaton engaged in sowing chaos.

Am I promoting Ellison as a simple multiculturalist? No: the road to *this* diversity leads directly through profound mechanization. Only those who have been most subject to mechanization can fulfill the "historical role of the Negroes" of "integrating the larger American nation and compelling it towards true freedom" (Ellison, "Editorial Comment" 1.4, 298).

Invisible Man contains numerous models of failed leadership. Bledsoe is the very image of bad "Negro leadership," deeply corrupt and self-serving, perhaps interested in advancing his people, but *more* interested in his own cause, and complicit in a counterproductive understanding of history. Brother Jack is most interested in wielding power for its own sake. The distant white leadership scarcely warrants mentioning: while Mr. Norton is not *entirely* unsympathetic, he needs no discussion as a leader, nor does the infinitely remote elder Mr. Emerson. For all the failures of "Negro leadership" and Brotherhood leadership, they at least have the tiniest shred of credibility, unlike the distant powers of white business and government.

Ras the Destroyer and Rinehart the Runner, as signaled by their semidivine titles, are less easily dismissed. They live *in* and *as* ritual, playing the roles of warrior and trickster, responding ritually to a technologically conditioned situation. The narrator's encounters with Ras and Rinehart show him new possibilities, a new way of understanding time.

In the prologue, the invisible man remembers listening to Louis Armstrong after smoking a reefer: "I not only entered the music but descended, like Dante, into its depths. And *beneath the swiftness of the hot tempo there was a slower tempo and a cave*" (9). Under Armstrong's music (outside ordinary time) he encounters ritual after ritual. First he sees slaveowners bidding for a naked girl, then enters a variation of the "Negro Church" Ishmael enters in *Moby-Dick,* where the text is the "Blackness of Blackness" in Ellison's version, or the "Blackness of darkness" in Melville's (*Invisible Man* 9; *Moby-Dick* 10). He encounters an old woman who loved and hated her master; her son attacks the narrator, nearly killing him. He then wanders into a dark tunnel where a tom-tom beats. He hears footsteps in the darkness:

> *"Hey, Ras," I called. "Is it you, Destroyer? Rinehart?"*
>
> *No answer, only the rhythmic footsteps behind me. Once I tried crossing the road, but a speeding machine struck me, scraping the skin from my leg as it roared past.*
>
> Then somehow I came out of it, ascending hastily from this underworld. (12)

Descending into the underworld, he expects to encounter Ras and Rinehart, especially after hearing the tom-toms associated with Ras's ritual primitivism and the trumpets associated with Rinehart's techno-ritual sophistication. Instead, he encounters the machine; his scrape with it returns him to the surface; in this Dantean scene, the machine is his Virgil, even his Beatrice. The violent collision of mechanical and ritual time leads to his emergence.

We can characterize the narrator's leadership in three ways. First, he is a "true" leader who does not betray his people in favor of his own interests, as do Rinehart and Bledsoe; he now takes direction from the people (e.g., at Clifton's funeral) rather than imposing a prefabricated ideology upon them. Second, he ultimately constructs himself not merely as a political leader but as a *techno-political* leader, a thinker-tinker whose power resides in his deployment of machines and electricity. His technical ability, like that of his fellow thinker-tinkers and Edison, leads seamlessly to cultural and political authority. Third, he is a ritual leader, forthrightly related to a long genealogy of literary and actual preachers, with Melville's preacher of "The Trap" as one model and Jonah himself as another. The narrator becomes the instantiation of "the Negro leader" whom Ellison had delimited, with further shaping by Raglan's meditation on ritual and history.

Rinehart is ritually and technologically oriented, but rather than integrating with the masses he preys upon them. Ras is oriented toward ritual and is arguably integrated with the masses, but he doesn't understand the relationship of the masses to technology, despite his selflessness. Because Ras and Rinehart both have two of the Negro leader's aspects, they are on the narrator's mind under the reefer's influence. No other character in the novel clearly fulfills even two aspects; Brother Jack, for instance, is at best a technological leader, but he is not integrated with the masses and does not understand ritual.

What is at stake in the recognition that the narrator's emerging leadership is equally characterized by integration, technology, and ritual? The three aspects together lead to power on the one hand and a realization, on the other, that the *story* of domination or mechanization, in which the history of technology is an upward spiral of power and subjugation, is false. The invisible man, like Louis Armstrong, appreciates the power of contemporary techniques, instruments, and mechanical reproduction while understanding that their origins and directions are complex; by using that power for and through ritual, he defies teleological history.

The invisible man's discovery of infinite possibilities, rooted in mechanically reproduced jazz and blues, is identical with his attacks on progress and the concept of technology-as-progress: "Of course Louis was kidding, *he* wouldn't have thrown old Bad Air out, because it would have broken up the music and the dance, when it was the good music that came from the bell of old Bad Air's horn that counted" (581). To return to Raglan's phrasing of a similar thought, "Ritual is far more to millions today than history has ever been to anyone" (156). The music and the dancing will go on, despite the abominations of history; to throw out old bad air would be to end ritual, displacing it for rationalized history—the way of the Brotherhood, that is, Stalin.

The narrator finds freedom rather than slavery in his mechanical identity by imagining technology without eschatology, that is, by freeing time from progress and by permitting ritual time and mechanical time to collide without resolution: he gives up temporal hierarchies. Yet this world—a jazz world—is never static. Ellison abandons a world in which there is a "forward" or "back," especially where technology is concerned; technological change represents a specific adaptation, not a general improvement, and American forms of oppression are not embedded within (and therefore necessitated by) the story of America's upward spiral. Technology, rather than being subordinate to or determinate of history's teleological movement, is an ongoing, changing aspect of human life, affiliated with ritual; Louis Armstrong is as much a thinker-tinker, as much a master of technology (technique), as Edison and Franklin. The affirmation of technology-as-ritual rather than technology-as-teleology is, strangely, an affirmation of the individual, who attains a degree of freedom, even power, through the ritual use of technology. Curiously, it's far easier to humanize technology than to humanize history.

Ellison's thought is akin to Nye's "electrical sublime," which is contrasted both to the Kantian sublime and the technological sublime, both of which are complicit with institutional racism: "Kant's sublime made the individual humble in the face of nature, the technological sublime exalted the conquest of nature. The electrical sublime represented a third kind of experience, as it dissolved the distinction between natural and artificial sites. In blurring or even erasing this line, it created a synthetic environment infused with mystery" (*Technological Sublime* 152). Nye's electrical sublime (following Mumford's neotechnics) is the reentry of mystery into life, specifically technological life. Yet the electrical sublime describes Rinehart's state more readily than the narrator's; Rinehart, though he could reject teleological history, by being *merely* sublime permits it to recapitulate itself. The narrator, although he learns from Rinehart, does not *merely* dwell in or partake of the electrical sublime, but radicalizes it. He recognizes that time as we know it, that is, history as technological progress (and the sublime itself), *is* political. Ellison understands the terrors of technological domination as well as any of the other major philosophical and literary figures who meditated upon it; like many of the rest of them, he owes much in this area to Mumford. But Ellison, who tries to imagine the possibilities as well as recounting the failures of black leadership, knows better than to indulge in the (often masked) nostalgic yearnings shared by figures from Heidegger and Marcuse to Cleanth Brooks; that would mean a return to domination, to slavery, not the nonexistent "middle state." Instead, he illustrates the continuity of life as ritual *and* as technology. Technological domination is an ongoing element of life, and "faith" in its "progress" is a political belief, contingent on a particular conception of history—one that generates a deeper domination.

Too often, Ellison's critics fail to recognize the thoroughness of his assault upon history-as-progress. My contribution is to show, through Ellison's simultaneous engagement with Mumford and Raglan, that Ellison attacks "progress" as radically in his time as the most cutting-edge historians of technology and philosophers of biology do today, and that this attack on progress is an attempt at an authentic liberating politics, based on a fusion of black experience and technological reality.

Ellison's attempt to recoup technology for the oppressed and anonymous, while abandoning the ideologies of progress which circulate around technology, is an explicit development of Melville's, Mumford's, and Faulkner's similar but less fully realized projects. Ellison, as their heir, offers a powerful political and intellectual antidote to the technological teleologies that seem to be always already given.

The question is not, How can we survive the technological *eschatos,* the automation of the self? The question is, How do we survive, at any particular moment, the ongoing reality of our struggle against mechanization and the particular dilemmas associated with it? How can we do better, by substituting change for teleological progress? Hoping for change, not progress, and for survival most of all, I turn to a brief meditation on biological thought, which will serve as a coda to this project and as a prologue to things to come.

Conclusion

Telos, Bios, Techne

In this book, which addresses the nearly universal teleological understanding of the relationship between time and technology and maps ways in which U.S. literary works reconceptualize that relationship, I have developed a revisionary understanding of this relationship within, and inspired by, American literature. This section is both a coda to this project in literary criticism and also a prolegomenon to possible future projects: a more theoretical work on time and technology and an exploration of the anti-teleological deployment of biological thought in contemporary literature.

I advocate the rejection of the idea of progress in all its forms. Change is real, and particular changes—for instance, the melting of the polar ice cap or the development of the microprocessor—may be viewed as positive or negative (although in reality large changes tend to be irreducibly complex), but the idea of *progress,* as appealing as it is, is a chimera. This argument is suggested by my analysis of "modern" technology (Bruno Latour's contention that "we have never been modern" hovers in the background), which is, after all, the point from which ideologies of progress supposedly originate.

I have emphasized the age and centrality of technology in human life. Any attempt to establish a moment at which humanity enters into a space-devouring, time-annihilating mechanical crisis from which it requires deliverance is deeply flawed and historically dishonest, which is not to deny that we find ourselves continually in crisis or to claim that our crisis is unrelated to time and technology. Any attempt, though, to look back to nature while simultaneously looking forward, with a sensation of vertigo toward the machine that ends time, is simply the projection of an emotion, albeit a forgivable one, into the world. We are threatened, even haunted, by automatism, by the threatened deadening of all possibilities; a machine threatens to cut off *our* time, and therefore all time. Finding ourselves in a technological crisis, we attribute the crisis to our time, understandably but incorrectly.

The threat of mechanization endures. It is real for us, as it was for Ellison, Faulkner, and Melville, and indeed for Hobbes, Shakespeare, and the pyramid builders. It is the *persistence* of this crisis that is absent from nearly all philosophical and theoretical accounts of mechanization, with the notable exception of Bergson's, and which is powerfully present, albeit sometimes hidden at depth, in the literary figures whom I have discussed. What to *do,* though, when we understand that the threat of mechanization endures?

We must recognize that there is no question of salvation, or at least leave such questions to theologians. Such hopes are traps, invitations to imagine and create a capstone to history—"grand ones [architects] leave the copestone to posterity. God keep me from ever completing anything," Melville writes (*Moby-Dick* 145). The hope of salvation from or through the machine is a greater danger than the mechanization of the self as such; the urge to fix or solve history ("What's wrong with this world is, it's not finished yet," proclaims Faulkner), especially to make it "natural" once more, is paradoxically a back door into the willing mechanization of world and self, as we see most profoundly in Heidegger (Faulkner, *Essays* 135).

Our particular culture, and human life in general, is not, however, unthreatened. Within his provocative book *The Inhuman,* which includes the essay-cum-science-fiction-story "Can Thought Go On without a Body?" Lyotard sarcastically demands that philosophy confront the world's literal death: "after the sun's death there won't be a thought to know that its death took place. . . . [That] is the sole serious question to face humanity today" (9). The sun's death, however, is an asymptote: our outer limit, not our expected life span. Most likely we will have been extinct long before. There have been numerous mass extinctions in the earth's history, which destroyed most existing species, including the most dominant; there is no particular reason to trust in our immunity to this process, which tends to weed out large, specialized surface dwellers first—even if we set aside the astonishingly dangerous changes we are making in our own environment. *Homo sapiens* nearly did, in fact, go extinct some seventy thousand years ago. Richard Dawkins explains that despite our vastly greater population, humans are less genetically varied than chimpanzees: "We can explain this human uniformity by guessing that our ancestors, but not the chimpanzees', passed through a genetic bottleneck not very long ago. The population was reduced to a small number, came close to going extinct but just pulled through. There is evidence of a fierce bottleneck—perhaps down to a population of 15,000, some 70,000 years ago, caused by a six-year 'volcanic winter' followed by a thousand-year ice age" (405). Humanity will have its end, whether in eighty years or ten million. But when we end, even if as a result of our technical ingenuity, we will not end because of our selves' sudden mechanization. We will, rather, die *with* mechanical selves, as we have lived *with* them. For we are not alone in turning the world into a machine or information system, despite the alacrity with which contemporary biology and computer science perform the latter task, opening the way for the radical forms of posthumanism Katherine Hayles discusses in *How We Became Posthuman*. To return to an earlier moment from the project: "Organisms do not experience environments. They create them" (Lewontin 109). We experience little that is not profoundly influenced by life. Lyotard acknowledges as much in his essay/story:[1] "technology wasn't invented by us humans. Rather the other way around. As anthropologists and biologists admit, even the simplest life forms, infusoria (tiny algae synthesized by light at the edges of tidepools a few million years ago) are already technical devices. Any material system is technological if it filters information useful to its survival, if it memorizes and processes that information and makes inferences based on the regulating effect of behavior" (12). I don't endorse Lyotard's understanding of technology as information processing (which aligns him roughly with those problematic forms of posthumanism to which Hayles's work has attended): following Mumford and Bergson, I associate technology with action, the shaping and mastering of a world that, as (principally) a collection of organisms, also acts upon us. Nonetheless, I wish to explicate it. *Bios* is not easily distinguished from *technē:* all life has techniques, and shapes the world; therefore I, unlike Lyotard, argue that all *bios* has techniques (*technē*), whereas Lyotard makes technique more strictly into life's identity. "It is perfectly possible to say that the living cell, and the organism with its organs, are already *tekhnai,* that 'life,' as they say, is already technique," writes Lyotard in "*Logos* and *Technē,* or Telegraphy" (*The Inhuman* 52).

Lyotard imagines humanity (and the inhuman that follows it; I would say, with Bergson, that the inhuman forever haunts the human) as the *logos* of *technē,* or *technologos* (which is related to but not identical with autopoiesis; Lyotard is less focused than Maturana and Varela on the organism as a monad), which he defines as "remembering, and not only habit. Its self-referential capacity . . . is exercised by remembering its own presuppositions and implications as its limitations. . . . [T]he *technologos* opens up the world of what has been excluded by its very constitution, by the structures of its functioning, at all levels. This is how new denotative linguistic genres are invented: arithmetic, geometry, analysis. This is how science is generated" (*The Inhuman* 53). As the *logos* of *technē,* we are distinguished by language, self-referentiality, reflection—by philosophy, though Lyotard does not invoke that term. Fair enough: we are seemingly the only philosophical animal. Other animals are also technical, but they are characterized by "habit" or the "received *technologos* of breaching," whereas we are characterized by a reflective *technologos,* called scanning (53). Lyotard's hope is that "new technologies" will empower scanning, enabling resistance to "clever programmes and fat telegrams"; he wonders, will "passage" be allowed by "the new mode of inscription and memoration that characterizes the new technologies? Do they not impose syntheses, and syntheses conceived still more intimately in the soul than any earlier technology has done?" (57). Lyotard looks to "new technologies" to allow new insight, a new ability to stand up to the "clear mirror, through the breaking" (56). His familiar hope is that modern technologies, led by information technologies, will lead to a kind of psychoanalytic break with the past. The breach between nature and culture becomes a matter of the psyche and its history. In the final essay/story of

The Inhuman, "*Domus* and the Megalopolis," Lyotard imagines a domestic scene, a manor or estate, where all is ordered, all is "right": the middle landscape purified: "It is the sphere of reference of the estate, a monad. A mode of space, time and body under the regime (of) nature. A state of mind, of perception, of memory confined to its limits, but where the universe is represented" (192). Again: "The past repeats itself in work. It is fixed, which is to say it is held back and forgotten, in legends. The *domus* is the space-time of this reiteration" (193). The domus's time is cyclic. But something "is capable of interrupting the cycles. The domestic monad is torn, full of stories and scenes, haunted by secrets. . . . In the lowest depths of the *domus,* rumour of anti-nature" (195). Lyotard argues that only "the thought suggested by techno-science" could imagine the domus's end (198). Why? Because a bigger monad, capable of great complexity, programming, and mediation, was necessary. Following Maturana and Varela, we might associate this bigger monad with a higher order of autopoiesis. And thus the inhuman looms, in this science-fiction story of our innermost selves: "The control is no longer territorialized or historicized . . . the big techno-scientific monad has no need of our terrestrial bodies, of passions and writings that used to be kept in the *domus.* What it needs is 'our' wonderful brains. When it evacuates our dying solar system, the big monad, which is now cosmically competitive, will not take the untameable along with it" (199). This is too brilliant a tale for me to wholly reject it. But I must make two skeptical notes.

First, we assume too easily that (human) language is the only true carrier of information and that we determine the destiny of all earthly information; yet the gene is far from being reduced to human language. We are utterances in a language that remains nearly incomprehensible; we know the genetic alphabet and can transcribe texts, but meaning is another matter. If we "understood" that language, whatever that entails, we would remain an utterance in it; our inhumanity is as inescapable as our humanity.

Second, Lyotard backtracks on the domus's historical reality: "Domesticity is over, and probably it never existed, except as the dream of the old child awakening and destroying it on awakening" (201). He follows "Baudelaire, Benjamin, Adorno" in asking "How to inhabit the megalopolis" and answering: "By bearing witness to the impossible work, by citing the lost *domus*" (200). Lyotard asks us to "bear witness . . . to thinking as disaster, nomadism, difference and redundancy," even in the full awareness that "suffering and the untameable are as if already destroyed" (203–4). Unlike his ancestors, Lyotard denies the domus's historical reality—which should make us question the value of citing it. Lyotard recognizes the unreality of the domus but does not follow that understanding through.

The anti-nature rising against the domus is untamable, as is the witness against the megalopolis that replaces the domus; Lyotard hints that domus and megalopolis are not as divided as they appear. Historically, even Lyotard admits, the domus may never have existed; as I have detailed at length, to pin a date on the arrival of the megalopolis is impossible. The megalopolis's horror is the mechanization of the self, which turns even rebellion into a resource. Lyotard's horror is understandable, but his shifting terminology is revealing.

The megalopolis is a sophisticated form of slavery, so ancient that it is not merely human: our cousins the ants and termites also dwell within it.[2] Like all life, but especially like the life of ants and termites, human life—a particular genetic utterance—imposes a new "final" order on its environment. Abandoning all claims to the historical reality of the domus should lead to doubts about the imminent final dominion of its twin, the megalopolis. Unenslaved, unexploited life is a mirage; there is no such life. The inhuman megalopolis does not *now* threaten to overtake human life, but continuously dwells within it, like the mitochondria and other incompletely assimilated "alien" life that our ancestors absorbed. We have been, for hundreds of millions of years, appropriated as a resource by mitochondria. And so, also, with the legions of bacteria inhabiting us: Are we their resource, or are they ours? Perhaps our relationship with them is peaceful symbiosis, the domus internalized (autopoiesis), but we can rest assured that the colonization of our ancestor's bodies was no painless or trivial matter; much raw material was destroyed to make our current selves.

In *Animal Rites,* in the process of discussing systems theory (beginning with Maturana and Varela) and Derrida's work on the animal, Carey Wolfe notes Beardsworth's argument (following Stiegler, who follows Heidegger) that time has been sped up and compressed under technoscience. Wolfe then elliptically raises the possibility that the acceleration of time may be "part of a larger evolutionary process of chronicities and periodicities in which all animals participate in a sort of shared passivity in the face of time's alterity" (76). That is, the experience of cruel, accelerated time might not be strictly a human experience; Wolfe argues that Derrida's work on the animal stresses "the *inhuman* rather than the *human* relation *to the inhumanity of time and technicity itself*" (77). The inhumanity of time, an important topic for Wolfe (and for Derrida before him), is something we like to explain dramatically, apocalyptically: it crushes us, mechanizes us, kills us, most particularly in *our* historical moment. As Wolfe implies, though, time's cruelty isn't our experience alone: all life experiences death.[3] Wolfe emphasizes Derrida's insistence on thinking of animals not in terms of "the animal" but in terms of *animals,* a true plurality: we (all animals, including humans) have our own time, our own techniques, our own automatism, our own death.

There is no stable way to divide *zoē* from *technē.* Such divisions are necessarily pragmatic and ad hoc, oriented toward action, without epistemological or ontological claims, although we need not, like Hobbes or Maturana, simply understand *zoē* as *technē.* We might, instead, recognize the *zoē* pervading *technē,* and vice versa. Many contemporary thinkers (including the founders of cybernetics), as documented in Hayles's *How We Became Posthuman,* among other works, have understood life differently in the light of contemporary technology: life, in short, becomes a form of information, even being reconceived as a form of computation. By way of clarification, *my* claim (rooted in figures from Bergson to Lewontin) is that *technē* is an aspect of life, but a *universal* one. *All* life manifests itself as *technē*—a weighty subject I'll discuss again briefly in the afterword to this book.

Lyotard's horror is a significant, representative historical response to "the Inhuman," but it isn't the only possible response. Science-fiction writers have anticipated the inhuman with zest: Isaac Asimov, Octavia Butler, and Samuel R. Delany have portrayed our fear of mechanization as continuous with our response to our enduring institution(s) of enslavement and domination, even while Wolfe, following Derrida, opens the experience of the inhuman to animals. Lyotard acknowledges this continuity only by implication: his domus, while opposed to the anti-nature that rises against it to form the great monad, "the Inhuman," is named domus for a reason. The name evokes Horkheimer and Adorno's "domination," which is nothing if not inhuman. The inhuman is not separate from the human any more than we are independent from the life-forms that colonize us. The inhuman, as Hayles eventually acknowledges of the posthuman, has always been with us.

It is dangerous to conceive of technological development or biological evolution as progress, but it is especially dangerous to imagine a turning point in either after which everything is different; insistence on radical division, on ruptures in time, have helped to maintain scientific racism in a species that is remarkably genetically uniform. Our own techniques have peculiar characteristics, as do, presumably, our genes, but our *technē* is as continuous with inhuman *technē* as our genes are continuous with inhuman genes.

The techniques of mitochondria blur into our own; we might, stretching the point, be regarded *as* their techniques. They shape and use us as vehicles for their own survival, while we could not exist without them. They do not own us, we might assert; but neither do we wholly own the dogs we have bred for millennia, as the Australian dingo shows. To alter Lyotard's story of the escape of the inhuman into space: Isn't it easier, and more resonant with the history of *zoē* as we understand it, to imagine human life mutually appropriating and being appropriated by the inhuman? Human and inhuman, nature and anti-nature are useful if dangerous metaphors for the conflicts that define life and its techniques. They are also an illusion: techniques are not only part of being human; they're also part of being a dog, an ant, or an octopus.

We can imagine ourselves, or all life, extinct, or we can imagine the survival of human techniques in a kind of mitochondrial coexistence within a future system. Varieties of life blur together; we can regard ourselves as unities or colonies (one great failing of Maturana's philosophy is that it makes it difficult to understand our disunity as well as our unity); technologies, techniques, are our inevitable but wildly varying attributes. Although technology defined narrowly (machine technology, etc.) is readily identified, more useful definitions—which, following Mumford, include techniques and containers as well as tools—blur into definitions of life itself. Life is haunted by automatism, and automatism by life, with no breach between. Time is not threatened, but always already permeated, by the automatism of life.

Teleology and eschatology fall by the wayside; the copestone is never added. Life and its techniques are unstable and ever-changing: there is no moment when life suddenly becomes technology, or vice versa. We *experience* those moments, but we experience them, like the domus's remembered embrace, as myth; the automaton has never arrived, because it is forever with us. We witness the arrival of megalopolis, yet it is as old as ants and termites. War, oppression, and slavery are, of course, real: one of these events one day will be a bottleneck too tight to pass, but this will not be an ontological crisis: it will be death. The crisis is real enough, but it is a condition of life as such and not of a particular, privileged historical moment.

Nor is the crisis of mechanization only a human experience. Opening "the beaver's tale," Richard Dawkins defines *phenotype* as "that which is influenced by genes," or the "external and visible manifestation of the hidden genotype" (*Ancestor* 186). A giraffe's phenotype would include its long neck and coloration. But the beaver's phenotype, the external manifestation of its genotype, is not bounded by its body: "Beavers have lake phenotypes, caused by dam phenotypes. A lake is an *extended phenotype,*" the extension of the phenotype from the body out into the world (187). More dramatically than most other animals' genes, the beaver's reach far beyond its body, which displays once again the limits of thinking of life only in terms of autopoiesis; doing so annihilates life's most interesting territory, where "inside" and "outside" are indistinguishable. For Dawkins, with Descartes looming behind him, the beaver is a machine of tremendous complexity:

> Dam-building behavior is a complicated stereotypy, built into the brain like a fine-tuned clockwork mechanism. . . . I have seen a remarkable film of captive beavers imprisoned in a bare, unfurnished cage, with no water and no wood. The beavers enacted, "in a vacuum," all the stereotyped movements normally seen in natural building behavior when there is real wood and real water. They seem to be placing virtual wood into a virtual dam wall, pathetically trying to build a ghost wall with ghost sticks. . . . One feels sorry

> for them: it is as if they are desperate to exercise their frustrated dam-building clockwork. (189)

The beaver's automatism, its insistence on reenactment or dramatization of its "natural" behavior, is pitiful. But is not our pity for the beaver also for ourselves, trapped under domination? The mastery of human movement to which the likes of Frederick Winslow Taylor aspired surely resembles the beaver's automatism. Bergson writes: "Our freedom, in the very movements by which it is affirmed, creates the growing habits that will stifle it if it fails to renew itself by a constant effort: it is dogged by automatism. The most living thought becomes frigid in the formula that expresses it. The word turns against the idea" (*Creative* 127). The beaver's phenotype, the expression of its genotype in the world, implies pure and hopeless automatism. Dawkins's comparison to "the history of clocks in the electronic age" is telling; as Michael Adas has documented, the developing clock and the temporal structure of the railroad which it enables have been central tools in the construction and teaching of Western ideologies: "Time became a factor to be controlled by the ascendant middle classes" (226, 251). Is the beaver in its frustrated clockwork movements middle class, or under middle-class tutelage/oppression? The question, while amusing, is not trivial: though we might protest that the order *we* impose on the world is more flexible and "self-aware" than the beaver's, our genetic differences from the beaver are rather subtle. We are close kin. We might, surely, compare the beaver's caged automatism to the automatism to which the prison system has always aspired. But, Dawkins might protest, the beaver is, unlike us, only a genetic machine.

Surely. Yet the beaver enacts a ritual; it takes part in a drama, a backwards look at the domus, before the arrival of the megalopolis (the cage). It expends energy in hopeless, pathetic protest (as political prisoners do). The beaver's resistance to its mechanization, the reinscription of its meaning in the cage, is itself mechanical. If the beaver's ritual, drama, and protest are only mechanical, then ours are also in danger of mechanization. Conversely, an attempt to save some fragment of human freedom from the consequences of biology, as in Lewontin's work, must also erode the pure hopelessness of the beaver's situation. Following Wolfe's reading of Derrida, the beaver does not simply represent "the animal," which is equivalent in Dawkins (as in Descartes) to "the machine"; it is one of many animals, including the human animal, each with its own potential. Wolfe makes the critical point that the philosophical wing of the animal rights movement has helped to clarify that, as science exposes the animality of "the human," animal rights are necessary, if nothing else, to secure human rights.

Early in *The Voyage of the Beagle,* the foundation of his work, Charles Darwin describes the hopeless resistance of black Brazilians to slavery: "This spot is notorious from having been, for a long time, the residence of some runaway slaves, who, by cultivating a little ground near the top, contrived to eke out a subsistence. At length they were discovered, and a party of soldiers being sent, the whole were seized with the exception of one old woman, who, sooner than again be led into slavery, dashed herself to pieces from the summit of the mountain. In a Roman matron this would have been called the noble love of freedom: in a poor negress it is mere brutal obstinacy" (19). One wonders what techniques the escaped slaves developed on their mountain. Darwin is silent on these matters, for the "brutal obstinacy" of the "negress" is hopeless automatism, not thought; it is a beaver's empty ritual in a cage without escape, to be pitied, not analyzed. The march of Western man has overtaken and eclipsed her. Yet the prisoner's automatism haunts us; under the gaze of the slave and the animal, our own clockwork automatically twitches in recognition, and "we" struggle in the web, poor flies, to escape the automatism "we" see in "them."

Perhaps the slave sees differently. After the end, after one's own automatism is revealed, much remains to be done. Something may come of this masquerade, at least once the story of progress has been destroyed. But we have seen that the story of progress, of eschatological change, insistently returns. I turn to Giorgio Agamben's *Homo Sacer* and, briefly, *The Open,* for an example of contemporary thought that is able to thoroughly demolish the notion of a true barrier between nature and culture yet remains enmeshed in eschatology; as with Haraway, Agamben reinscribes the *eschatos* while destroying it.

In Agamben's *Homo Sacer,* an analysis of Western culture and politics ranging from Hobbes to Heidegger and Rome to Dachau, we find the double assertion that, first, the state's sovereign power is rooted in a particular understanding of nature, and second, that this state of nature, following Hobbes, "did not necessarily have to be conceived as a real epoch, but rather could be understood as a principle internal to the State" (36). The state of nature with which the state justifies itself exists only *theoretically,* yet creates the state of exception through which sovereign power is exercised: "the *nomos* is necessarily connected with both the state of nature and the state of exception. . . . [They] are nothing but two sides of a single topological process in which what was presupposed as external (the state of nature) now appears, as in a Möbius strip or a Leyden jar, in the inside (as state of exception), and the sovereign power is this very impossibility of distinguishing between outside and inside, nature and exception, *physis* and *nomos*" (37). "*Not simple natural life, but life exposed to death (bare life or sacred life) is the originary political element,*" Agamben argues, in an analysis of Rome (88). *Bios,* political life, is rooted in, contrasted to, and threatened by reduction to bare life. In *The Open,* Agamben extends the argument, claiming that in the West the conflict "which governs every other conflict, is that between the animality and the humanity of man. . . . Western politics is also biopolitics" (80). The reduction of human to animal is the end of history, which terminated roughly with Heidegger: "post-history was beginning to knock on the doors of a concluded metaphysics" (75).

Agamben is concerned with interlocked crises in the state and philosophy, in which the (concentration) camp (which I connect to the beaver's cage) "signals the political space of modernity itself" (*Homo Sacer* 174). The traditional order collapses: "Something can no longer function within the traditional mechanisms that regulated this inscription [of bare life], and the camp is the new, hidden regulator of the inscription of life in the order—or, rather, the sign of the system's inability to function without being transformed into a lethal machine" (175).

Although Agamben struggles to avoid analyzing modernity in mechanistic terms, he plummets into this language in due course. The camp is created when the inscription of bare life into the political order fails; it is created as a machine for destruction, a machine equated with modernity itself. Inevitably, once the machine's specter is conjured, the shade of nature appears as its rival, despite Agamben's earlier critique of the reality of the "state of nature":

> Just as the biopolitical body of the West cannot be simply given back to its *natural life* [emphasis added] in the *oikos,* so it cannot be overcome in a passage to a new body—a technical body or a wholly political or glorious body—in which a different economy of pleasures and vital functions would once and for all resolve the interlacement of *zoē* and *bios* that seems to define the political destiny of the West. This biopolitical body that is bare life must itself instead be transformed into the site for the constitution and installation of a form of life that is wholly exhausted in bare life and a *bios* that is only its own *zoē.* Here attention will also have to be given to the analogies between politics and the epochal situation of metaphysics. (*Homo Sacer* 188)

Once we had a natural life in the *oikos,* but we can neither return to it nor replace it with a new, technological body; we have arrived at a political and metaphysical *telos* in which the natural order of the *oikos* has been replaced by the camp's mechanical order.

It's a curious ending for Agamben, who convincingly argues that the state of nature is a theoretical category imposed on history, not a truly historical category. The story of civilization as movement from state of nature to mechanized and mechanizing nation-state, from *arche* to *telos,* is precisely the imposition that *is* history. Agamben falls, eyes wide open, into the trap, reinscribing the teleological story of the technological nation-state, the locomotive that has, yet again, arrived at our very moment, the *telos,* the hinge upon which history turns.

For Agamben, brilliantly following Benjamin, we cannot escape messianic thinking, which is connected to the state of exception and the formation of the state on the most intimate level, and yet defies it. Messianism is the point where religion "passes beyond itself and calls itself into question insofar as it is law (hence the messianic aporias concerning the Law that are expressed in both Paul's Epistle to the Romans and the Sabbatian doctrine according to which the fulfillment of the Torah is its transgression)" (*Homo Sacer* 56). In the state of exception, as with the Messiah's arrival, the execution and transgression of the law blur. Thus, the law is "fulfilled and consummated. But this fulfillment does not signify that the old law is simply replaced by a new law that is homologous to the old. . . .

What is implied instead is that the fulfillment of the Torah now coincides with its transgression" (57). Agamben's parenthetical reference to Paul's epistle to the Romans is almost too subtle. Agamben refers, most directly, to Romans 10:4: "Telos gar nomou kristos eis dikaiosunē panti tô pisteuonti"; in the New Revised Standard translation: "For Christ is the end of the law so that there may be righteousness for everyone who believes." The translation is beautiful but necessarily incomplete; it inevitably fails to capture the complexity of *telos* ("end," which, ironically, *begins* the Greek sentence): Christ is the end-as-cessation *and* end-as-fulfillment of the law. The law dooms us, devours us, and yet is just. We can only escape the law through the law. "For the letter kills, but the Spirit gives life" (2 Corinthians 3:6). Thus the frustrating ambiguity of Paul's relationship to the Roman state, which he both endorses and surely hopes to see pass away. For Paul, life is a conflict between kinds of slavery: "with my mind I am a slave [*douleuô*] to the law [*nomos*] of God, but with my flesh [*sarki*] I am a slave to the law of sin [*amartias*]" (Romans 7:26). To understand Agamben's theology, it helps to note that when Paul affirms his flesh's enslavement to sin, he uses the same word for flesh as John 1:14: "And the Word [*logos*] became flesh [*sarx*] and lived among us, and we have seen his glory [*doxan*], the glory as of a father's only son, full of grace and truth [*aletheias*]." One might even speculate that the author of John intended this as a development of Paul's theology: the *precise* flesh enslaved to the law of sin is the *precise* flesh that the *logos* becomes. Thus the extremity of the messianic transgression of which Agamben speaks; abused and abusing, enslaved and brutalized matter *is* the messiah. There is a difficulty in the relationship Agamben establishes between *bios* and *zoē:* given that his work engages the history of Judaism and Christianity as well as the history of philosophy, where is *sarkis,* flesh, in this transaction? This is a whole theological dimension of the text that speaks only through its absence (Paul, the ex-torturer, is already familiar, I submit, with bare life, and would have much to say regarding our own "state of exception").

My attempt to force Agamben from Paul to John is significant to my own text. I have demonstrated that the history of attitudes toward "modern technology" is a history of eschatology, an eschatology that makes Darwin's Negro into a savage and a slave, the beaver into clockwork,

Melville's sailor into a pendulum, and which leads to the eschatological dread of mechanization (partially because the master sees his own mechanism laid bare in the slave), which leads, for example, to Heidegger's Nazism. Agamben asserts that "there is no return from the camps to classical politics," as there is no return from technics to a pre-technical existence (*Homo Sacer* 188). But the experience of Dawkins's beaver is already the experience of the camp; one need not be human to both be an automaton and to struggle wildly against automatism. There never was a *bios* or a *zoē* that was not already *technē* and *sarkis*. We all, as Wolfe acknowledges, must submit to the inhumanity (which perhaps should be "inanimality") of time.

The *eschatos* has always already come. I have presented this argument from my readings of Melville, Faulkner, and Ellison, and now more theoretically: the technological crisis that threatens life is the crisis that, following Bergson, constitutes life as the vital force struggling against inevitable automatism. Life shapes and is shaped by the life around it. If it shapes or is shaped wrongly, it dies. Life is nothing but change, which is nothing but the exercise of technique.

How do we survive an *eschatos* always already past, which renders us as *technē-sarkis-zoē*? The answer in Melville, Faulkner, and Ellison is that we find a new way of understanding time, one in which the erasure of our original innocence of the machine (or freedom from it) renders it unsurprising that we have survived the "eschatos" which in reality constitutes us. Refusing a technological Eden, we undermine the technological *eschatos*. The masquerade continues.

I turn to the words of Victor Frankenstein, under his father's care as he is transported from colonized, brutalized Ireland, where he lost his beloved Henry, to Switzerland, where he will lose his sister-wife and father: "My father, who was watching over me, perceiving my restlessness, awoke me; the dashing waves were around; the cloudy sky above; the fiend was not here: a sense of security, a feeling that a truce was established between the present hour and the irresistible, disastrous future" (Shelley 188). What Victor doesn't know, with the threat of inhuman antinature looming on the domus's horizon, is that the *monster* has grown sick of violence and has declared a unilateral truce, which he will ultimately violate because Victor dares to return to the compulsory heterosexuality of union with Elizabeth. It is only Victor's absolute rejection of the monster, and his absolute obligation to marry his sister-wife, which keep the truce from being permanent. Victor's "irresistible, disastrous future" is brought on by his insistence on the absolute divide between nature and artifice, as demarcated by him, *no matter how loathsome he finds the obligations of a nature which he has already proven not to exist, by making the monster.* Frankenstein's disastrous future prefigures those of Ahab, Sutpen, and the Brotherhood, futures that can only be survived by slaves and confidence men. Technology does not destroy Victor Frankenstein, nor blackness Sutpen, nor violent nature Ahab. Frankenstein is destroyed by his own border war, his insistence on the reality of the border between nature and culture *which he himself has annihilated;* Sutpen and Ahab similarly insist on the boundaries they have erased. The Confidence Man, Ishmael, and the invisible man endure, however. They have witnessed the "the breaking-up of the icebound stream of Time," in which teleology exists in the teeth of chaos, and all things are subject to change, as well as to destruction, but not to any *end* (*Moby-Dick* 13).

Science fiction is the field that may further develop this masquerade; the art form most mesmerized by technical progress is the field in which progress may be fully debunked. Darko Suvin argues in *The Metamorphoses of Science Fiction* (1979) that one task of science fiction is to think of history without ending: "[cognitive] validation for SF [is] being based on science as an open-ended corpus of knowledge, which . . . [is] anchored to the bedrock fact that there is no end to history, and in particular that we and our ideologies are not the end-product history has been laboring for from the time of the first saber-toothed tigers and Mesopotamian city-states. It follows that SF will be the more significant and truly relevant the more clearly it eschews final solutions" (83). Suvin argues that secular science fiction is dominated by the temporality of Revelation, a temporality reproduced even by Agamben and Lyotard (83). Suvin, of course, does not reject progress, but only *endings,* and implicitly favors a Kantian teleology over one directly rooted in Revelation. I find the potential for a broader abandonment of progress in Octavia Butler's science fiction, which I will discuss by way of Donna Haraway.

Although Haraway insistently reinscribes the salvation history that she attempts to overthrow, her work remains critical for me: she recognizes that acknowledging continuity among human, animal, and machine (particularly in the problematically messianic figure of the cyborg) is necessary for an alternative to salvation history. One of my project's origins is Haraway's brief commentary at the end of her book *Primate Visions* (1989) on Octavia Butler's *Xenogenesis* trilogy. Haraway, for all of her insight in her commentary upon Butler, characteristically errs by reinscribing Butler as salvation history. Butler begins, however, by satirizing salvation history; the remainder of *Xenogenesis* concerns humanity's struggle to think beyond it.

Whereas Faulkner imagines the world post-*eschatos,* and Ellison imagines the *beginning* of a liberating post-eschatological politics, Butler struggles with the hard question: What do life and politics look like when they are stripped of *telos* and *eschatos*? Who are we, after abandoning our *ends*? Her answers, although only a beginning, go even further than Ellison's. A detailed exploration of that answer and its importance must wait for another project, but I will make an initial gesture now, by way of Haraway.

The first book of the trilogy, *Dawn,* begins with a masquerade, a false *eschatos:* humanity has seemingly been annihilated by nuclear war. But "coincidentally" the Oankali, a "species" characterized by the ability and need to manipulate the genes of themselves and others, ambiguously rescue the remnants of humanity. As Haraway succinctly explains, "their nature is always to be midwife to themselves as other" (*Primate* 379). The Oankali make little use of "machines" in the sense of metal and plastic artifacts. Rather, they sculpt *life* to suit all their needs; their *technē* operates only upon *bios.* They intend a "trade" with humanity wherein humanity will become both Oankali and raw material for Oankali exploitation: we are simultaneously freed for future projects and turned into perfect automatons by the very process that rescues us from the *eschatos.*

Haraway, characteristically, both accepts and rejects *Xenogenesis* as salvation history. Traditional messianism is eschewed, but something else is substituted for it in Haraway's reading: "Butler writes not of Cain or Ham, but of Lilith, the woman of color whose confrontations with the terms of selfhood, survival, and reproduction in the face of repeated ultimate catastrophe presage an ironic salvation history, with a salutary twist on the promise of a woman who will crush the head of the serpent. Butler's salvation history is not utopian" (*Primate* 378). *Dawn* chronicles humanity's discovery of itself as standing-reserve for the Oankali, while detailing ongoing intrahuman conflict. The trilogy's second book, *Adulthood Rites,* is the story of the first male human-Oankali "construct," who convinces his elders that humanity ought to survive genetically unaltered, to reenact its *telos,* if it can do nothing else (the image of the *telos* haunting this remnant seems like an Ellisonian ritual). This seems like a victory for humanity and its teleological history. But the third book, *Imago,* is the story of the first human-Oankali construct ooloi (a third sex, which manipulates genes but does not pass its own genes on), who in something like a messianic moment confronts the most intransigent of purely human settlements; these resisters fall over themselves to be seduced by it into inhumanity. The repeated, disastrous future for an unaltered humanity that was offered in the second book is withdrawn in the third, in favor of humanity's willing embrace of the inhuman; humanity chooses to become "itself as other," to become standing-reserve and survive.

Pure humanity wills itself out of existence. Its future as Oankali, spreading across the galaxy, is to continually breed with other life-forms. The Oankali's changes and adaptations, their technologies, are endless. All Oankali may eventually die, but they will die one by one, on different sides of the galaxy, for endlessly varied reasons. There is no scent of ideology, of "progress," in what the Oankali do. Their drive to change, to adapt, is essentially sexual: as, perhaps, is our own.

Like Ellison and Melville, but also meditating on the same consequences of contemporary biology that spawned Lewontin's and Gould's rejection of evolutionary progress, and parallel to Pacey's, Edgerton's, and Basalla's rejection of technological progress, Butler presents the Oankali as the unshamed and exaggerated mirror of earthly life, which is nothing but change, adaptation, and appropriation of life as standing-reserve.

In Butler's novels *Parable of the Sower* and *Parable of the Talents,* the main character, a young black woman who passes through the destruction of her family, the death of her husband, the loss of her child, rape, and slavery to establish a new religion, builds that religion on a simple premise: "God is Change"; that very idea, incidentally, is among Bergson's assertions in *Creative Evolution:* the only prescription against automatism is change. Butler, unlike Bergson, refuses to make that change (which both writers identify literally as God) into progress. It is life as *process,* which is neither progress nor bare life.

American literature has been marked, as Leo Marx and Lewis Mumford prominently understood, by the conflict between nature and culture. The genuine contrast between what was easily (but problematically) understood as frontier on the one hand and intensive mechanization on the other hand has made this contrast prominent in American thought. Unlike the metaphysicians, various American artists understood that the eschatological confrontation between nature and culture, human and machine, is theoretical, not historical, and were thus able to understand life as process, not progress, in advance of the historians of biology and technology.

I reject salvation history; there is no "crisis in modernity," no domination that particularly privileges our historical moment. We confront no crisis in time (although many in the world) other than that which continually constitutes all life. Technology has not suddenly become ascendant over life; life is technological. The relationship between *bios* and *technē* is not, therefore, a sudden metaphysical or ontological problem, but it opens endless pragmatic *ethical* problems, related to the problems of "the human" and "animals" addressed by Wolfe, as well as Agamben's tension between *bios* and "bare life." This is the business of life, but it is also the business of science fiction, which is—not only in our age of the cyborg, as Donna Haraway argues, but in all ages—really the same thing.

Afterword

My favorite definition of the novel, although perhaps not the most accurate one, is "a long prose narrative with something wrong with the ending." As with the novel, so with criticism, perhaps doubly so: endings disappoint. Endings do not disappoint only through their individual failures: a plot thread neglected, an argument forgotten, a critical source uncited. They disappoint structurally: they must simultaneously close one text and open possibilities for others; apocalyptic narratives, in criticism and in fiction, tend to avoid *opening,* which is one source of their appeal to both readers and writers. Simultaneously closing and opening is a task few endings even approximate.

All ways of ending are problematic: ending abruptly and gradually, singly and multiply, are equally fraught with peril. My own choice, to end doubly, appropriately has a double goal: first, to explain the path I have taken through a particular maze of topics, by way of acknowledging discourses I have, to greater or lesser extents, neglected; and second, somewhat perversely, to show the very lack of faith in *ends* which the project has pursued from the beginning. In my case, it was suggested to me as a way of positioning the book within contemporary discourses, which explains my first goal; the very alteration in the structure, though, is useful for the second goal.

I have attempted to explain how, in American culture and in Western culture more broadly, the dominant understanding of technology sees it as a teleological force, one continually on the brink of ending time and history as we know them, of bringing the *eschatos,* perhaps not with the arrival of God or the literal end of the world, but with the mechanization of the *self.* My argument is that this understanding of time and technology is both incorrect and disastrous, and that a line of thought articulated in American literature exposes its errors.

This argument has necessitated that I discuss the teleological, eschatological aspects of mainstream thinking on technology, detail a literary alternative, and demonstrate the errors of the mainstream. My detailing of the literary alternative is, in fact, the heart of the book. For better or worse, this is essentially a book of literary criticism: when analyzing its strengths and weakness, inclusions and omissions, this fact is, I think, critical. My critique of the mainstream, teleological understanding of the relationship between time and technology has often become deeply involved in theoretical and philosophical issues, but it has always been rooted in the empirical claims of historians of technology. While I have spent much time and energy discussing philosophy and theory, and my interest in it is genuine, my strategy has been to conduct an empirical critique of philosophy and of mainstream ideology, one rooted in the history of philosophy as well as in a literary tradition, as well as in Bergson's distinctive philosophy, which is uniquely rooted in Darwin. Speaking simplistically, I have deployed literature and history (with the history verifying the literature, although the historians have operated in literature's wake) to conduct a critique on a hegemonic ideology, one that has subverted precisely those philosophers and theorists who try to critique it. From my own point of view, in fact, the book's greatest flaw is that it could be more empirical than it is—but such a shift would be fundamental, demanding a new book.

This talk of history leads me to one of the academic discourses I have discussed, but not as deeply as I might have. The discipline of world-systems analysis, as articulated by Immanuel Wallerstein and anticipated by Braudel, is significantly congruent with my project. This is a discipline, essentially historical but with theoretical roots, that draws upon Bergson and thus resists our habitual ways of thinking about history. Wallerstein analyzes the "capitalist world-system" in terms of the *longue durée:*

a system does not form or change as suddenly as we think, but *endures,* in this analysis. Without detailing either my interest in or my disagreements with Wallerstein, I need to at least position my project in relation to his important (and itself enduring) project. My essential difference from Wallerstein and his followers, and the reason I return directly to the Bergson of *Creative Evolution,* is that I never want to step too far away from analyzing humanity in terms of *bios* and *technē:* understanding humanity as existing within a system (in some ways, almost an autonomous system) is not illegitimate, but to my way of thinking it downplays the *biological* nature of change (earlier I explained my skepticism toward explaining life in terms of autopoiesis; this skepticism applies equally to larger, allegedly autopoietic social systems): my frequent connection of biology to technology is deliberate, and this particular deployment of Bergson and Basalla is not ultimately compatible with Wallerstein's thought. Without presenting a detailed argument, I argue that Wallerstein's approach, which has many virtues, nonetheless takes a teleological turn itself (precisely because of its distance from evolutionary thought). For Wallerstein, as for so many others, our moment is at least a fulcrum of history, the moment when the world-system is on the brink of transformation for the first time in centuries. At the end of his *World-Systems Analysis: An Introduction,* Wallerstein turns to the question of "constructing the successor system (or systems) to our existing one, [wherein] we shall be opting either for a hierarchical system . . . or for a relatively democratic, relatively egalitarian system" (89). The claim that the world-system is less stable now than in the depths of World War II is remarkable, and ultimately ideological: our moment *must* be the turning point. Thus, ultimately, I eschew extensive use of systems analysis (despite my great admiration for Wallerstein) for a more (to my mind) empirical approach.

Although I have touched on my skepticism of Maturana and Varela's autopoiesis, which is important to the foundation of systems analysis, in order to clarify one of my own central positions I must briefly discuss my objection to thinking of life as strictly an autopoietic machine. Thinking in terms of autopoiesis (a useful term, which helps us to analyze the homeostatic characteristics of all organisms), focusing strictly on *internal* processes, may help us to discard teleology, but in the process we turn life into an automaton once more, albeit now a purposeless one.

The one defining characteristic of life, in terms of autopoiesis, is that it is a self-producing machine. It is what it *is* and not what it *does,* or, at best, it is what it does *internally* rather than in the world. I submit that finding some kind of freedom against automatism (following Bergson) involves focusing on what life *does:* its creativity, its changeability, its being-in-the-world. Hence, the importance of understanding *technē* as an aspect of *bios,* not *bios* as a variety of *technē.* My objection to systems analysis, autopoiesis, cybernetic varieties of posthumanism, and so forth is ultimately Bergsonian: life *acts.*

Many readers will find it questionable that I have written a book about literature and technology yet say little about computers, and only tangentially deal with cybernetics and posthumanism. To explore my choices fully would have led me astray from my main purpose, but I can offer a brief explanation. The assumption of cybernetic thought and its descendants (which Hayles details in *How We Became Posthuman*) is that life, or even the universe itself, *is* information. More modest thinkers have disagreed or treated the issue with more nuance, but I would argue that posthumanist and cybernetic thought has treated our historical moment as the *eschatos,* where *bios* stands revealed as a form of *technē.* My position, again, is precisely the opposite: that *technē* has always been an aspect of *bios,* of *all* life, not merely our own.

From another angle, I disagree with the implicit premise that our current information technologies are a revolutionary force that opens a fundamentally new way of understanding the world. Daniel Headrick's *When Information Came of Age* wonderfully analyzes the long development (*longue durée*) of the "information age." Richard Lewontin provides in *Biology as Ideology* a detailed critique of the tendency to see DNA as software, which is a prerequisite for an intellectually plausible attempt to understand life as information. On a more personal note, as someone who worked for several years in Dilbert's world, writing C and SQL code with accountants and financial aid processors as my clients, I find myself intensely skeptical of those who see computation as a kind of underlying reality rather than as a crude but powerful prosthesis. I may, in time, have more to say to say about teleologies that revolve around computation, but at this point I don't think they require any special attention or that there is anything generally revolutionary about our information technologies (despite the many revolutions they have wrought in particular professions).

I turn, finally, to a discourse I have addressed little but which, to my mind, is closely connected to my work. Serious ecocriticism, as well as forms of posthumanism (Wolfe's development of Derrida is exemplary) that focus on animals rather than computation, have a certain kinship with my work. My hardly unique difficulty with much of ecocriticism is the common, implicit assumption that there is some original "nature" that we can imagine or access. Despite this difficulty, and the perhaps greater difficulty that I find much ecocriticism to be uncritically eschatological (I speak not of rhetoric attending to particular material crises, which are usually real enough, but to more generalized and spiritualized rhetorics), I believe that the intellectual and political work of ecocriticism can be advanced through adopting an anti-teleological understanding of the relationship between time and technology. Technology does not kill time; the wrong technologies at the wrong time do, however, kill animals, ecosystems, and very likely us. I hope, in short, that my work (to say nothing of the historians of technology upon whom I draw) can be useful to ecocriticism, although I have made only an initial gesture in that direction myself.

On this note, which indicates the political as well as the intellectual possibilities that I hope this work will open, I end again. There is more to be said, but these things are beyond the scope of this, my second ending.

Notes

Introduction

1. Critiques of the anthropic principle abound; N. Katherine Hayles dissects it in some detail in *My Mother Was a Computer* (220).

Chapter 1

1. The four gospels have differing concepts of time, from the already-finished nature of time in John to the intense *nowness* of time's crisis in Mark. Only in Revelation does "our" notion of a prolonged supervision of time emerge.

2. "The Monad, of which we will speak here, is nothing else than a simple substance, which goes to make up composites" (Leibniz 251).

Chapter 2

1. On Father Mapple's logocentrism see Eric Wilson's "The Nomad, the Pilgrim, and the White Whale."

2. See Daniel Headrick's *The Tools of Empire* on the central role of specific military technologies in Western colonialism, and Manuel De Landa's *War in the Age of Intelligent Machines* on the mechanization of the self necessary for the prosecution of Western-style wars.

3. Mayr 119. One of the most interesting sections in Mayr's book is his discussion of an ongoing proxy debate between Newton and Leibniz about whether or not the world is essentially clockwork: Newton says nay, Leibniz says yea. Hobbes, of course, makes an analogy between the state and a clockwork automaton.

4. See David Mitchell's "'Too Much of a Cripple'" and Kris Lackey's "More Spiritual Terrors," as well as C. L. R. James's *Mariners, Renegades, and Castaways.*

5. One way to make this argument would be to connect *Moby-Dick* and *A Connecticut Yankee in King Arthur's Court* with the development of scientific management and the assembly line, using Siegfried Giedeon's *Mechanization Takes Command* (1948) and David Noble's *America by Design* (1977). Giedion argues that the assembly line was developed early in the nineteenth century by the Cincinnati (later Chicago) meatpacking industry; although he doesn't mention whaling specifically, that seems like a natural extension of his argument. Twain's engineer, of course, is equally an inventor and a manager, who makes factories to produce goods but metaphorizes his project as a whole as "a man factory." The complexity in Twain's work is that the engineer sees the manufactured men as free and authentic men.

Chapter 3

1. Lynn White and others also emphasize the medieval origin of power machinery. The "industrial revolution" as we know it describes changes in management techniques (epitomized by Taylor's scientific management and the rise of formalized engineering) more than a sudden shift in technologies.

2. *Technics and Human Development* 229. Mumford anticipates De Landa and parallels Deleuze in some respects. See also Victor Hanson's *The Western Way of War* on this subject. Hanson—now a neoconservative pundit—emphasizes the shocking, inhuman horror of phalanx warfare and the near-total lack of skill of Greek soldiers. Submission to total discipline was far more important than any particular combat skills.

3. This point would take a book to elaborate. Mumford's story of the development of technics in *The Myth of the Machine* is rooted in *Technics and Civilization,* and his account of medieval history has parallels to Lynn White's account (Mumford draws guarded praise in White's *Medieval Religion and Technology*). Whether or not *The Myth of the Machine* is sound, it has its origins in sound scholarship; if it is mad, it's mad like Ahab, who is mad in his purpose but utterly sound in his method.

4. Michael Zuckerman details this consensus and his opposition to it in "Faith, Hope, Not Much Charity: The Optimistic Epistemology of Lewis Mumford." He focuses on the element of hope in the late Mumford, but I argue that Mumford is fun-

damentally pessimistic because he envisions a humanity fallen into posthuman servitude, even if that servitude is still not inescapable.

5. It is important to note that Melville was personally and psychologically important to Mumford while Mumford was writing a book (*Technics and Civilization*) *seemingly* unrelated to Melville.

6. Raymond Weaver *was* a Nietzschean reader of Melville. In a discussion of the public's failure to recognize Melville, he writes: "The herd must always be intolerant of all who violate its sacred and painfully reared traditions" (18). Weaver uses Nietzsche to discuss the humor in *Moby-Dick* (332). He considers Melville is both a tablet smasher, as idealized in Nietzsche's *Thus Spake Zarathustra,* and an advocate of the "gay science." Weaver's biography has been badly mistreated, beginning with Mumford's attack on it, but that's a subject for another time.

7. Spark 258. The letter she quotes is printed in Mumford, *My Works and Days* 292–93.

Chapter 4

1. *Light in August* is not as directly concerned with cotton as with timber, but the cotton industry—because it exhausted the soil—also existed on a relatively short clock. The fundamentally temporary nature of cotton farming is one reason behind the westward spread of the United States. *Absalom, Absalom* and the Snopes trilogy take up this theme.

2. Note also the role of machinery in the plantation system. A focus on the United States obscures this point, but the heart of the plantation system, the sugar-growing areas of the Caribbean and Brazil, involved sugar mills, which were complex and expensive mechanical systems. For details see Philip Curtin's *The Rise and Fall of the Plantation Complex: Essays in Atlantic History.* Also see Wallerstein and Nye's *Electrifying America,* respectively, on the early integration of the South into the capitalist world-system and the ways in which mechanization often *preceded* agriculture in the United States.

3. Similarly, Theresa Towner argues in *Faulkner on the Color Line* that one of the central effects of the Snopes trilogy, especially through its conscious use of a nearly all-white cast, is to lay bare an ideology of whiteness (79).

Chapter 5

1. I make this attribution partially because of Jackson's authority as Ellison's biographer but also because the editorial's style is thoroughly Ellisonian, unlike Herndon's transparent lucidity in the following article.

2. For lack of any evidence to the contrary, I attribute this editorial to both Herndon and Ellison. The style is distinctly Ellisonian, but its Marxism and internationalism, although hardly anti-Ellisonian, seem to bear Herndon's mark.

3. Dostoyevsky's text responds to Chernyshevsky's 1863 utopian novel *What Is to Be Done?* (a major influence on Lenin); Ellison deploys Dostoyevsky's antisocialist nationalism to support his own.

4. Ellison critics often confuse science with technology. In "'Riffing' and Paradigm Building" (1987), John Callahan emphasizes Ellison's interest in "the theory and practice of science and technology" (93). He silently accepts science's hegemony over technology, perpetuating what Giedion calls the anonymity of technology, which, I assert in the spirit of *Technology and the African-American Experience,* in turn silently perpetuates and mirrors racial hierarchies.

5. See Portia James's "'To Collect Proof of Colored Talent and Ingenuity': African-American Invention and Innovation, 1619–1930." Black inventors weren't always fully silenced; see Bruce Sinclair's "Pictures from an Exhibition," which discusses Thomas Calloway and W. E. B. Du Bois's exhibit in the Palace of Social Economy at the 1900 Paris Exposition. See also *The Negro Artisan* (1902), edited by Du Bois, which argues that "Negro machinists were also becoming numerous before the downfall of slavery." Many southern railroads had all-black crews, excepting only the conductor (17). Although Trueblood sharecropped, his grandfather or great-grandfather might have been an engineer.

6. Ellison also refers to Freudian automatism, which is, as Freud acknowledges in *Wit and Its Relation to the Unconscious,* indebted to Bergson's idea of automatism (761). There is no conflict between Freudian and Bergsonian automatism; Ellison invokes them simultaneously.

Conclusion

1. While Lyotard's acknowledgment that humans are, in a sense, created by technology might seem to place him in the same realm as Maturana and Varela, who argue that life is best defined as an autopoietic machine, Lyotard's emphasis is on information filtered *into* the organism; Lyotard, unlike Maturana and Varela, focuses on the information an organism processes, not on the information that, in a sense, it *is.*

2. E. O. Wilson's *Sociobiology* is a relevant text, but exploring this issue in depth must wait for another book.

3. The omnipresence of death, in fact, points to what may be most problematic in Maturana and Varela's work: their notion of life as autopoiesis does nothing to explain the universality of death, and more particularly of organisms that are mortal

by their nature. They allow for the external disruption of life but not for the *universal* failure of *mere* autopoiesis: no organism (let alone the complex organisms such as ourselves, which are autopoietic at the second or third order), even in an ideal environment, can produce its systems indefinitely, for reasons that are surely evolutionary. Their attempt to subordinate evolution to autopoiesis, in other words, is an interesting failure.

Bibliography

Abromeit, John. "Marcuse's Critical Encounter with Heidegger." *Herbert Marcuse: A Critical Reader.* Ed. John Abromeit and W. Mark Cobb. New York: Routledge, 2004. 131–51.

Adams, Henry. *The Education of Henry Adams.* New York: Mariner, 2000.

Adas, Michael. *Machines as the Measure of Men: Science, Technology, and Ideologies of Western Dominance.* Ithaca: Cornell UP, 1989.

Adler, Joyce. *War in Melville's Imagination.* New York: New York UP, 1981.

Agamben, Giorgio. *Homo Sacer: Sovereign Power and Bare Life.* Trans. Daniel Heller-Roazen. Stanford: Stanford UP, 1998.

———. *The Open: Man and Animal.* Trans. Kevin Attell. Stanford: Stanford UP, 2004.

Aland, Barbara, Kurt Aland, Johannes Karavidopoulos, Carlo Martini, and Bruce Metzger, eds. *The Greek New Testament.* 4th rev. ed. Stuttgart: United Bible Societies, 1983.

Andriano, Joseph. "Brother to Dragons: Race and Evolution in *Moby-Dick.*" *ATQ* 10 (1996): 141–53.

Arac, Jonathan. "Toward a Critical Genealogy of the U.S. Discourse of Identity: *Invisible Man* after Fifty Years." *boundary 2* 30 (2003): 195–216.

Ausband, Stephen C. "The Whale and the Machine: An Approach to *Moby-Dick.*" *American Literature* 47 (1975): 197–211.

Basalla, George. *The Evolution of Technology.* New York: Cambridge UP, 1988.

Bell, Sarah. "William Faulkner's Creative Evolution: The Influence of Henri Bergson's Philosophy upon Three Major Novels." Diss. U of Georgia, 1990.

Benesch, Klaus. *Romantic Cyborgs: Authorship and Technology in the American Renaissance.* Amherst: U of Massachusetts P, 2002.

———. "Technology Writ Large: The Machine, the Body, and the Text in Melville's Shorter Narratives." *Weber Studies* 14.3 (1997): 61–72.

Benjamin, Walter. *Illuminations.* Trans. Harry Zohn. New York: Schocken Books, 1968.

Bergson, Henri. *Creative Evolution.* Trans. Arthur Mitchell. Dover: Mineola, 1998.

———. *Duration and Simultaneity, with Reference to Einstein's Theory.* Trans. Leon Jacobsen. Indianapolis: Bobbs-Merrill, 1965.

———. *Time and Free Will: An Essay on the Immediate Data of Consciousness.* Trans. F. L. Pogson. New York: Dover, 2002.

———. *The Two Sources of Morality and Religion.* Trans. R. Ashley Audra and Cloudesley Brereton. Westport: Greenwood P, 1935.

Berthold, Michael C. "The Prison World of Melville's *Pierre* and 'Bartleby.'" *ESQ* 33 (1987): 237–252.

Birk, John F. "Unsealing the Sphinx: The *Pequod's* Egyptian Pantheon." *ATQ* 5 (1991): 283–99.

Blake, Casey. "Mumford and Politics after Liberalism." *Lewis Mumford: Public Intellectual.* Ed. A. C. Hughes and T. P. Hughes. New York: Oxford UP, 1990. 283–300.

Blake, Susan L. "Black Folklore in the Works of Ralph Ellison." *PMLA* 94 (1979): 121–36.

Blotner, Joseph. *Faulkner: A Biography.* 1-vol. ed. New York: Random House, 1984.

Braudel, Fernand. *Afterthoughts on Material Civilization and Capitalism.* Trans. Patricia Ranum. Baltimore: Johns Hopkins UP, 1977.

———. *Capitalism and Material Life: 1400–1800.* Trans. Miriam Kochan. New York: Harper and Row, 1973.

Brevda, William. "Neon Light in August: Electric Signs in Faulkner's Fiction." *Faulkner and Popular Culture.* Ed. Ann Abadie and Doreen Fowler. Jackson: U of Mississippi P, 1990. 214–41.

Brooks, Cleanth. *William Faulkner: The Yoknapatawpha Country.* New Haven: Yale UP, 1963.

Buell, Lawrence. "Faulkner and the Claims of the Natural World." *Faulkner and the Natural World.* Ed. Ann Abadie and Donald Kartiganer. Jackson: UP of Mississippi, 1999. 1–18.

Bull, Malcolm. "On Making Ends Meet." *Apocalypse Theory and the Ends of the World.* Ed. Malcolm Bull. Cambridge, MA: Blackwell, 1995. 1–16.

Burke, Kenneth. "Ralph Ellison's Trueblooded *Bildungsroman.*" *Ralph Ellison's* Invisible Man: *A Casebook.* New York: Oxford UP, 2004. 65–79.

Butler, Octavia. *Adulthood Rites.* New York: Warner, 1988.

———. *Dawn.* New York: Warner, 1987.

———. *Imago.* New York: Warner, 1989.

———. *Parable of the Sower.* New York: Warner, 1995.

———. *Parable of the Talents.* New York: Warner, 1998.

Callahan, John. "'Riffing' and Paradigm Building: The Anomaly of Tradition and Innovation in *Invisible Man* and *The Structure of Scientific Revolutions.*" *Callaloo* 30 (1987): 91–102.

Carlyle, Thomas. *A Carlyle Reader.* Ed. G. B. Tennyson. New York: Cambridge UP, 1984.

Carney, Judith. "Landscapes of Technology Transfer: Rice Cultivation and African Continuities." *Technology and the African-American Experience: Needs and Opportunities for Study.* Ed. Bruce Sinclair. Cambridge: MIT P, 2004. 18–49.

Clipper, Lawrence J. "Folkloric and Mythic Elements in *Invisible Man.*" *CLA Journal* 30 (1970): 229–41.

Colatrella, Carol. *Literature and Moral Reform: Melville and the Discipline of Reading.* Gainesville: UP of Florida, 2002.

Cook, Jonathan. *Satirical Apocalypse: An Anatomy of Melville's* The Confidence-Man. Westport: Greenwood P, 1996.

Cowley, Malcolm. Introduction. *The Portable Faulkner.* Ed. Malcolm Cowley. New York: Penguin, 1977. vii–xxxi.

Curtin, Philip D. *The Rise and Fall of the Plantation Complex: Essays in Atlantic History.* New York: Cambridge UP, 1998.

Dale, Corinne. "*Absalom, Absalom!* and the Snopes Trilogy: Southern Patriarchy in Revision." *Mississippi Quarterly* 14 (1992): 323–37.

Darwin, Charles. *The Voyage of the Beagle.* New York: Modern Library, 2001.

Dawkins, Richard. *Ancestor's Tale: Pilgrimage to the Dawn of Evolution.* Boston: Houghton Mifflin, 2004.

De Landa, Manuel. *War in the Age of Intelligent Machines.* Swerve Editions. New York: Zone Books, 1991.

Deleuze, Gilles. "Bartleby; Or, the Formula." *Essays Critical and Clinical.* Trans. Daniel W. Smith and Michael Greco. Minneapolis: U of Minnesota P, 1997. 68–90.

Deleuze, Gilles, and Félix Guattari. *A Thousand Plateaus: Capitalism and Schizophrenia.* Trans. Brian Massumi. Minneapolis: U of Minnesota P, 1987.

———. *What Is Philosophy?* Trans. Hugh Tomlinson and Graham Burchell. New York: Columbia UP, 1994.

Descartes, René. "Discourse on the Method." *Selected Philosophical Writings.* Trans. John Cottingham. New York: Cambridge UP, 1988. 21–56.

Dimitri, Carl. "*The Hamlet* and the Modernist Critique of Reason." *Renaissance and Modern Studies* 41 (1998): 47–59.

Dimock, Wai-Chee. *Empire for Liberty: Melville and the Poetics of Individualism.* Princeton: Princeton UP, 1989.

Dorn, Harold, and James E. McClellan III. *Science and Technology in World History: An Introduction.* Baltimore: Johns Hopkins UP, 1999.

Dostoevsky, Fyodor. *Notes from Underground.* Trans. Richard Pevear and Larissa Volokhonsky. New York: Vintage, 1993.

Douglass, Paul. *Bergson, Eliot, and American Literature.* Lexington: UP of Kentucky, 1986.

———. "Deleuze's Bergson." *The Crisis in Modernism.* Ed. Frederick Burwick and Paul Douglass. Cambridge: Cambridge UP, 1992. 368–88.

Du Bois, W. E. B., ed. *The Negro Artisan: Report of a Social Study Made Under the Direction of Atlanta University; Together with the Proceedings of the Seventh Conference for the Study of the Negro Problem.* Atlanta: Atlanta UP, 1902.

Edgerton, David. *The Shock of the Old: Technology and Global History since 1900.* New York: Oxford UP, 2007.

Ellison, Ralph Waldo. *The Collected Essays of Ralph Ellison.* New York: Modern Library, 1995.

———. "Editorial Comment." *Negro Quarterly* 1.2 (1942): i–v.

———. "Editorial Comment." *Negro Quarterly* 1.4 (1943): 295–302.

———. *Invisible Man.* New York: Vintage, 1995.

———. *Juneteenth.* Ed. John Callahan. New York: Vintage, 1999.

Ellison, Ralph Waldo, and Angelo Herndon. "Editorial Comment." *Negro Quarterly* 1.1 (1942): i–v.

Faulkner, William. *Absalom, Absalom! The Corrected Text.* New York: Vintage, 1986.

———. *As I Lay Dying.* In *Novels, 1930–1935: As I Lay Dying, Sanctuary, Light in August, Pylon.* New York: Library of America, 1985.

———. *Collected Stories.* New York: Vintage, 1995.

———. *Essays, Speeches, and Public Lecture.* Ed. James B. Meriwether. New York: Modern Library, 2004.

———. *Go Down, Moses.* In *Novels, 1942–1954.* Ed. Joseph Blotner and Noel Polk. New York: Library of America, 1985.

———. *Light in August.* In *Novels, 1936–1940.* Ed. Joseph Blotner and Noel Polk. New York: Library of America, 1985.

———. *Pylon.* In *Novels, 1930–1935: As I Lay Dying, Sanctuary, Light in August, Pylon.* New York: Library of America, 1985.

———. *Snopes: The Hamlet, the Town, and the Mansion.* New York: Modern Library, 1994.

Feenberg, Andrew. *Heidegger and Marcuse: The Catastrophe and Redemption of History.* New York: Routledge, 2005.

Ford, Douglas. "Crossroads and Cross-Currents in *Invisible Man.*" *Modern Fiction Studies* 45 (1999): 887–904.

Foucault, Michel. *Discipline and Punish: The Birth of the Prison.* Trans. Alan Sheridan. New York: Vintage, 1977.

———. *Madness and Civilization: A History of Insanity in the Age of Reason.* Trans. Richard Howard. New York: Vintage, 1965.

Fowler, Doreen. *Faulkner: The Return of the Repressed.* Charlottesville: UP of Virginia, 1997.

Fox, Richard. "Tragedy, Responsibility, and the Intellectual." *Lewis Mumford: Public Intellectual.* Ed. A. C. Hughes and T. P. Hughes. New York: Oxford UP, 1990. 323–37.

Franklin, Benjamin. *The Autobiography.* In *Writings.* New York: Library of America, 1987.

Frazer, James G. *The Golden Bough: A Study in Magic and Religion.* Abridged ed. New York: Macmillan, 1951.

Freud, Sigmund. *Wit and Its Relation to the Unconscious.* In *Basic Writings.* Trans. A. A. Brill. New York: Modern Library, 1995.

Friday, Krister. "Miscegenated Time: The Spectral Body, Race, and Temporality in *Light in August.*" *Faulkner Journal* 16 (2000–2001): 41–63.

Garrity-Blake, Barbara. "Raising Fish with a Song: Technology, Chanteys, and African-Americans in the Atlantic Menhaden Fishery." *Technology and the African-American Experience: Needs and Opportunities for Study.* Ed. Bruce Sinclair. Cambridge: MIT P, 2004. 109–17.

Gidley, Mick. "The Later Faulkner, Bergson, and God." *Mississippi Quarterly* 36 (1984): 377–84.

Giedion, Siegfried. *Mechanization Takes Command: A Contribution to Anonymous History.* New York: Oxford UP, 1948.

Gimpel, Jean. *The Medieval Machine: The Industrial Revolution of the Middle Ages.* New York: Barnes and Noble, 2000.

Godden, Richard. *Fictions of Labor: William Faulkner and the South's Long Revolution.* Cambridge: Cambridge UP, 1997.

Gould, Stephen Jay. *Full House: The Spread of Excellence from Plato to Darwin.* New York: Three Rivers P, 1996.

———. *The Mismeasure of Man.* Rev. ed. New York: Norton, 1996.

———. "On Replacing the Idea of Progress with an Operational Notion of Directionality." *The Philosophy of Biology.* Ed. Michael Ruse. New York: Oxford UP, 1998. 650–68.

Griffiths, Frederick T. "Ralph Ellison, Richard Wright, and the Case of Angelo Herndon." *African American Review* 35 (2001): 615–36.

Habermas, Jürgen. *The Future of Human Nature.* Trans. William Rehg, Max Pensky, and Hella Beister. New York: Polity, 2003.

Hahn, Stephen. "What Leaf-Fring'd Legend Haunts about Thy Shape? *Light in August* and Southern Pastoral." *Faulkner Journal* 10 (1985): 30–40.

Hammett, Dashiell. *Red Harvest.* New York: Vintage, 1992.

Hanson, Victor. *The Western Way of War: Infantry Battle in Ancient Greece.* Berkeley: U of California P, 1989.

Haraway, Donna. *Primate Visions: Gender, Race, and Nature in the World of Modern Science.* New York: Routledge, 1989.

———. *Simians, Cyborgs, and Women: The Reinvention of Nature.* New York: Routledge, 1991.

Hawthorne, Nathaniel. *The House of the Seven Gables.* In *Collected Novels.* New York: Library of America, 1983.

———. *Tales and Sketches.* New York: Library of America, 1982.

Hayles, N. Katherine. *How We Became Posthuman: Virtual Bodies in Cybernetics, Literature, and Informatics.* Chicago: U of Chicago P, 1999.

———. *My Mother Was a Computer: Digital Subjects and Literary Texts.* Chicago: U of Chicago P, 2005.

Headrick, Daniel R. *The Tools of Empire: Technology and European Imperialism in the Nineteenth Century.* New York: Oxford UP, 1981.

———. *When Information Came of Age: Technologies of Knowledge in the Age of Reason and Revolution, 1700–1850.* New York: Oxford UP, 2002.

Hearn, Lafcadio. "The Genius of Japanese Civilization." *Kokoro: Hints and Echoes of Japanese Inner Life.* 1896. New York: ICG Muse, 2001. 7–33.

Heidegger, Martin. *Being and Time: A Translation of* Sein und Zeit. Trans. Joan Stambaugh. Albany: State U of New York P, 1996.

———. *Introduction to Metaphysics.* Trans. Gregory Fried and Richard Polt. New Haven: Yale UP, 2000.

———. "The Question Concerning Technology." *The Question Concerning Technology and Other Essays.* Trans. William Lovitt. New York: Harper, 1977. 3–35.

Heilbroner, Robert L. "Do Machines Make History?" *Does Technology Drive History? The Dilemma of Technological Determinism.* Ed. Merritt Roe Smith and Leo Marx. Cambridge: MIT UP, 1994. 53–66.

Herndon, Angelo. "Frederick Douglass: Negro Leadership and the War." *Negro Quarterly* 1.4 (1943): 303–29.

Himes, Chester. *Blind Man with a Pistol.* New York: Vintage, 1989.

Hobbes, Thomas. *Leviathan.* New York: Oxford UP, 1996.

Horkheimer, Max. *Eclipse of Reason.* New York: Oxford UP, 1947.

Horkheimer, Max, and Theodor W. Adorno. *Dialectic of Enlightenment: Philosophical Fragments.* Trans. Edmund Jephcott. Stanford: Stanford UP, 2002.

Hungerford, Harold. "Past and Present in *Light in August.*" *American Literature* 55 (1983): 183–98.

Jackson, Lawrence. *Ralph Ellison: The Emergence of Genius.* New York: Wilkey, 2002.

James, C. L. R. *Mariners, Renegades, and Castaways: The Story of Herman Melville and the World We Live In.* Hanover: UP of New England, 1953.

James, Portia. "'To Collect Proof of Colored Talent and Ingenuity': African-American Invention and Innovation, 1619–1930." *Technology and the African-American Experience: Needs and Opportunities for Study.* Ed. Bruce Sinclair. Cambridge: MIT P, 2004. 49–70.

Johnson, Susie Paul. "*Pylon:* Faulkner's Waste Land." *Mississippi Quarterly* 38 (1985): 287–94.

Kasson, John. *Civilizing the Machine: Technology and Republican Values in America, 1776–1900.* Penguin: New York, 1977.

Kazin, Alfred. "The Stillness of *Light in August.*" *Faulkner: A Collection of Critical Essays.* Ed. Robert Penn Warren. Englewood Cliffs, NJ: Prentice-Hall, 1966. 147–62.

Kermode, Frank. *The Genesis of Secrecy: On the Interpretation of Narrative.* Cambridge: Harvard UP, 1979.

Kleitz, Dorsey. "Questioners of the Sphinx." *Melville "Among the Nations."* Ed. A. C. Christodolulou and Sanford Marovitz. Kent, OH: Kent State UP, 2001. 455–62.

Kuhn, Thomas. *The Road since* Structure: *Philosophical Essays, 1970–1993.* Chicago: U of Chicago P, 2000.

———. *The Structure of Scientific Revolutions.* Chicago: U of Chicago P, 1970.

Krasteva, Yonka. "Chaos and Pattern in Ellison's *Invisible Man.*" *Southern Literary Journal* 30.1 (1994): 55–72.

Lackey, Kris. "More Spiritual Terrors: The Bible and the Gothic Imagination in *Moby-Dick.*" *South Atlantic Review* 52 (1987): 37–50.

Latour, Bruno. *We Have Never Been Modern.* Trans. Catherine Porter. New York: Prentice Hall.

Leibniz, Gottfried Wilhelm. *Discourse on Metaphysics, Correspondence with Arnauld, Monadology.* Trans. George Montgomery. La Salle: Open Court Classics, 1902.

Lennox, James G. "Plato's Unnatural Teleology." *Aristotle's Philosophy of Biology.* New York: Cambridge UP, 2001. 280–302.

Lewis, Bernard. *What Went Wrong? The Clash between Islam and Modernity in the Middle East.* New York: Perennial, 2003.

Lewontin, R. C. *Biology as Ideology: The Doctrine of DNA.* New York: Harper, 1991.

Lukács, Georg. *The Theory of the Novel.* Trans. Anna Bostock. Cambridge: MIT P, 1996.

Lutz, John. "That Texas Disease: Commodity Fetishism and Psychic Deprivation in *The Hamlet.*" *Literature Interpretation Theory* 13 (2002): 69–90.

Lyotard, Jean-François. *The Inhuman: Reflections on Time.* Trans. Geoffrey Bennington and Rachel Bowlby. London: Polity P, 1991.

———. *Postmodern Fables.* Trans. Georges Van Den Abbeele. Minneapolis: U of Minnesota P, 1997.

Marcuse, Herbert. "From Ontology to Technology." *Critical Theory and Society: A Reader.* Ed. Stephen Eric Bronner and Douglas MacKay Kellner. Routledge: New York, 1989. 119–27.

———. *One-Dimensional Man: Studies in the Ideology of Advanced Industrial Society.* Boston: Beacon P, 1964.

———. "Some Social Implications of Modern Technology." *Technology, War, and Fascism: Collected Papers of Herbert Marcuse.* Vol. 1. Ed. Douglas Kellner. New York: Routledge, 1998. 39–66.

Marx, Karl. *Capital.* Vol. 1. Trans. Ben Fowkes. New York: Penguin, 1976.

Marx, Leo. "The Idea of 'Technology' and Postmodern Pessimism." *Does Technology Drive History? The Dilemma of Technological Determinism.* Ed. Merritt Roe Smith and Leo Marx. Cambridge: MIT P, 1994. 237–58.

———. "Lewis Mumford: Prophet of Organicism." *Lewis Mumford: Public Intellectual.* Ed. A. C. Hughes and T. P. Hughes. New York, Oxford UP, 1990. 164–80.

———. *The Machine in the Garden: Technology and the Pastoral Ideal in America.* New York: Oxford UP, 2000.

Matthews, John T. "*As I Lay Dying* in the Machine Age." *boundary 2* 19 (1992): 69–94.

Matthiessen, Francis Otto. *American Renaissance: Art and Expression in the Age of Emerson and Whitman.* New York: Oxford UP, 1941.

Maturana, Humberto, and Francisco Varela. *Autopoiesis and Cognition: The Realization of the Living.* Boston: D. Reidl, 1980.

Mayr, Otto. *Authority, Liberty, and Automatic Machinery in Early Modern Europe.* Baltimore: Johns Hopkins UP, 1986.

McMurry, Andrew. *Environmental Renaissance: Emerson, Thoreau, and the Systems of Nature.* Athens: U of Georgia P, 2003.

Meeks, Wayne, gen. ed. *The HarperCollins Study Bible: New Revised Standard Version.* New York: HarperCollins, 1993.

Melville, Herman. "Bartleby, the Scrivener." *Pierre, Israel Potter, The Piazza Tales, The*

Confidence-Man, Uncollected Prose, and Billy Budd. New York: Library of America, 1984. 635–72.

———. "The Bell-Tower." *Pierre, Israel Potter, The Piazza Tales, The Confidence-Man, Uncollected Prose, and Billy Budd.* New York: Library of America, 1984. 819–31.

———. *Clarel: A Poem and Pilgrimage in the Holy Land.* Ed. Harrison Hayford, Alma A. MacDougall, Hershel Parker, and G. Thomas Tanselle. Evanston and Chicago: Northwestern UP and The Newberry Library, 1991.

———. *The Confidence-Man: His Masquerade.* In *Pierre, Israel Potter, The Piazza Tales, The Confidence-Man, Uncollected Prose, and Billy Budd.* New York: Library of America, 1984.

———. *Correspondence.* Ed. Lynn Horth. Chicago: Northwestern UP and the Newberry Library, 1993.

———. *Israel Potter.* In *Pierre, Israel Potter, The Piazza Tales, The Confidence-Man, Uncollected Prose, and Billy Budd.* New York: Library of America, 1984.

———. *Journals.* Ed. Howard C. Horsford and Lynn Horth. Chicago: Northwestern UP, 1989.

———. *Mardi: and a Voyage Thither.* In *Typee, Omoo, Mardi.* New York: Library of America, 1982.

———. *Moby-Dick, or, the Whale.* Evanston and Chicago: Northwestern UP and Newberry Library, 1988.

———. *Omoo: A Narrative of Adventures in the South Seas.* In *Typee, Omoo, Mardi.* New York: Library of America, 1982.

———. "The Paradise of Bachelors and the Tartarus of Maids." *Pierre, Israel Potter, The Piazza Tales, The Confidence-Man, Uncollected Prose, and Billy Budd.* New York: Library of America, 1984. 1257–79.

———. *Pierre: or, the Ambiguities. Pierre, Israel Potter, The Piazza Tales, The Confidence-Man, Uncollected Prose, and Billy Budd.* New York: Library of America, 1984.

———. *Poems of Herman Melville.* Ed. Douglas Robillard. New Haven: College and UP, 1976.

———. *Redburn: His First Voyage.* In *Redburn, White-Jacket, Moby-Dick.* New York: Library of America, 1983.

———. *Typee: A Peep at Polynesian Life.* In *Typee, Omoo, Mardi.* New York: Library of America, 1982.

———. *White-Jacket: or The World in a Man-of-War.* In *Redburn, White-Jacket, Moby-Dick.* New York: Library of America, 1983.

Miller, Donald. *Lewis Mumford: A Life.* Pittsburgh: U of Pittsburgh P, 1989.

Mitcham, Carl. *Thinking through Technology: The Path between Engineering and Philosophy.* Chicago: U of Chicago P, 1994.

Mitchell, David. "'Too Much of a Cripple': Ahab, Dire Bodies, and the Language of Prosthesis in *Moby-Dick*." *Leviathan* 1 (1999): 5–22.

Mularkey, John. *Bergson and Philosophy.* Edinburgh: Edinburgh UP, 1999.

Mumford, Lewis. *Art and Technics.* New York: Harcourt Brace, 1952.

———. *The Brown Decades.* New York: Dover, 1971.

———. *The City in History.* New York: Harcourt Brace, 1961.

———. *The Condition of Man.* New York: Harcourt Brace, 1944.

———. *The Conduct of Life.* New York: Harcourt Brace, 1951.

———. *The Culture of Cities.* New York: Harcourt Brace, 1938.

———. *Findings and Keepings.* New York: Harcourt Brace, 1975.

———. *The Golden Day.* New York: Horace Liveright, 1926.

———. *Herman Melville.* New York: Harcourt Brace, 1929.

———. *The Highway and the City.* New York: Harcourt Brace, 1953.

———. *The Myth of the Machine: Technics and Human Development.* New York: Harcourt Brace, 1967.

———. *The Myth of the Machine: The Pentagon of Power.* New York: Harcourt Brace, 1970.

———. *My Works and Days: A Personal Chronicle.* New York: Harcourt Brace, 1979.

———. *Sketches from Life.* New York: Dial P, 1982.

———. *Sticks and Stones.* New York: Dover, 1955.

———. *The Story of Utopias.* New York: Viking P, 1922.

———. *Technics and Civilization.* New York: Harcourt Brace, 1963.

Nadel, Alan. *Invisible Criticism: Ralph Ellison and the American Canon.* Iowa City: U of Iowa P, 1988.

Neal, Larry. "Ellison's Zoot Suit." *Ralph Ellison's* Invisible Man: *A Casebook.* Ed. John F. Callahan. Oxford: Oxford UP, 2004. 81–108.

Neighbors, Jim. "Plunging (outside of) History: Naming and Self-Possession in *Invisible Man*." *African American Review* 36 (2002): 227–42.

New, Elisa. "'Bible Leaves! Bible Leaves!' Hellenism and Hebraism in Melville's *Moby-Dick*." *Poetics Today* 19.2 (1998): 281–303.

Noble, David F. *America by Design: Science, Technology, and the Rise of Corporate Capitalism.* Oxford: Oxford UP, 1979.

———. *The Religion of Technology: The Divinity of Man and the Spirit of Invention.* New York: Knopf, 1997.

Nye, David E. *American Technological Sublime.* Cambridge: MIT P, 1994.

———. *Consuming Power: A Social History of American Energies.* Cambridge: MIT P.

———. *Electrifying America: Social Meanings of a New Technology, 1880–1940.* Cambridge: MIT P, 1990.

———. *Narratives and Spaces: Technology and the Construction of American Culture.* New York: Columbia UP, 1997.

O'Meally, Robert G. *The Craft of Ralph Ellison.* Cambridge: Harvard UP, 1980.

Pacey, Arnold. *Maze of Ingenuity.* Cambridge: MIT P, 1992.

———. *Meaning in Technology.* Cambridge: MIT P, 1999.

———. *Technology in World Civilization.* Cambridge: MIT P, 1991.

Pierce, Charles W. "How Electricity Is Taught at Tuskegee." *A Hammer in Their Hands: A Documentary History of Technology and the African-American Experience.* Ed. Carroll Pursell. Cambridge: MIT P, 2005. 136–41.

Poe, Edgar Allan. *The Fall of the House of Usher and Other Writings.* Ed. David Galloway. New York: Penguin, 2003.

Polk, Noel. *Children of the Dark House.* Jackson: UP of Mississippi, 1996.

Porter, Roy. *Blood and Guts: A Short History of Medicine.* New York: Norton, 2002.

———. *The Greatest Benefit to Mankind: A Medical History of Humanity.* New York: Norton, 1997.

Puchek, Peter. "William Faulkner's *Light in August:* Epiphany, Eternity, and Time." *Southern Quarterly* 36 (1997): 25–36.

Pursell, Carroll, ed. *A Hammer in Their Hands: A Documentary History of Technology and the African-American Experience.* Cambridge: MIT P, 2005.

Quinby, Lee. *Anti-Apocalypse: Exercises in Genealogical Criticism.* Minneapolis: U of Minnesota P, 1994.

Radloff, Bernhard. *Cosmopolis and Truth: Melville's Critique of Modernity.* New York: Peter Lang, 1996.

Raglan, Lord. *The Hero: A Study in Tradition, Myth, and Drama.* Mineola, NY: Dover, 2003.

Reed, Brian K. "The Iron and the Flesh: History as Machine in Ellison's *Invisible Man.*" *College Language Association Journal* 37.3 (1994): 261–73.

Riasanovsky, Nicholas Valentine. *A History of Russia.* 3rd ed. New York: Oxford UP, 1977.

Rio-Jelliffe, R. *Obscurity's Myriad Components: The Theory and Practice of William Faulkner.* Lewisburg, PA: Bucknell UP, 2001.

Rochberg-Halton, Eugene. "Megamachine and Organicism." *Lewis Mumford: Public Intellectual.* Ed. A. C. Hughes and T. P. Hughes. New York: Oxford UP, 1990. 127–51.

Rogin, Michael Paul. *Subversive Genealogy: The Politics and Art of Herman Melville.* Berkeley: U of California P, 1985.

Rozelle, Lee. *Ecosublime: Environmental Awe and Terror from the New World to Oddworld.* Tuscaloosa: U of Alabama P, 2006.

Safranski, Rüdiger. *Martin Heidegger: Between Good and Evil.* Trans. Ewald Osers. Cambridge: Harvard UP, 1998.

Said, Edward. *Culture and Imperialism.* New York: Vintage, 1994.

———. *Orientalism.* New York: Vintage, 1979.

Sartre, Jean-Paul. "On *The Sound and the Fury:* Time in the Work of Faulkner." *Literary and Philosophical Essays.* Trans. Annette Michelson. New York: Collier, 1962. 84–93.

———. "William Faulkner's *Sartoris.*" *Literary and Philosophical Essays.* Trans. Annette Michelson. New York: Collier, 1962. 78–83.

Schafer, William J. "Ralph Ellison and the Birth of the Anti-Hero." *Ralph Ellison: A Collection of Critical Essays.* Ed. John Heresy. Englewood Cliffs, NJ: Prentice-Hall, 1974. 115–26.

Schueller, Malini Johar. *U.S. Orientalisms: Race, Nation, and Gender in Literature, 1790–1890.* Ann Arbor: U of Michigan P, 1998.

Shakespeare, William. *The Norton Shakespeare.* 5th ed. Ed. Stephen Greenblatt, Walter Cohen, Jean E. Howard, and Katharine Maus. New York: Norton, 1997.

Shelley, Mary. *Frankenstein.* New York: Penguin, 1985.

Sinclair, Bruce. "Integrating the Histories of Race and Technology." *Technology and the African-American Experience: Needs and Opportunities for Study.* Ed. Bruce Sinclair. Cambridge: MIT P, 2004. 1–18.

———. "Pictures from an Exhibition." *Technology and the African-American Experience: Needs and Opportunities for Study.* Ed. Bruce Sinclair. Cambridge: MIT P, 2004. 119–30.

Sinclair, Upton. *The Jungle.* New York: Bantam, 1981.

Singer, Marc. "'A Slightly Different Sense of Time': Palimpsestic Time in *Invisible Man.*" *Twentieth-Century Literature* 49.3 (2003): 388–419.

Smith, M. R. Introduction. *Does Technology Drive History? The Dilemma of Technological Determinism.* Ed. Leo Marx and M. R. Smith. Cambridge: MIT P, 1994. ix–xv.

Snead, James. *Figures of Division: William Faulkner's Major Novels.* New York: Methuen, 1986.

Spanos, William V. *The Errant Art of* Moby-Dick: *The Canon, the Cold War, and the Struggle for American Studies.* Durham: Duke UP, 1995.

———. "Pierre's Silence: Melville's Unmapping of American Space." *Melville "Among the Nations."* Ed. A. C. Christodolulou and Sanford Marovitz. Kent, OH: Kent State UP, 1997. 367–83.

Spark, Clare L. *Hunting Captain Ahab: Psychological Warfare and the Melville Revival.* Kent, OH: Kent State UP, 2001.

Spenser, Edmund. *The Faerie Queene.* New York: Penguin, 1988.

Spiller, Robert E., ed. *The Van Wyck Brooks–Lewis Mumford Letters.* New York: Dutton, 1970.

Sten, Christopher. "Melville's Cosmopolitanism: A Map for Living in a (Post-) Colonialist World." *Melville "Among the Nations."* Ed. A. C. Christodolulou and Sanford Marovitz. Kent, OH: Kent State UP, 2001. 38–48.

Stiegler, Bernard. *Technics and Time, 1: The Fault of Epimetheus.* Trans. Richard Beardsworth and George Collins. Stanford: Stanford UP, 1998.

Sundquist, Eric J. *Faulkner: The House Divided.* Baltimore: Johns Hopkins UP, 1983.

Suvin, Darko. *The Metamorphoses of Science Fiction: On the Poetics and History of a Literary Genre.* New Haven: Yale UP, 1979.

Taketani, Etsuko. "*Moby-Dick:* Gnostic Re-writing of History." *American Transcendental Quarterly* 8 (1994): 119–35.

Taylor, Frederick Winslow. *The Principles of Scientific Management.* New York: Dover, 1998.

Towner, Theresa. *Faulkner on the Color Line: The Later Novels.* Jackson: UP of Mississippi, 2000.

Trafton, Scott. *Egypt Land: Race and Nineteenth-Century American Egyptomania.* Durham: Duke UP, 2004.

Twain, Mark. *A Connecticut Yankee in King Arthur's Court.* New York: Oxford UP, 1996.

United States, Office of the Federal Register. *Weekly Compendium of Presidential Documents.* 4 Oct. 2004.

———. *Weekly Compendium of Presidential Documents.* 18 Oct. 2004.

Wagner, Vivian. "Gender, Technology, and Utopia in Faulkner's Airplane Tales." *Arizona Quarterly* 49 (1993): 79–97.

Wallerstein, Immanuel. *The Modern World-System II: Mercantilism and the Consolidation of the European World-Economy, 1600–1750.* San Diego: Academic P, 1980.

———. *The Modern World-System III: The Second Era of Great Expansion of the Capitalist World-Economy, 1730–1840s.* San Diego: Academic P, 1989.

———. *World-Systems Analysis: An Introduction.* Durham: Duke UP, 2004.

Wardrop, Daneen. "The Signifier and the Tattoo in Melville's *Typee.*" *ESQ* 47 (2001): 135–61.

Washington, Booker T. *Working with the Hands: Being a Sequel to "Up from Slavery" Covering the Author's Experiences in Industrial Training at Tuskegee.* New York: Doubleday, 1904.

Weaver, Raymond M. *Herman Melville, Mariner and Mystic.* New York: George H. Doran, 1921.

Weinstein, Philip M. *Faulkner's Subject: A Cosmos No One Owns.* New York: Cambridge UP, 1992.

White, Lynn. *Medieval Religion and Technology.* Berkeley: U of California P, 1978.

———. *Medieval Technology and Social Change.* London: Oxford UP, 1962.

Whitman, Walt. *Song of Myself* (reproduction of 1st ed.). Mineola: Dover, 2001.

Williams, Rosalind. "Lewis Mumford as Historian of Technology in *Technics and Civilization.*" *Lewis Mumford: Public Intellectual.* Ed. A. C. Hughes and T. P. Hughes. New York: Oxford UP, 1990. 43–65.

Wilson, E. O. *Sociobiology: The New Synthesis.* Cambridge: Belknap, 1975.

Wilson, Eric. "Melville, Darwin, and the Great Chain of Being." *Studies in American Fiction* 28 (2000): 131–50.

———. "The Nomad, the Pilgrim, and the White Whale." *Colby Quarterly* 28 (1998): 226–42.

Winner, Langdon. *The Whale and the Reactor: A Search for Limits in an Age of High Technology.* Chicago: U of Chicago P, 1986.

Wolfe, Carey. *Animal Rites: American Culture, the Discourse of Species, and Posthumanist Theory.* Chicago: U of Chicago P, 2003.

Wright, John. "The Conscious Hero and the Rites of Man." *Ralph Ellison's* Invisible Man: *A Casebook.* Ed. John F. Callahan. New York: Oxford UP, 2004. 221–52.

———. "Ellison's Experimental Attitude and the Technologies of Illumination." *The Cambridge Companion to Ralph Ellison.* Ed. Ross Posnock. New York: Cambridge UP, 2005. 157–71.

———. "'Jack-the-Bear' Dreaming: Ellison's Spiritual Technologies." *boundary 2* 30 (1993): 175–94.

Young, Philip. "The Machine in Tartarus: Melville's Inferno." *American Literature* 63 (1991): 208–24.

Zamyatin, Yevgeny. *We.* Trans. Mirra Ginsburg. New York: Viking P, 1972.

Zeitlin, Michael. "Faulkner's *Pylon:* The City in the Age of Mechanical Reproduction." *Canadian Review of American Studies* 22 (1991): 229–40.

Zimmerman, Michael E. *Heidegger's Confrontation with Modernity: Technology, Politics, and Art.* Bloomington: Indiana UP, 1990.

Zuckerman, Michael. "Faith, Hope, Not Much Charity: The Optimistic Epistemology of Lewis Mumford." *Lewis Mumford: Public Intellectual.* Ed. A. C. Hughes and T. P. Hughes. New York: Oxford UP, 1990. 361–75.

Index